ENLIGHTENED OR MAD?

DAVID Y. F. HO

ENLIGHTENED OR MAD?

A PSYCHOLOGIST GLIMPSES INTO
MYSTICAL MAGNANIMITY

Dignity Press
World Dignity University Press

Published by Dignity Press
16 Northview Court
Lake Oswego, OR 97035, USA
www.dignitypress.org/enlightened-or-mad

Cover art: Deeds of the Zen Masters Hanshan and Shide. Handscroll, 35.0 x 49.5 cm. Ink on paper, Tokyo National Museum, Tokyo.

Printed on paper from environmentally managed forestry: http://www.lightningsource.com/chainofcustody

print version: ISBN 978-1-937570-51-4
ebook (epub): ISBN 978-1-937570-54-5
ebook (Kindle): ISBN 978-1-937570-55-2

CONTENTS

6

FOREWORD

I've never experienced David Ho in his professional roles as professor and clinical psychologist. I wish I had, since Dr. Ho would have undoubtedly proven to be a most provocative goad. However, I've been blessed to know him, albeit briefly, as a thoughtful, ever-curious and caring pilgrim in our beloved community called *Tapestry*.

This book will assist every one of us frail yet valiant travelers on our own peculiar journeys. The operative word is "assist."

Why? Because it's the brutally honest portrait of a fellow human being who, above all else, strives to build bridges rather than barriers in his oft-tormented, personal odyssey. Ho *is* a relentless bridge-builder. Actually, he doesn't only build bridges; Ho *is* a bridge himself. David/YF are literal bridges between East and West, between psychiatry and spirituality, between poetry and prose, between internal struggle and cultural evolution. What makes this book so powerfully relevant is that all of the aforementioned bridges are center stage in the life of our 21st century universe. They are contemporary chasms that need to be boldly spanned, if we are going to have any chance of prevailing as a species.

This book isn't an easy read. There are parts of it I neither understand nor want to hear. Clearly, it isn't for anyone who doesn't choose to undertake the spiritual practice of discomfort. So, you've been given a fair warning: only tackle it if you desire to plumb the depths of your own interior while engaging the infuriating diversity in the greater globe. Only read it if you're fully dressed in courage.

Hence, I make no promises and offer no guarantees. All I can say is that my soul has grown after tackling this difficult, risky book. Maybe yours will too.

Rev. Dr. Tom Owen-Towle

PREFACE

This book tells the story of my life as a journey of spiritual discoveries in the East and the West.

"Enlightened or mad?" This is a question well-nigh impossible to answer. By what means could the answer be known? Psychologists may be less equipped to answer the question than Buddhists, who have long pondered questions of enlightenment and spirituality. But what does madness have to do with either enlightenment or spirituality? Everything. This audacious assertion I will defend.

I had no history of psychiatric disturbance prior to age fifty-eight. Then something happened that profoundly changed my life. For about two weeks, I listened to music in a way I had never listened before. Music came to life, evoking emotions that brought me to the lofty realm of spirituality. And it was not just music. As I listened, I began to move—first my arms, then my whole body. I entered into a state of selfless-oblivion, like a trance. I experienced disinhibition as I had never experienced before. Released from overcontrol, a long-standing problem I had struggled with, I became spontaneous, liberated. My mind exploded. Creative thoughts and flashes of insight rained down faster than I could record them in writing. I was on my way toward a rediscovery of my artistic and literary bent. People around me said I had become strange—stranger than my usual self. Then, this brief episode of exuberance ended as unpredictably as it came.

What happened? Even as a clinical psychologist, I was—and I am still—perplexed. I knew I showed hypomanic symptoms, such as unusually elevated mood, during the episode, but I didn't think I suffered from psychiatric disturbance. After all, I enjoyed the episode immensely. It caused me or others no harm.

Since then, more episodes have occurred, two of which approached the severity of mania. I experienced symptoms like inflated self-esteem, racing thoughts, and excessive talkativeness. I acted in ways that went beyond the bounds of social acceptability. People around me were bewildered and became very concerned about my mental condition. Yet, my mind retained its logicality and self-reflectiveness with undiminished prowess. At no point was there any threat of my losing contact with reality or of acting in destructive or violent ways. What's more, I had glimpses of enlightenment, a mystical state of magnanimity, tranquility, and freedom from inner turmoil. I became a more colorful person, more sensitive, generous, and loving *during* episodes of madness.

I was forced to ask myself, "Am I enlightened or mad?" The response to this question is a self-study of my life. I dig deep into my past to better understand the present and future. I struggle to harness the creative forces of madness without incurring unnecessary social costs, which is quite a feat even if it is only partially successful.

Altogether, I have had fifteen episodes—all of exuberance, none of depression. This defies the typical pattern seen among patients who have had hypomania or mania. This intriguing fact alone would occasion a rewriting of psychiatric textbooks. Further, the deeper I delved into my case, the more I became aware how limited psychiatric approaches to understanding and coping with abnormality are. Fundamentally, psychiatry has failed to address the creative forces of madness.

The episodes of exuberance afforded me precious opportunities to gain unhindered access to the unconscious, experience the extraordinary, and glimpse into mystical magnanimity. All the good things are present, in enhanced magnitudes. Gone are fixations, prejudices, obsessions. Life is sweet, meaningful, and fulfilling. Above all, the enlargement of love dominates my being, leading me to act in selfless ways for the betterment of humankind. I say "glimpses of enlightenment" because that is exactly what they are—only glimpses. Unfortunately, they are extinguished at the exit from an episode.

They remain experiences to be treasured, acting as a beacon for the remainder of my journey through life.

Writing this book affords me the opportunity to fulfill one of my lifelong aspirations: to be an agent of East-West understanding. I take advantage of my bilingual-bicultural background to tell select tales of intercultural encounter along the way of my spiritual journey. I draw upon the religious-philosophical traditions of the East, Confucianism, Daoism, and Buddhism, to enlarge our understanding of spirituality.

Throughout this book are imaginary interviews between David and YF. David is my Christian name, representing my Western self; YF are the initials for my given Chinese name, Yau Fai, representing my Chinese self. In essence, these interviews are internal dialogues between my two selves, one Eastern and the other Western. They give concrete illustrations of how I have struggled to achieve an integrated identity in response to the question "Who am I?" They also demonstrate the process of self-healing at work.

In many ways, my personal transformation parallels the historical transformation of the Chinese nation as a whole. Thus, the interviews are as much oral history as self case study of a psychologist with a bicultural-bilingual background. The oral history covers a period of unprecedented turmoil, as well as hope, in Chinese society. My experiences of East-West encounters are put within the context of this historical period; my personal pains and rewards are linked to those of collective others. The oral history reveals to the reader my intimate thoughts and reflections on a wide range of psychological issues on intercultural fertilization and personal identity. In a sense, then, a glimpse into my life is also a case study in psychohistory.

So this book is not meant to be just a report on my bouts of madness, extraordinary experiences, and glimpses of enlightenment. It is about my personal journey in quest of an integrated identity, sense of self-mastery, and new directions to lead a good life—in short, spiritual fulfillment. The journey is at once arduous and rewarding. Often I see no end in sight; I may come close to facing despair. Along the way, however, hope invites me to go on, and I also experience tranquility, interspersed with intense feelings of exhilaration and ecstasy.

Spirituality then provides the unifying theme and context to interpret all my experiences, normal and abnormal, in China and the United States. What have I learned? Madness has the potential to energize spiritual journeys. Spirituality derives creative energy from madness to reach new heights; madness receives the healing, calming effects of spirituality to become benign. Wedded to ecumenicity, spirituality dissolves ethnic or cultural boundaries, fosters universal love, and promotes world citizenship.

This book results from the blessing of circumstance. In separation, being a psychologist steeped in a bilingual-bicultural background, experiencing glimpses of enlightenment, or having episodes of madness may not be that uncommon. But the confluence of all these is rare, if not unique. My encounters with madness have enabled me to gain firsthand experiences of abnormality, a valuable resource for probing into the patient's mind. In my case, I am both doctor and patient. Taking advantage of my specialty, I can do a self case study of abnormality.

Confronting episodes of madness one after another is a process of consecutive learning. Gradually I learn to view these episodes as high points in my journey of spiritual discoveries, where the dynamics of spirituality and spiritual emptiness play out. The benefits, both professional and personal, I have derived from my encounters with madness are immense. This realization propels me to share my spiritual discoveries with fellow travelers in search of a good life.

Writing this book is the closest experience to conception, and getting it published the closest to giving birth to a baby I will ever have. This new life is my karma. Fortunately, I have help from competent and encouraging "obstetricians." One is the Reverend Tom Owen-Towle, a Unitarian Universalist minister, who activates

song she had composed just for her nemesis, "I don't want to be a parasite in the world...."

Years later, during psychotherapy workshops I conduct in Confucian-heritage communities, when I mention marital strife caused by antagonism between the wife and her mother-in-law, women participants immediately recognize the phenomenon and describe their own experiences with it.

David   Control and ownership of the most important man in their lives underlie perennial battles between mothers-in-law and daughters-in-law. What can men caught between two women do? Poor men folk!

By the ethic of filial piety, a man is supposed to side with his mother and persuade his wife to accede. But not all wives are docile or open to persuasion. Some may be fearsome and prone to strike back, as did your mother against her mother-in-law.

Psychological illiteracy appears to be more pronounced in men than in women. In the final analysis, psychotherapy for Chinese families is basically limited in what it can hope to achieve. We need to redefine the role of women and of male-female relationships in Chinese societies. Again, I see individual struggles in a larger context; they must be linked to collective struggles involving society as a whole.

YF   In my own family, quarrels between my parents seemed endless. Eventually they were separated when my mother left Hong Kong to live in the United States. I was then ten years of age. So I grew up in a broken family, pained, but unbroken.

From Childhood to Grandparenthood: What is Filial Piety?

David   Overall, traditionally Chinese children are socialized to be obedient, timid, controlled, inhibited, and dependent. Like their counterparts in the West, they love to play and make noise. But their childhood impulses are increasingly subdued as they grow older.

While children in the West climb up trees, Chinese children tend to sit still to avoid physical risk, having been reminded constantly of the filial injunction:

> The body, hair and skin, have all been received from one's parents. One does not dare to do them harm. That's the beginning of *xiao* [filial piety].

YF   Right, sit still they do, at home and in school—too much, especially in the presence of authority figures. It's quite a sight to see an entire class of kindergarten or primary schoolchildren sitting still, with both hands held firmly behind their back. Meanwhile, the teacher looks over them like an owl.

David   Like other children of your generation, you would have been expected to be respectful and obedient toward your elders and stay out of trouble. Misbehavior that reflected poorly on the family invited shaming. So, did you sit still?

YF   Generally, I was well behaved. But I didn't sit still. One of my childhood memories, of age eleven, stand out. Once I ran down a hilly path at "lightning" speed, to the horror of my onlooking uncles and aunts, who showed great disapproval of my unruly behavior. Inwardly, I harbored delight in having horrified them with my physical agility.

David   Understandably, hyperactive children cause formidable difficulties to their parents and teachers. Of special interest here is a cross-cultural comparison between Western and Chinese standards of hyperactivity. Many a child considered normal in the West would be regarded as a hyperactive trouble-maker in a Chinese context.

YF   And so it is painful to witness the deadening developmental path of Chinese children: lively in nurseries and kindergartens, overcontrolled in primary schools, half-dead in secondary schools, and brain-dead by the time they enter universities.

David   The reader will surely forgive you, driven by moral indignation, for making such hyperbole.

Let's touch on another cross-cultural comparison. The difference in reaction to animals between Western and Chinese children is dramatic. While Western children delight in seeing small animals, dogs in particular, Chinese children are prone to retreat in fear to hide behind their mothers.

YF   Why? Because the mothers, afraid of dogs themselves, frequently frighten their children with the remark, "Watch out! The dog will bite you."

Another scare tactic that adults use to control children is to say to them, "If you continue to misbehave, I will take you to the police station." This reinforces the generalized fear of authority figures typical of Chinese children.

Elderly women are fond of reminding young girls, "Men are not to be trusted."

David   Women might rebut that the reminder to young girls is based on reality. Still, it is an overgeneralization, not helpful to maidens in courtship for developing skills to discriminate between suitors who can or cannot be trusted.

Can you be trusted?

YF   Being trusted by a woman imposes on the trusted man heavy responsibilities not to betray her trust. Wouldn't you rather be released from all bondage, on occasion, and plunge with abandon into the "pleasures of cloud and rain" (Chinese euphemism for sexual union)?

David   Back to psychohistory. Unwittingly, the adults create an unsafe world full of dangers in the minds of the young. How can trust and security be established?

YF   The unsafe world extends into the home when mothers deal with their misbehaving children with the threat, "Wait till your father comes home."

David   In translation, this threat implies three messages. One, I have failed to discipline control you by myself. Two, the real authority resides in your father. Three, in our home your father is the fearsome person you should be afraid of.

The first two messages undermine the mother as a disciplinarian. The last one is pernicious, for it drives a wedge into the father-child relationship emotionally and predisposes the child toward a generalized fear of authority figures.

The child has reasons to be fearful of the father, who is more likely than the mother to administer harsh discipline. A popular Chinese saying sums it up: "Stern fathers, softhearted mothers." No wonder Chinese children tend to be emotionally attached to their mothers, but detached from their fathers.

YF   All these I have seen and heard, all too frequently, in my professional practice as well as daily life. Even as a child, I thought to myself: With such emphasis on impulse control, obedience, and fear inducement, our traditional upbringing produces enslaved nations!

After becoming a psychologist, I was determined to bring about changes in upbringing children for the better through parental education. It was an uphill battle—to put it bluntly, against centuries of psychological illiteracy. To begin with, being a psychologist invited people to look upon me with circumspection. I had to earn their trust, before I could begin to educate.

David   It is pleasing to witness how generally Chinese parents have become more democratic and sensitive to the child's psychological needs, with far reaching consequences for Chinese society as a whole.

YF   After becoming a father, I went to an extreme to give my daughters what I was deprived of in my childhood. I engaged them in dialogues. I encouraged them to express their own opinions, even to argue with me. A dialogue with my elder daughter at age seven ran like this:

> **Father**   "Is there a God?"
> **Daughter**   "Yes. If there is no God, who made you? Grandma?"
> **Father**   "Who made God?"
> **Daughter**   "Chemical liquids."

At age seventeen, after a day of job hunting, she said, "I discovered something today. Everybody wants to know if I can type, take shorthand, and so forth. Nobody asked me about philosophy. I don't see anything like 'Philosopher Urgently Needed' in the newspaper ads. I am angry."

At age four, my younger daughter gave me a lecture: "You taught us to do…. Why haven't you done so yourself?" I didn't interrupt her. The lecture lasted some twenty minutes, as recorded by my stopwatch, after which she resumed her usual sweetness.

In her first year of primary school, I went to receive her report card. Her teacher complained, "She talks too much." Intimidated, I dared not reveal I was a psychologist. Back home, I asked her, "Why do you like to talk so much?" She replied, "The mouth is not just for eating, but also for talking."

David   Like daughter, like father!

YF   Apprehensive, I let my paternal protectiveness take over: "You are right, of course. Fortunately, you have only one mouth. What matters the most is not so much what you say, but where. You can say what you want at home. But you need to be more careful at school. I don't want you to get into trouble with your teacher." She didn't argue with me.

Now she is a teacher herself. I asked once, "How do you keep the kids under control?" She replied, "I have learned from all your mistakes." Suddenly, I was at a loss for words.

She is now a mother of two children, making me a grandfather. Noah is the first born, followed by Harper. In this case, the fruit arrives before the flower. My troubles fly away when these babies smile in response to my stimulation.

David   No less than fatherhood, grandfatherhood requires new learning.

YF   In the traditional pattern, there is a dark side to grandparenting, in the form of extreme indulgence. In particular, grandmothers tend to mollycoddle, pamper their grandsons beyond belief, to the point of smothering them with excessive care that leaves little room for independence. Enforcement of discipline by male adults would be sabotaged, rendered virtually impossible. The Chinese term, "drowning love," captures aptly the essence of such extreme indulgence—even plants may wither from too much watering.

Drowning love reinforces infantilization. Thus, women have the awesome power to turn the very boys they love into good-for-nothing men.

My guiding principle for grandparenthood: "Just enjoy it. Be helpful, without interfering. Avoid giving advice or expressing too many opinions." Surprisingly, I find it quite easy to do, for a professor who has been expounding a lot of opinions on parenting.

David   Grandparents and their grandchildren form a natural alliance, against their common "enemies." Why not indulge Noah and Harper a little? That's your grandparental privilege.

YF   Harper is in her infancy, having just reached her first birthday. So, it makes little sense to speak of spoiling her yet. Noah is four years of age, old enough to be mischievous. We love to walk our grandpa-grandson walks, hand in hand, through a grove near his home where we can play hide-and-seek—away from parental surveillance.

Noah is rather willful. Once, at age four, he grabbed a stick that I had picked up and started to pull hard to get it out of my hands. He yelled, "Gong Gong [grandpa on Mom's side], don't pull so hard." I thought it was time for me to teach him lesson one in the Taiji school of martial arts rooted in Daoism. I let go of the stick. Naturally, Noah fell to the ground. Before he had time to complain, I said, "You are the one who was pulling. Not me."

David   It wasn't a fair fight! But it was an innovative way to temper his willfulness.

YF   I can't help compare the superb quality of parenting and material abundance (baby strollers, books, toys, etc.) that my grand-children enjoy with what most children of my generation received.

Family life has been turned upside down, from traditional elder-centeredness to modern child-centeredness. Everything revolves around my grandchildren's needs; their sleeping and feeding sched-ules dictate adult schedules. In the words of my daughter, they are "the center of the universe for us."

David   So, in place of filial sons and daughters, nowadays you find plenty of filial parents. One baby commanding the attention of two parents and four grandparents: This is the modern reality. We belong to a sandwiched generation, expected to be filial sons and daughters to our elder generations and filial parents to our children. What's more, we can't expect the same filiality from our children that our parents expect from us.

YF   Some years ago, my younger daughter asked, "Dad, what research are you doing?" I replied, "Filial piety." She shot back, "What's that?"

David   The times have surely changed. Changes you have witnessed in your own family are just a few examples of changes in the Chinese family as an institution and are symptomatic of changes in the wider society.

The period of adolescence and early adulthood is when you are most susceptible to the impact of changes, biological and socio-cultural, on the development of your personality. We need to revisit this period of special significance.

The Age of Turbulence: Adolescence and Early Adulthood

YF   Adolescence and young adulthood were the most turbulent years of my life. I had more than the usual adolescent angst concerning sexuality.

When I was around fourteen, my father told me that masturbation was damaging to the body, like "cutting your artery open and letting the blood flow out"; worse, it would lead to intellectual deterioration. Naturally I was terrified. Conflicts between sexual impulses and control over them reached intensities that brought me great distress and turmoil.

David   You fell victim to a culturally induced psychoneurosis.

YF   In 1955 I left Hong Kong for university study in Canada at an early age. With trepidation, I sought advice from a psychology professor, Harold Breen, who set me straight about the normality of masturbation. I felt much relief after talking with him.

Before going to Canada, I had never traveled away from home for a distance of more than twenty miles or so. I was academically and emotionally unprepared. Living in a foreign culture added complications, especially to heterosexual relations. All these propelled me to enter into adulthood prematurely; my life as an adolescent was shortened.

David   But the life of your adolescent playfulness and sentiments was not; so a belated adolescence would pop up now and then in your later years—as your friends trying to make fun of you might say. Your youthful naiveté combined with fearlessness served you well. You welcomed the opportunity to explore new frontiers. An intrepid traveler, that's what you were. On the front page of your 1958 diary were these words:

In this little book, I will give my most honest account of passion, lamentations, and joy; laziness and industry;

shame and pride; hatred and love; action and thought; endless intellectual explorations. Let this be an adventurous tragic song, and pages of glory, for these are the years of foundation. Holding my present fast, upon the past shall I build my future, in the service of mankind.

Your diaries and correspondence with friends and relatives written during your student days in North America are revealing of your state of mind.

YF   Reading these materials again today refreshes my memory on some forgotten aspects of my youth, most notably my inclination toward spirituality and my desire to write poetry.

Writing was one way of satisfying the yearnings for expression of my "lonely soul." I felt the sentiments of a "poet in love, in ecstasy." Writing to a friend, I wrote, "If I were a poet, I would ... immortalize our friendship" (18 Dec 1962).

David   But your proficiency in the English language was simply no match for the demands of expressing your thoughts and sentiments.

YF   In those days, the difference between words like *circumcision* and *castration* were fine distinctions I was ignorant of.

Once I asked a Jewish friend of mine, "Is it true that Jewish infant boys are castrated?" Fortunately, my friend distinguished between linguistic goof and social inaptitude. Much of what I wrote now strikes me as rather uncouth or melodramatic. It has taken me decades of hard work to approach meeting the demands of poetic expression.

David   Nonetheless, the dynamism, passion, and resolute determination of a young man in search of himself leap out of the diaries and correspondence. So do the idealism and extremism characteristic of youthful minds.

YF   "I am a person of extremes," I wrote in my diary (31 Jan 1959). This terse statement summed it up well. There were fluctuations between supreme self-confidence and self-doubt, and between elation and sorrow.

Ideas of striving toward "spiritual beauty" and "a finer inner being" may be found in abundance. Often, however, the emotional tone was very negative: "[I suffered from] spiritual disease" (1 Jan 1960); "My soul drowns in anguish.... My spiritual emptiness is very acute" (28 Aug 1960).

David   I can't help but notice the theme of spirituality in your writings. It is significant that you expressed your inner turmoil in the language of spirituality rather than of psychology. Thus your articulation of a dynamic conception of spiritual fulfillment versus spiritual emptiness years later should come as no surprise. You have acquired the requisite firsthand experience of struggle and emotional foundation for articulating the dynamic conception.

The highly charged negative tone reflected your feelings of frustrated spiritual striving. What saved you from collapse?

YF   My love of life remained unshakable: "My passionate love of life never dies" (20 Feb 1958). I maintained an intense sense of purpose. My writing was replete with expressions like "meaning," "destiny," "transcendence," "self-discovery," and "quest for the ultimate truth."

David   Your fighting spirit would not allow you to surrender; you were ready to "plunge into battle."

But I must also say that you were neurotically driven, overwhelmed by ambition. You were a tormented soul. There was a pressing sense of urgency: Expressions like "make haste to live, to love" dotted your diaries everywhere. Constantly reproaching yourself for "wasting time," you pushed yourself to the limit.

To excel was the only way you knew how to deal with your self-doubt and feelings of inferiority. Psychologists call it compensation. So you exploited your intellectual endowment to the fullest—at a terrible psychological cost to yourself.

YF   Yes, I wanted to know, to learn everything, to be schooled in scholarly pursuits as well as martial arts. To equip myself, I took violin, singing, dancing, and fencing lessons. I wrote a short story, "On the Other Side of Hate" (19 April 1959), for submission to a literary contest. My notebooks were filled with all kinds of ideas for writing projects, such as an autobiography (9 June 1960) and "The Future of Mankind" (25 Aug 1960).

One was to write "The Outline of Philosophy" (27 Dec 1959), even though I had taken only an introductory course in philosophy. I had the audacity to make assertions like God is "the origin of evil." Another project was "The Great Dialogue between Reason and Faith" (28 Dec 1959). In it, I find this statement: "Faith has its beginning where reason ends" (a paraphrase of Voltaire's famous dictum "Faith consists in believing when it is beyond the power of reason to believe," of which I had not heard then).

David　This provides proof that many of your present thoughts have their origins in your early adulthood.

YF　The fact that I was uninformed of the topics I wrote about was of no concern to me. I wanted to give my imagination free rein. I protested against "the creative writer [being] forced to write as a scholar." This was a presage of my career as an academic author in the decades to come. Amazing!

Occasionally, however, I was unsettled by reality checks. I would write, "Damn it. There is not much of value in what I have written."

Poor me, as I look back: I had the makings of a Renaissance man, but without the requisite genius to generate momentous knowledge or objects of beauty. Was my maker playing a trick on me? It is a good thing that I know, and accept, my limitations. Otherwise, my ambition would have consumed me in the awful predicament of endless frustrations.

David　You say to your students not to dwell on the final outcome or achievement, but to enjoy of the process of creating. Revisiting your turbulent age has deepened our understanding of subsequent periods of your life, particularly the golden age, to which we shall turn shortly.

In all, literary-artistic-spiritual aspirations during your energetic student days in North America match those of your golden age, but they were also intertwined with neurotic entanglements. Or, to put it differently, your golden age may be viewed as a distillate of your former aspirations, more mellowed and less turbulent than before.

There was yet another challenge that you had to face in your age of turbulence. Prejudices and discrimination against Asians in North America during your student days were more pronounced and overt than they are today. Readers would like to know how you faced them.

YF   I had my share of unpleasant experiences. One, in particular, threatened my personal safety. In 1956, a summer job landed me on a construction site in Canada, working as a laborer. Immediately I found myself met with unconditional rejection and hostility. The workers ganged up to bully the teenage Asian, alone in their midst, with menacing threats of physical violence. I stood my ground, although I knew I could have been hurt seriously. Fortunately, physical violence did not materialize; unfortunately, I was fired.

In my freshman year in Canada, a female student refused to sled down a slope on the same toboggan with me during a group outing in the snow. (Other students disapproved of her behavior.) I tasted the first rejection by the opposite sex.

David   To a teenage boy, rejection by males is no comparison with rejection by females.

YF   A few years later, upon learning that my elder brother had found a Canadian girl he intended to marry, I wrote him a letter (30 March 1959): "You know I have never been against interracial marriage…. It demands exceeding firmness and courage, especially when you may find yourselves alone against society…. We need pioneers to open the way toward … material progress, spiritual well-being, and universal brotherhood."

David   Significantly, you saw interracial marriage as a natural avenue for achieving all kinds of good things for humankind.

YF   At the same time, I sensed that the marriage would be opposed and run into difficulty. Sure enough, my apprehension was not groundless. Subsequently I received a letter from my brother (3 March 1960), informing me of "a tremendous change" in his life: "[My girlfriend] told me that we should part. The reasons: 1) She is not mentally strong enough to be insulated from violent family opposition and social pressure, 2) I am 'too good' for her in 'every way'; she is incapable of 'catching up' with me."

David   Did you experience racism in academic-professional circles?

YF   Yes, an example of racism is the use of medical term "mongolism" or "Mongolian idiocy," a misnomer with pointed racist overtones. The term has been largely replaced by Down syndrome.

One of my most memorable experiences speaks to this very point. In a clinic for children with mental retardation, where I had my first job as a psychologist, I examined hundreds of children with Down syndrome and counseled their parents. One day, during a consultation session, the head of the clinic suddenly asked me how I felt about the term "mongolism," which was still commonly used. Mentally unprepared, I lied and told her that I didn't care—to avoid further embarrassment. To this day, I still feel embarrassed that I resorted to lying.

As a budding psychologist, I formulated a relationship: As understanding approaches infinity, condemnation and bitterness drop to zero. The rationale: There are always reasons that account for why people act in foolish, destructive, or self-destructive ways; once the reasons are fully understood, it would be pointless to condemn (oneself or others) or to be embittered.

David   This formulation acknowledges that there are fools who do foolish things in the world. The important thing is to remind oneself not to be one of them: "I am the one who might become no less of a fool, when I dwell on the negativity of fools and suffer unnecessarily"; and equally, "I will become more of a fool than I am now, if I persist in dwelling how much of a fool I have been."

YF   Now this formulation strikes me as a workable way to approximate enlightenment, although I did not think of it as such then. It has evolved into forgiveness as a coping strategy for those who have to face life's misfortunes I have articulated in my late professional life.

David   Needless to say, the formulation does not always work because our understanding is nowhere near infinity.

YF   Nevertheless, I have benefited greatly when I do apply it. My unpleasant experiences from prejudices have not made me bitter, diminished my faith in universal brotherhood, or derailed me from my path to world citizenry. I say to myself, "There are always bad or uninformed people in any ethnic or national group who need to be educated."

I simply define prejudices against me as an educational problem, to be linked to the larger context of intercultural understanding. In a letter to a Canadian friend (1 Feb 1961), I wrote, "I see bridging the gulf of misunderstanding between the East and the West as a sacred mission…. We need people who are well acquainted with both sides."

David   "Gulf of misunderstanding" and "sacred mission" are emotionally laden expressions. I sense a deeper psychological meaning here. You came from a broken family; your parents had been separated since you were a child of ten years. You have two cultural parents, Chinese and American. Certainly you don't want to relive the pain of separation, this time between your cultural parents.

So you "transform pain into strength," as a Chinese saying puts it, to preserve their marriage, a marriage of cultures. In doing so, you deal with an internal psychological conflict through directing your energy outwards for a worthwhile cause.

To understand more fully how you prepared yourself for this process, tell us something about your educational history.

Education in and out of the Classroom

YF   My childhood education was mostly uneventful and unin-spiring. It did not prepare me well for anything. Reflecting on my educational history now, however, helps me to understand more deeply how education shapes the destiny of nations and is, there-fore, a critical component of psychohistory. I have two educational parents, Chinese and American, a comparison of which demands attention across the Pacific.

First, my childhood education was imbued with British colo-nialism. Hong Kong, where I was born and raised, was under British colonial rule. In my schooldays, students spent endless hours on arithmetic problems involving guineas, pounds, crowns, half-crowns, shillings, and pence—sterling units, now antiquated, they had never seen or touched. Do you know 1 half-crown = 2 shillings 6 pence = 1/8.4 guinea? That was surely an infamous chapter in the history of mathematics education.

In contrast, modern Chinese history was given truncated coverage by design. What was not in the syllabus was not examined and, therefore, would not be taught. Most young people, even if educated, had no or only fuzzy knowledge of Chinese history after 1911. Even today, you can find university students confusing the founding of the Republic of China in 1912 with that of the People's Republic of China in 1949.

David   Depriving a people of knowledge of its history is a powerful instrument of colonialism: It multiplies the effects of individual memory loss, even if reversible; it warps the normal development of selfhood and identity, at both individual and collec-tive levels.

Colonialism and missionary schools often go together. To what extent were you exposed to Christian education?

YF   I attended a Jesuit school for boys for six years. Its approach to religious education was dogmatic and impoverished through and through. I can still recite parts of the Catechism of the Catholic Church that provided me with the main diet of religious education in those years.

David   So, such religious education did nothing to awaken your spirituality. What were you like as a schoolboy?

YF   I was rather mischievous. The youngest and the smallest in my class, I horsed around and cracked jokes that caused the entire class to burst into laughter. This brought punishment upon me by humorless or, worse, sadistic teachers.

David   Chinese schoolchildren commonly have tales of horror to tell about their teachers and principals, don't they?

YF   In one therapy case I worked on, the school principal made a schoolboy stand in the hallway, wearing a humiliating placard for all to see. On the placard was written: "I received a zero-egg [literally, a zero mark]." The schoolboy became utterly resentful of all authority figures.

Chinese schoolchildren react to their teachers typically with fear, docility, silence, negativism, resentment, and outward compliance (but inward defiance) in front of their teachers; disrespect, noncompliance, and passive-aggression behind their backs. When they grow up, they react to authority figures likewise. Is the Chinese nation condemned to be made up mostly of people without guts?

Under ordinary circumstance, resentment and aggression are held in check or expressed indirectly. Students would ventilate anger in the form of passive or displaced aggression. They would "dare to be angry but not to voice a protest" and "forbear and swallow one's voice."

David   Under extraordinary circumstances, however, control mechanisms break down and aggression might erupt into the open. During the Great Cultural Revolution, aggression did erupt, this time in the form of unprecedented collective violence. Prompted by MAO Zedong, students revolted against institutional authority. Many got out of control, humiliated and acted with physical violence toward their teachers and professors.

In terms of psychohistory, your personal experiences both as a student and as a therapist make it easier to understand the phenomenon of student violence during the Great Cultural Revolution.

But there must have been some exceptional teachers whose good words or deeds made enough of a difference to your life to be remembered.

YF   Yes, a Jesuit teacher who taught us the true meaning of manhood comes to mind. In a self-study class, many students, including myself, were reading books outside of the curriculum (e.g., novels) we weren't supposed to read. We did it surreptitiously, hiding the books under desk covers. The teacher stood up and said to the class:

> Bring your books out, into the open. It's all right. Don't act like you have something to hide, as if you were a scoundrel. I'd rather see you act with openness and courage.

Unfortunately, most of the teachers were uninspired and uninspiring, morally or intellectually. Yet, they had great talent for reducing joyous learning to painful drudgery. They habitually repeated the same boring lessons time and again. Incredibly, the thought of boredom reduction seemed to have never once occurred in their minds. They have forgotten the days when they themselves were students.

So, to bring some life into the classroom, I made fun of teachers, targeting those and only those I held in low regard. What else was there to do? Intellectually speaking, those years were the "Dark Age" of my life. Never once, however, was I destructive or openly defiant.

David   Years later, you became a teacher yourself. What have you learned from the teachers of your "Dark Age"?

YF   I've learned that there is a connection between cowardice and being boring. So, as a teacher I shall summon all the courage to be true to myself—inspired and inspiring, never to bore.

David   One of the myths about Asia is that learning and education are highly valued in their own right. This is a romanticized ideal that falls short of reality. Closer to the truth is that academic qualifications are more highly valued than are learning and education per se. Pains have to be endured to secure the promised rewards of education—earning a better living and gaining upward social mobility.

Confucian-heritage education is dominated by examination superstition: examination results = academic performance = academic achievement = future academic achievement = occupational success or failure = socioeconomic status = personal and familial achievement = personal worth and glory/disgrace to the family.

What was your experience like?

YF   Academic achievement brought praise, more than anything else. During family gatherings, a favorite topic of conversation at the dinner table was the children's academic performance.

Children and, by proxy, their parents were pitted against one another. Those who excelled were singled out for praise; naturally, their parents gained face. Those who did not were ignored, left in silent resignation. Or, they might be hit with pointed remarks made by adults (including their own parents who felt they had lost face), such as, "Your cousin ranks first in his class. Why can't you learn to be more like him?" Not so subtly, academic ranking translated into social and personal ranking.

There was little encouragement for the development of independence, individuality, or creativity. And little or no attention to hands-on learning of practical, mechanical, or self-help skills (e.g., cooking).

In my childhood, my mother drove me out of the kitchen because she thought it was no place for her children to be. I was expected to excel in school; nothing else seemed to matter much. This explains, at least in part, my lifelong ineptitude in practical skills.

David   So you had a personal taste of examination superstition. Entrenched to the present day, this academic golden rule remains:

"Passing exams is the most important thing in one's education. In order to do well in exams, one has to do lots of homework." Chinese schoolchildren spend an inordinate amount of time on homework. But does quantity mean quality?

Here then is another myth: Repeated practice and doing a great amount of homework is the key to academic success. Reality: Stressing quantity, at the expense of quality, takes the joy out of learning; it leads schoolchildren to associate learning with drudgery, even punishment; and it would backfire, resulting in the extinction of intellectual curiosity and the thirst for knowledge.

Diligence is highly valued in Confucian-heritage education, but it is all too commonly equated with monotonous, repetitive practice. Perseverance is a Chinese virtue, but I sometimes wonder if the cost is numbness to boredom.

Perhaps I now understand why you feel so strongly about fostering creativity, personally and professionally.

YF   Are Chinese people incapable of feeling bored? That's a horrible specter.

Looking back, I can't see much lasting benefit from the untold hours I spent on homework as a schoolboy. My intellectual development would have been enhanced, had I been allowed to read materials (e.g., novels) outside of the prescribed, narrow syllabus. As a father of two daughters, I resented the excessive amount of homework they had to do, which robbed me of playful hours I could have spent with them.

As a therapist, I can testify that getting children to do their homework, or doing it for them (as is often the case), is a major burden in the life of Chinese parents. Doing homework is a major source of strain in parent-child relationships. Is it worth it?

In a nutshell, children are robbed of their childhood and of the joys of learning. The harmful effects of pushing too hard and too early are evident. To play the academic game, students study only what is set out in the curriculum. Having survived competitive exams, they are intellectually exhausted upon entering university; many feel they may now "relax."

David   Presumably, upon graduation obtaining a diploma means "academic success."

YF   But graduates may be hardly prepared for life and work. There is great irony in this educational failure. My students, for instance, have gone through highly structured systems, with rigidly defined paths. Yet, they are at a loss when they reflect on why they have chosen their concentration of study and on what they have really learned.

To prevent being misunderstood, I must make clear that I am not condemning examinations per se. Exams may be beneficial when they help students to find out what they don't know. The discovery of ignorance is the mother of gaining knowledge. The question is: Do exams serve to advance or to subvert the goals of education?

In sum, examination superstition subverts the goals of whole-person education in Confucian cultures. It renders educational systems to function like huge machines that sort students into hierarchical institutions according to exam results and warp their development in the process.

David   MAO Zedong, a fierce critic of Chinese education, minced no words:

> At present, there is too much study going on, and this is exceedingly harmful.... the burden is too heavy, it puts middle-school and university students in a constant state of tension.... The students should have time for recreation, swimming, playing ball, and reading freely outside their course work....
>
> Our present method of conducting examinations is a method for dealing with the enemy.... I am in favor of publishing the questions in advance and letting the students study them and answer them with the aid of books.... Whispering in other people's ears and taking

examinations in other people's names used to be done secretly. Let it now be done openly....

At present, we are doing things in too lifeless a manner....

The present method of education ruins talent and ruins youth.

It is most ironic that MAO's words are as relevant today as they were in his day. When will educators take his words seriously and confront the bane of examination superstition?

YF   We can't trust educators enough to put our children in their hands. Repeated calls for reforming education in Asia have been voiced for more than a century. In terms of reducing pressure, not much has been accomplished. If anything, academic pressure has intensified and has extended into even nursery schools. Even the unborn child is not left alone: Antenatal training (e.g., listening to English) for a head start is often practiced by parents among the urbanized middle class in mainland China.

Bookstores in East Asia are filled with titles pitched to parents on how to improve their children's IQ, academic performance, and so forth. The most ludicrous are titles on educational programs that confuse creative teaching with teaching creativity (uncreatively).

David   To me, creativity begins with undoing most of what we as adults have internalized in our educational history. For young children, creativity is as natural as breathing. All that educators and parents need to do is to respect the Dao of human development and refrain from crushing it.

FY   Examination superstition continues to grip students, parents, and teachers in an academic rat race with no diminishing force, sometimes with tragic consequences. Committing suicide is one way to exit from the rat race. Moreover, an alarming trend is that suicide is committed by younger and younger children.

A case in point is a 10-year-old Singaporean girl who committed suicide because she was stressed with schoolwork. The girl is reported to have said that she did not want to be reincarnated as a human being because it would mean going to school, doing homework, getting scolded. Among the youngest victims of education was a 7-year-old boy in Hong Kong, who failed an exam in Chinese dictation, went home and leaped out of his high-rise apartment.

As an educator and therapist, I have been a witness and participant in these education-induced tragedies. One student in mainland China, of whom I have served as mentor, puts it this way:

> I am scared my examination marks will not be high enough to earn me a place in a top university like Peking or Tsinghua. If I fail to get into Peking or Tsinghua, there will be no future for me. I may as well kill myself.

David   Alas, examination superstition and, more generally, perverted Confucian educational values are creeping into America. Witness the publication of Amy Chua's *Battle Hymn of the Tiger Mom*, in which she advocates harsh, even cruel parenting. Achievement at any cost?

Incredibly, she has a following. How gullible can Americans get? Nowadays, some Americans are also flocking to cram schools that were once a notorious Asian preserve. Do they really want to import the Asian education pressure cooker into American society?

YF   Relax! In mainland China, it is not unusual to see secondary school students assembled in their classrooms to study until after 10:00 p.m. or so, only to resume attending class by 7:00 a.m. the next morning. They are prepared to sacrifice their weekends, and much more, to prepare for exams. Are Americans prepared to do that? I doubt it.

I am optimistic that the Asian educational model from hell will be Americanized, rendered less pernicious, if and when it is transplanted across the Pacific.

David   Schools in America are generally happy places—barring senseless mass shootings by disgruntled individuals with access to lethal weapons. I see boys and girls participating actively in the classroom and running around, sometimes boisterously, in the school playground. They show little fear of teachers or other authority figures. In these respects, I wish Chinese schoolchildren could be more like them.

But I also wish that American schoolchildren could be more like traditional Chinese schoolchildren in other respects: more serious about studying, more steadfast in facing hardship, more respectful of teachers and other authority figures.

Why can't we have the best of both worlds? But, first you must tell the reader how you took step one to leap out of your intellectual "Dark Age."

Across the Pacific on My Way to Discover a New World

YF   At age sixteen, I went overseas to study in Canada together with my elder brother. We traveled by ship and train, as it was rather expensive to travel by plane in those days. I still remember *President Cleveland*, the ocean liner that took us to continental America, with nostalgia. The voyage took eighteen days across the Pacific to reach its destination, San Francisco, from where we continued to Canada.

David   You are the reincarnate of Columbus—from the East. I bet you were highly conscious of being among the lucky minority who had the privilege of studying overseas. Full of hope, you looked forward to getting the most out of not only a university education but also Western culture.

YF   That's right. The voyage marked a turning point in my life. It was not until twelve years later that I would set foot on Chinese soil again.

There were more than a hundred students on board *President Cleveland*, enough to create much excitement. Playing around and mingling with these fellow passengers for the entire voyage, I put to the back of mind my intention to study.

I wrote in my diary (circa Aug 1955):

> A huge fish jumping out of the surface of the sea, swimming faster than the ship; watching sunrise at four a.m., together with some female passengers; a risqué burlesque in Japan; watching the hula dance and using the surf board in Hawaii: These are all my first experiences, which I enjoy.

I remember how exhilarating it was to watch a snowfall and other natural wonders of a Canadian winter for the first time.

David Don't you now envy the youthful you who had such capacity for delight in the simple, wondrous things of the world? I also sense that the original emotions you had are being reawakened in the present as you describe the past. It is in your being to preserve youthfulness for as long as you can. It is part and parcel of spiritual striving.

What was your first exposure to university education in a foreign land like?

YF I found myself among giants, physically speaking, something I experienced initially as rather bewildering. I was the youngest student at Carleton College (now Carleton University). On one occasion, a bus driver issued me a ticket for a primary schoolchild. It was amusing.

I was awfully unprepared academically. My major was physics. I learned more in the first physics lecture than in the previous three years combined.

English was my major headache. I still remember the textbook I had for freshmen English. It was bulky, many more times thicker than the texts I had in Hong Kong. In it, close to half of the words on every page were words I had never before seen. Naturally, I failed freshman English, and had to take a supplementary exam.

My self-esteem suffered little loss. I simply construed the failure as a discovery of ignorance.

Then, I had the audacity to go to the dean and asked for permission to take a survey course in English literature in place of the required course in geology in my sophomore year. I argued with him until permission was granted. In hindsight, I feel that I made the right choice. I took to the survey course in English with a level of keenness that would have well-nigh impossible to attain for geology.

David   What kind of grades did you get generally?

YF   Being academically unprepared was not the main reason why my grades were bad: Unlike other Chinese students, I was not a "good" student. Attending university was like a child entering a playroom full of intriguing toys. Finally, I thought to myself, I was out of the dark age of my secondary school days in Hong Kong. Homework was no longer doing repetitive exercises; composition was no longer drudgery; and learning was no longer unrelated to life, but joyous and meaningful.

Mingling with Canadian students in extracurricular and social activities was an eye-opening experience. They worked together, they practiced democracy, and they knew how to have fun.

In sharp contrast, my fellow Chinese students, all of whom were from Hong Kong, did not know how to work together. Most of them were reluctant to assume leadership positions, but treated those who did as targets of animosity. During meetings, they bickered endlessly among themselves, with nothing much accomplished in the end. I felt ashamed of being Chinese.

David   They were not just "a pile of loose sand," as Dr. SUN Yat Sen, the founder of the Chinese republic, used to say, but an assembly of warring cliques. Defying stereotypes (unwittingly reinforced by cross-cultural psychologists), the Canadians were behaving like "collectivists" and the Chinese like "individualists."

Back in the 1950s, studying psychology was virtually unheard of among overseas Chinese students. How did you become a psychologist?

YF   Although my major was physics, I could not resist the temptation of exploring other subjects. I roamed the library and read books unrelated to physics. I sat in courses in which I had not registered and made diagnostic assessments of professors on the inspiring-boring spectrum.

The psychology professor Harold Breen, who brought me relief from my conflicts over sexual impulses, was particularly fascinating. He had deep-set blue eyes and a mustache, looking rather like the philosopher Friedrich Nietzsche. I followed him around, looking for opportunities to talk with him. Sensing that I had an interest in psychology, he invited me to audit his Personality Dynamics course.

That was my very first exposure to psychology; it took place during my freshman year. There were no lectures, only discussions. No syllabus, no lecture notes, and no formal examination. Textbook learning was not emphasized.

David   To a Chinese student, this must have been strange indeed!

YF   The students did not appear knowledgeable, even to one as ignorant as I was. Yet the remarkable thing was that most of them seemed genuinely interested in the subject matter and participated actively in discussions. They struggled to apply psychological principles to understand life better. They expressed their opinions freely, arguing with one another and even with the professor.

At first, I was hesitant to speak. One day, I marshaled enough courage to open my mouth. No one laughed at me. Professor Breen encouraged me to speak up more. Since then, I have found it difficult to keep my mouth shut. This got me into lots of trouble after I returned to Chinese societies many years later.

I was not sure what I had learned, probably not much that could be measured in a traditional examination. Nonetheless, I began to ponder questions I had never before thought of. The seeds for a lifelong quest had been sown.

David   What was your experience of graduate studies? What special training did you receive? What have you learned about yourself through psychology?

YF   At age twenty, I left Canada and moved to the United States. After obtaining a degree in physics, I decided to enter graduate school to study psychology—to the dismay of my parents and the bewilderment of other Chinese students. That is why I am a psychologist today.

David   Had you been deprived of these opportunities in North America, you would have suffocated under the Hong Kong educational system or have been eliminated altogether by it.

YF   That's why I remain grateful to Canada and the United States to this day.

I took to psychology as a fish to water. My specialization was clinical psychology. Studying psychology was like eating the forbidden fruit of knowledge. Eyes opened, I read the psychopathology within my own family. I became critical of the repressive, conservative, and authoritarian aspects of Chinese culture.

My mother complained that I had become a bad, unfilial son after I began studying psychology. "It's largely on account of you that I have decided to study psychology. I want to know how to deal with my mother," I informed her.

David   So knowledge can lead to, or accentuate, conflicts. Psychological knowledge, in particular, can be outright dangerous. But for you the pursuit of knowledge is a cardinal drive that has seen no diminished intensity for more than half a century.

I bet you were eager to apply the knowledge you had acquired.

YF   I engineered a revolution in a mental hospital (Elgin State Hospital in Illinois), where I did my internship and later worked as a staff psychologist in the 1960s. The hospital was a monstrosity, with over 5,000 mental patients. It was like a small town unto itself, with its own electric generator, canteens, laundries, staff quarters.

David   Like other total institutions, such as prisons and concentration camps, it encompassed the inmates' whole being, subjected them to regimentation and undermined their individuality and dignity. Institutionalization rendered patients increasingly dependent on the hospital, and turned them into chronic patients with nowhere else to go. It was a place of hopelessness. Much like the setting of the film *One Flew Over the Cuckoo's Nest*.

YF   Soon after completing my internship, I conducted milieu therapy in the hospital. I declared that the first target of treatment was none other than the hospital itself, not the patients. I challenged the hierarchical authority structure of the institution. I wrote an article, one of the earliest I ever published, entitled, "Staff Too Can Be Institutionalized," which ruffled feathers.

I introduced democracy to a ward of chronic patients, some of whom had been hospitalized for more than thirty years: I empowered the patients to organize themselves, elect their own leaders, and insofar as possible make their own decisions. I organized the staff, and won them over to participate in the process of democratization.

David   You also stepped on people's toes, when you challenged their habitual ways of operation or threatened their vested interests.

YF   My supervisor said I took on a job he wouldn't have for a million dollars. However, statistics spoke to the fruits of my labor: Within a few months, discharge rate went up three times. Not that the discharged were cured; it went up largely because the discharged patients were reconnected with their families, deinstitutionalized. The milieu therapy continued, even after I left the hospital; by that measure, I regard the therapy as having its greatest success.

David   Like a dreadnought battleship in World War I, you were a force to be reckoned with; and like a bull in a china shop, you were fearless.

YF   As a Chinese saying puts it, "A new born calf does not fear the tiger"—because it is too ignorant or stupid to fear. Acquiring knowledge was not enough; I wanted action.

It is ironic that what I succeeded in doing in a mental hospital I couldn't even begin to try in an institution of higher learning, namely, the University of Hong Kong, where I spent most of my professional life after returning to Hong Kong.

David   Your experience at Elgin State Hospital speaks to an admirable feature of American society: its receptivity to new ideas.

There is still more room than probably most other places for an individual, through heroic effort, to make a difference.

YF   More action: Back in 1964, I took part in a demonstration against the war in Vietnam. A group of protesters sat down in the middle of a street, right in the heart of downtown Chicago. Among them I was the only Asian.

Arrested, I was locked up in a crowded prison cage, together with other male protesters, for some thirty-six hours. I cherish that experience, for now I know what it means to lose one's freedom, if only for a short time.

David   Speaking about the Vietnam War, horrors come to mind: napalm that consumed human flesh and bones; "saturation bombing of suspected targets"—in translation, indiscriminate bombing in the absence of reliable intelligence; Buddhist monks who set themselves on fire, as a *non*-final act of protest.

Remember Agent Orange? A chemical agent dropped by the tons to defoliate forests, so the North Vietnamese and Vietcong (Vietnamese communists) had nowhere to hide. Now, by the third generation, deformed children continue to be born.

YF   I lived through those exciting years—of the civil rights movement, Martin Luther King, protest against the war in Vietnam—as a graduate student in the United States. While other Chinese students were preoccupied with getting a Ph.D., a job, and a wife/husband, nearly always in that unchanging order, I became an activist.

Sad to say, America seems to have lost its sense of direction, its compassion for the needy or the oppressed, and its place in the world of nations as a beacon of hope, as it enters into the twenty-first century. Some say that the American Dream is dead or dying. I feel that one-half of my being is under threat.

David   So the actions you took on your path to personal liberation were linked to social conflicts in America, not China. In effect, you were saying: Personal liberation derives greater meaning and potency when it is enlarged to include liberation for all humanity.

But actions for liberation typically invite suppression. Did you get into any trouble?

YF   I suspected that the FBI opened a file on me. After I became naturalized, I exercised my right to request access to surveillance information gathered on citizens. The FBI sent me a copy of my file. How disappointing: There was nothing in it about myself that I didn't already know!

David   Nonetheless, it was a concrete demonstration of how the United States is run by the rule of law, and how the individual may stand undiminished against the might of government.

YF   The place where I lived was Hyde Park in Chicago, where the University of Chicago is located and where the streets were (are still?) infested with crime. It is a place with unmatched intellectual intensity. I understand Obama a little better, after discovering that he lived for many years in Hyde Park. Bittersweet reminiscence of me running around Hyde Park as a wayward young man still lingers in my mind.

Some years ago, I visited Vietnam. I fired an AK-47; none of the bullets hit their target. I crawled into a tunnel where the Vietnamese used to live for extended periods of time and fought the Americans with untold sacrifice; I felt extremely uncomfortable after only some twenty minutes.

I made it a point to go around asking how people felt about the war and Americans. This is what Chinese people call octogrammic (*bagua*, meaning nosy) investigation. I found no trace of hatred or animosity toward Americans! The people actively practice forgiveness. I suspect that being Buddhist has much to do with it.

David   Your extracurricular activities, such as engineering a revolution in a mental hospital and being jailed for antiwar protest, are integral to your education in America.

YF   However, they pale in comparison with cultural uprooting. A long time ago, I made a drastic decision: to uproot myself from Chinese culture.

I thought it was an essential step I had to take to become a serious psychologist. I was then at Elgin State Hospital. For several years, I had no contact with Chinese people. I spoke only English, even in my dreams. The psychology I absorbed into my being was devoid of Chinese content.

David   Uprooting oneself from one's culture is not something I would recommend to other people without great caution. It is probably irreversible. Moreover, it does not mean rooting oneself in another culture. Neither Eastern nor Western: That makes a marginal person.

YF   For years, I walked on tight ropes, continually trying to balance myself between conflicting demands. After much anguish, I acted to transform marginality into strength. I began to look at the East and the West alike with both attachment and detachment. I worked to absorb the best and discard the worst from both worlds, even to create an East-West synthesis.

Since then, I stand in and out of the two worlds with greater ease. Values are no longer anchored in any one culture. To serve as an agent for intercultural understanding has become a cardinal motive that impels my lifework. Still rootless, I have become a world citizen.

Reverse Culture Shock in an Anachronistic University

David   After an unbroken absence of twelve years, you returned to Hong Kong as a liberated, transformed person, imbued with democratic, egalitarian values strengthened by your North American experiences. You cherished the opportunity to serve as an agent of East-West understanding. The stark reality, however, was that Hong Kong remained what it had always been: mercantile and colonial. I sense trouble.

YF That's right. Going overseas for higher education was no culture shock. My student days in North America were formative of my worldviews. In contrast, my reentry into Hong Kong was traumatic. The society where I was born and raised had become alien to me. Nothing had prepared me for the shock of reentry. My academic career was marked by contradictions and agonies.

David The University of Hong Kong, where you worked, was dense with anachronism. Hoity-toity Oxbridge pretensions and Mandarin scholasticism (some say academic warlordism) were marital partners made in heaven. External examiners, mostly from the U.K., descended on the local scene, to be treated like overlords.

American scholarship was treated with condescension, as second class ("The American doctorate is equivalent to the British master's degree" was uttered with predictable regularity—a defensive reaction to the threat of increasing American dominance and corresponding decreasing British status). Chinese language and learning were relegated to third-class status.

YF An English lecturer in philosophy once asked, "Is there such a thing as philosophy in Taiwan?" Status distinctions were nonnegotiable, as in the glorious days of Empire. Even washrooms were differentially marked for "gentlemen" (reserved for senior staff) and for "boys" (reserved for minor staff).

Pomp and circumstance received more attention than intellectual pursuits. I saw precious little evidence of universities functioning as centers of East-West learning or intercultural exchange.

Most expatriates led self-imposed ghetto-like lives, with little or no meaningful interaction with the local people, as if they had never left their home country. They had no need and were unable to converse in the local language (Cantonese), even after having lived in Hong Kong for decades.

David All these factors make good material for a case study of how intelligent and knowledgeable people can be self-encapsulated.

YF The University of Hong Kong was a place of racial separation and thinly disguised racial discrimination. Entering the Senior

Common Room, into which minor staff were not admitted, you would find with few exceptions the expatriates in one quarter and the local Chinese in another.

Expatriate (mostly British) staff had generous perks (e.g., heavily subsidized housing, paid long-term leave) that local (i.e., Chinese) staff did not have. Of course, such discrimination was rationalized on high principles that most people today would find blatantly hypocritical.

David   Thus, colonialism corrupted academic institutions, which corrupted the academic staff, who in turn, acting as negative role models, corrupted the students.

YF   Even by design, it would be difficult to achieve the efficiency with which these institutions produced students with a turtle-like syndrome: refusing to stick their necks out, speak up, or act like young adults with a vision or passion for living.

David   Inequality in political, military, and economic power between ethnic groups produces unhealthy intergroup relations and breeds prejudices. What were the relations like?

YF   Unhealthy intragroup relations as well. I had never encountered so much emotional masking, distancing, and frigid embitterment. On the face of a self-proclaimed "world-class" professor was written his untold story: Every maxillofacial muscle was twisted, betraying inner rage. I shuddered when I saw him, even though we never exchanged a word.

When I first arrived at the university, I had the habit of greeting colleagues spontaneously. Some responded with a mixture of hesitation, embarrassment, condescension; some with autistic-like avoidance of eye contact. Some people showed determination not to allow collegial relationships to move an iota closer, no matter how sincerely I tried.

David   You experienced unconditional rejection, without being given any opportunity for interaction—possibly because you did not belong to their clique.

YF   Academics at the University of Hong Kong excelled in games of one-upmanship. One such game was peculiarly popular: treating you as if you did not exist. On quite a few occasions, I interacted with some expatriate colleague at a party, only to find later that the same colleague behaved as if he had never seen me before.

A scholar from Japan invited some expatriates to a banquet; on the next day, one of them did not "recognize" his Japanese host from the evening before. Chinese colleagues played the game as well, apparently having acquired the requisite mind-set from their expatriate counterparts. To an educator, most disconcerting was to witness students emulating their teachers—pretending upon seeing their teachers that they did not exist, especially after graduation.

David   Were there moments when you doubted your sanity?

YF   Social validation reassured me that I was not the one insane. Friends, both Chinese and non-Chinese, shared with me similar experiences they had. Painfully I learned to adjust my emotional temperature in the midst of a refrigerator. I learned to value the resilience of many of my colleagues and students; they were exemplars of being sane in "insane" places.

Before turning to a more pleasant topic, I must make clear my intent: to indict evil conditions that produce toxic relations in which human nature is warped. Nothing I have said implicates individuals, expatriate or local, as evil.

As an interesting postscript, Hong Kong, unlike Singapore and India, shows little vestige of Anglophilia after the end of colonial rule.

David   Now times have changed. There are indications of exchange on a more egalitarian basis and an increasing flow of knowledge in the East-to-West direction. These indications reflect a changing global balance of economic prowess. If history is a guide, political and military power will eventually follow.

YF   To conclude:

East is East, and West is West.
Excesses in one mirror deficiencies in the other, and vice versa.
Each has something from which the other needs to learn,
And something that the other should reject.
East is West, and West is East:
The world will be a better place.

The Golden Age of My Life

David   Fast forward to the years from 2003 to 2007, which may be said to be the golden age of your life. The age was golden not because it came during the "golden years" of old age, but because of three developments. First, your work environment could not have been better; your relations with coworkers were warm and mutually satisfying. Second, you derived great joy from teaching and felt affirmed as an educator. Third, your literary-artistic impulses, long repressed, found expression.

Of great significance is the fact that the golden age is also the period during which four of your episodes of madness occurred. This runs counter to the usual pattern wherein abnormal conditions occur during periods of stress, traumatization, or depression. Now, tell us more about your golden age.

YF   In the summer of 2003, I was invited to join the faculty in a teaching and research center at the University of Hong Kong. Thus began the golden age of my life, at least as far as work was concerned. I was freed from administrative duties and conflicts arising from vested personal interests that abound in academia. I was above the fray of backstabbing and petty power struggles that were all too common elsewhere in the university.

David   For decades, your working environment could be described as an emotional refrigerator, with temperatures sometimes dropping to those of a freezer. There, one could observe self-contained individualism in a not-so-collectivist Chinese society: academics locked in their offices, caring little about their colleagues, passing each other by in the hallway often without greeting or acknowledging the other's existence.

YF   Here, in contrast, the atmosphere at work couldn't be better. So coming to the center was like diving into a hot spring from an icy cave.

I have had many appointments in diverse locations: Canada, the continental United States, Hawaii, the Philippines, Taiwan, mainland China, and, of course, Hong Kong. The center surpassed them all. It was like a family, where people really cared for one another. At lunch, we would eat together, making jokes. I never laughed so much, so heartily in all my life. If laughter be the measure, then it was surely the happiest time I have had.

My relations with coworkers were excellent. I maintained no distinctions based on status or age.

David   Generally, you find putting on professorial airs, all too common by academics in Chinese societies, to be distasteful....

YF   My spontaneous, mischievous ways were a source of collegial joviality. My coworkers viewed me as humorous, scholarly, and talented. I didn't mind being the object of laughter, most often because of my well-known gullibility. I was not easily offended.

In short, my coworkers, most of whom were much younger than I was, viewed me as a jovial, harmless father figure they could trust. To many, I was their unofficial mentor. (By mutual consent, they refer to me privately as their Black Market Mentor.) Each day, I would look forward to going to work—actually to "play" while working.

David   I can't resist saying the obvious. In some ways, you match the stereotype of a nerdy professor. For instance, you don't normally dress like a professor, do you? How did your coworkers react to your nerdiness?

YF   I attach more importance to what's underneath the clothes I wear than to clothing. I hate shopping, especially for clothing. That's enough to prompt many a student to buy me articles of clothing as gifts. I feel rich, not impoverished, no matter what I wear.

However, my work at the center involved meeting VIPs, local and overseas. So it was fitting for me to pay more attention to my attire. My coworkers were all too ready to help. A trendy research assistant volunteered to accompany me for a shopping excursion. The end result: Not a trace of nerdiness could be found anymore.

David   I wish attaining enlightenment could be that easy. What about your role as a teacher?

YF   As a teacher, I felt liberated and affirmed. In a message to several of my close relatives about workshops I conducted (22 May 2005), I wrote:

> People were moved to tears, transformed. They gained self-respect. They learned to communicate more effectively, and less defensively. They dared to do things they had never done before (like speaking before a large audience, confronting their hidden selves). They began to face life with renewed conviction.

In no small measure, they were touched by my intellectual, moral, and spiritual presence. It gives me great comfort that I have brought greater happiness to the world through my actions.

David   It sounds as if you were self-liberated. In teaching, as in therapy, one cannot liberate others unless one is self-liberated first. Self-liberated from perfectionism, you encourage your students to accept and not to conceal their imperfection at the expense of authenticity. Having greater courage to be yourself, however imperfect, you insist on their being authentic.

YF   In a message I wrote to my students (27 Sept 2006), I stated:

You are what you are, always. Everything you say or do reveals what you are as a person, imperfect, with your strengths as well as foibles. In a sense, therefore, it is impossible not to "self-disclose." Better to be an imperfect, but real, therapeutic agent than to play the phony role of a counselor.

David   Acceptance of imperfection facilitates authenticity by reducing the need to conceal one's imperfection behind a facade. That's a central idea implied in your message. You abhor spurious role playing among helping professionals. Authenticity ranks no less in ordinary life as in therapy.

But I must also ask: Do you know how much students may be scared of you?

YF   Of course. They come into my office like scared rabbits or mice seeing a cat, formal, stiff, uneasy. But I am no cat. I dislike status distinctions, and I don't humiliate students, ever. Those who are not afraid of me have no problem.

David   Your standards are high. Your logic is as sharp as a knife. And you speak your mind. That makes you enough of a cat to make a student feel like a little mouse.

YF   On top of that, one of my teaching assistants once said to me point-blank: "You look too solemn. You don't smile much. So students find it hard to approach you, even though you are actually approachable. Remember to smile!"

I listened, and I was thankful. She was one of those who weren't afraid of me.

David   So you like those who aren't afraid of you. What about those who are? As a psychologist, you ought to know how strong an emotion jealousy can be.

YF   Oh, yes. Some years ago, I became aware of a strange "scale of favor" my clinical psychology students once invented. It was like the Hang Seng Index, except that instead of tracking the Hong Kong stock market it purported to track the favor I showed to specific students on a daily basis. This home-made scale came to me as a wake-up call.

I do have a problem of being too transparent. When I like someone, I make no effort to hide my feelings. That can be a problem for a group I interact with intensively. Recently, a student gave me this wise counsel: "In a group situation, it's best if members feel that your attention is evenly divided." It could have come only from a woman.

After much reflection, I changed some of my ways. But it is liberation from guilt and self-doubt that has truly enabled me to seize the opportunity to educate, now that external circumstances have changed for the better.

David As a high-impact teacher, you have heavy responsibilities. You must remain sensitive to the fact that many students yearn for your recognition—just as your daughters need their father's approval.

Finally, you have mellowed, much like a fully-flavored fruit asking to be plucked from a tree. This enables you to become far more effective, influential, and inspirational as a teacher. The courage to be your true self, in and out of the classroom, holds the key.

YF I maintain correspondence with my students after formal teaching has terminated. Here is one of the email messages I received: "It's always a pleasure to read your emails (and of course a bigger pleasure and honor to attend your class) … I am so impressed by your knowledge, wit, and heart." Another one says, "You already are our master-mentor-friend. I do not have any doubt about it." And another, "Indeed, your teaching has touched my life and I will always bear that in mind."

These are messages that have sustained me, even in my darkest moments.

David You define a facilitative teacher-student relationship as *the relational context in which the student and the teacher discover, apply, and generate knowledge.* This relationship forms the source from which teaching and learning proceed. A facilitative relationship has to be created; it is not present at the beginning. Creating this relationship is a joint endeavor. The act of creation transforms its creators. In an important sense, then, learning is self-learning, and education is self-transformation.

YF   My priorities are to be, in ascending order, a clinical psychologist, psychologist, social scientist, scientist, educator, thinker, writer, person of integrity. I want to be a member of the human family dedicated to ecumenical ideals, an educator committed to whole-person development, a social scientist with broad intellectual interests, a psychologist with research and clinical skills. Humility comes from knowing how far I have fallen short of realizing my ideals.

David   Your golden age is an age of generativity during which you direct your energy to guide and nurture younger generations, such as mentoring budding colleagues and touching the lives of students.

There is still another side of you, long unrecognized. "Be the artist that you are": That's the inner voice you have been hearing, most loudly during your golden age.

YF   Actually, I heard this inner voice no less loudly in my student days in North America. It subsided after I returned to Hong Kong and became absorbed in my academic career. For years, I did not think of myself as artistic in temperament.

A visit to my historical self, however, contradicts this assessment. As a Chinese student in the United States, I did many things that were singularly unusual. I went dancing on the south side of Chicago, where I found myself the only non-African-American present. I also took up folk dancing. The music of the Middle East gets into my blood after a while. Once I went to a folk dance camp and danced for three days and nights, with little rest. My body was dead tired, but the music drove me onwards.

I love music and dancing, but I never thought I had much artistic talent. And I still don't think I have. Fortunately, talent is not necessary for reveling in the performing arts, as I have said to my students:

> I would rather be a third-rate musician or performing artist than a first-rate psychologist. But, without talent,

what could I do? This is why I stand before you today as your psychology teacher. Please don't look at this negatively. For, to know and accept one's limitations is the beginning of wisdom.

David   The episodes of madness, in which heightened aesthetic sensibilities, self-expression, and ecstasy figure prominently, have reawakened my artistic impulses.

YF   On account of this alone, I would have reason to be grateful. But there is more: the artistic impulses have joined forces with my literary bent, which I discovered only several years before my first episode. It was as late as December 1995 that I attempted to wrote my very first poem.

Rewriting the Golden Rule

Pronominal reversals
Are symptomatic of infantile autism.
What audacity it is,
Therefore, to rewrite
The Golden Rule, "Do unto others
As you would have others do unto you,"
By a humble pronominal reversal,
And end up with "Do unto others
As *others* would have *you* do unto them."
Yet, this humility brings forth
The karma of selflessness.
And self-consciousness, now wedded
To the Dao of empathy,
Has taken a quantum leap.

Untutored, I was groping in the dark. A few more years brewed before I took writing poetry seriously, and many more meandered before I began to take myself seriously as a writer. Actually, however, my literary bent had been present, though not cultivated, long before that. I have always loved Chinese poetry. But I never dreamed that I had the ability to write poetry, in Chinese or English.

My interest in literary pursuits, creative writing in particular, is negatively correlated with my interest in academia. Increasingly, I find writing for scholarly journals unbearably dreary. It drains me of the energy and time that I would rather spend on more meaningful activities, such as writing this book.

During Mania 2, I did a free association in which I wrote down everything as it occurred in my mind without censorship; it represented an escape from the compulsive perfectionism I have long suffered from when it comes to writing.

David   Ordinarily, you impose on yourself the task of making everything easier for the reader: to connect and organize ideas in ways that allow them to flow smoothly and logically; to anticipate the reader's reactions, queries, or doubts; to save the reader time by high-density writing, to pack as much as possible in the least number of words; to double check the factual accuracy of contents; and so forth. Readers of this book may have sensed this perfectionism by now.

In all, the episodes have forced you to realize that temperamentally you are much closer to the artist than to the academic. To that extent, you have not been leading an authentic existence. Your desire to be an artist in living and relating has found expression in your golden age. Surely this is a milestone in your personal journey of spiritual discoveries.

YF   I did worry that the golden age would not last long. It was simply too good to last. I was determined to enjoy it as much as possible while it lasted. And in fact, by the summer of 2005, the environment at work began to decline. Some left the center under unhappy circumstances. By the summer of 2007, when I left the center, also under unhappy circumstances, the golden age had ended.

Confucianism, Shame, and Thought Liberation

David   Now that you have given your life account from child-hood to golden age, it's time to reflect. Your account strengthens the impression that you are not a typical Chinese: To pursue a career in clinical psychology, to be politically active, to be immersed in American culture, for instance, were almost unheard of among overseas Chinese students in the 1960s.

Why are you so atypical? Not by choice, I suppose, for atypicality typically makes life more difficult. You simply accept it as a fact of your existence. Perhaps you can even exploit it to your advantage.

YF   Not typical of anything, anywhere. I have always been a minority among minorities, being different, wherever I find myself.

The typical Chinese is one oversocialized, subdued in Confucian culture. For as long as I can remember, I have had instinctive antipa-thies to Confucianism. It strangles the Dionysian spirit. I discern no dialectical thinking in the *Confucian Analects*. Confucius says—end of dialogue. In contrast, the Daoist philosophers Laozi and Zhuangzi come across as dialectical thinkers. They have inspired me in my journey of spiritual discoveries.

Daoism underlies the golden age of my life, particularly with regard to removing psychological barriers stemming from differences in status. Zhuangzi speaks of the equality of all things: "The great Dao is all-embracing without making distinctions."

David   Equality ascends when no categorical distinctions among people are made. This strikes at the heart of Confucian societal order founded on well-defined status hierarchies, which you regard as a barrier to bidirectional communication and the formation of egalitarian relationships.

YF   I recall the apprehensive thought I had when I obtained my doctoral degree: "The degree transforms my social identity. It can place a distance between me and other people. Beware." Does "Ph.D." stand for "permanent head damage," in a manner of speaking?

David   An important point you make is that Confucianism has inculcated in the Chinese mind not just a sense of shame, but also feelings of shamefulness. As Mencius declared, "Those who do not have a sense of shame and dislike are not human," that is, no different from beasts.

That's why you say one of your goals in life is to become "shameless"—getting rid of not the sense of shame (i.e., the capacity to feel repugnance toward things evil), but feelings of shamefulness about oneself. Your thoughts about shame are captured in one of your epigrams (3 Jan 2009):

> The sense of shame has been a shackle on the Chinese soul. Ridding ourselves of it would open the door to creativity. Alas, the sense of shame is now eclipsed by avarice in mainland China in its blind quest for economic development. On the other hand, strengthening the sense of shame would restore time-honored standards for conduct in American society, especially for celebrities and politicians.

And in a poem you wrote (March 2004):

Shamefaced

I dreamt I was on stage, naked,
In front of a thousand piercing eyes, staring
At me. My face is a face that does not dare
To show itself. Nowhere to hide,
Not even from myself.
But what have I done wrong?

YF   Being Chinese, I have an entrenched sense of shame. To become shameless is a most formidable goal, which I have yet to reach after a lifetime of self-therapy. Only in episodes of madness do I find total relief.

David   That said, I wish to add that in many ways what America lacks China has in abundance, and vice versa. Strengthening the sense of shame would be good for American society, just as loosening thought control would be for Chinese society.

YF   Central to the Confucian tradition is to have no depraved thoughts—think not what is contrary to propriety. Underlying propriety is the basic virtue of sincerity. Because sincerity means purity of thought, "impure" thoughts must be purged. Not only impulse, but also thought control! No wonder we had the campaign against "spiritual pollution" in China not long ago.

David   Confucian thinking on morality has always assumed that there is a fundamental distinction between right and wrong, that the human mind is able to grasp this distinction and to act accordingly. The distinction cannot be disputed, because it is an extension of the cosmic principle into the social realm. Of course, Confucian scholars are anointed to decide what constitutes right versus wrong. You have traced some of your negative personal experiences to Confucian origination.

YF   I draw on my multicultural experiences that span decades in North America, Hawaii, and Asia (mainland China, Taiwan, Hong Kong, Singapore, the Philippines). At every turn, I see pernicious traces of Confucianism in Chinese family life: paternalism, prejudice, and discrimination against women; overprotection, overindulgence, infantilization of children, especially of males, by mothers and grandmothers.

In the midst of my mother's funeral in New York, a Chinese funeral director proclaimed, "Chinese people do not include the names of female descendents in elegiac couplets." My sisters and I protested. The funeral director, who saw himself as a defender of tradition, became nasty and began using foul language. It was one of the most painful experiences I have had in my life. The legacy of Confucius lingers in the land of the free.

David   The contrast between the Confucianism and psychoanalysis is most explicit with regard to thought control. Psychoanalysis is predicated on the total eradication of *all* restrictions on thought: Nothing is unthinkable. It makes a fundamental distinction between thoughts and actions. Thoughts are, in themselves, harmless and innocent. Only in the realm of actions is the exercise of control relevant.

To dare to think the unthinkable is the fountainhead of creativity. Internalized thought control suffocates the will to defy oppression. You have made these points in writing and in speech.

YF   Yes, I openly declare, in the spirit of Thomas Jefferson, eternal hostility to all forms of oppression over freedom of thought and speech. This is a celebration of my way to personal liberation. Unfortunately, however, I am also all too aware that the battle for freedom in China is far from over.

From Marginality to World Citizenship: The Will to Master

David   Of the things you have said, cultural uprooting stands out, because it is so drastic. Yet you don't reject yourself as a Chinese, and you are not anti-Chinese. In fact, you are proud of the treasure trove of Chinese history and culture; you practice Chinese martial arts, and you love Chinese poetry.

This has to be pointed out, if only to rectify the misleading impression of being anti-Chinese you might have given on account of your critical comments about Confucianism. Please expand and clarify on this point.

YF   To be precise, I was uprooting myself from Confucianism, rather than Chinese culture per se. After my return to Hong Kong,

I dug deep into my cultural roots. The result: I felt more holistic as a Chinese person. By then, however, being Chinese is only a part of my identity as a world citizen; being American figures prominently in that identity.

David   The will to master marginality leads only to world citizenship. World citizens live in appreciation of diversity.

YF   But I also tend to be more critical of the "ugly Chinese" when I live in China and of the "ugly Americans" when living in the United States.

In the midst of one of my episodes of madness (Hypomania 8, chap. 2), I wrote: "I sometimes get the feeling that Americans treat dogs better than humans. In the past I have also heard remarks made by Chinese people that they would rather be a dog in America than a human in China" (9 April 2010).

David   Such musing is indicative of the comfort you feel in being a Chinese-American. So is this is a happy answer to the question of who you are, Chinese or American, raised in the beginning of our interview? Have you achieved an integrated identity?

YF   Not quite entirely happy. Being bicultural magnifies my being atypical and different from others. It is certainly an asset, but it also complicates my life, particularly in terms of interpersonal relationships.

I don't mean I have a fragmented identity, with divergent aspects of itself in uneasy coexistence. I do have one foot rooted comfortably in Chinese culture and the other in Euro-American culture. These two cultures are synthesized in my mind, such that the specter of a schism between them would not arise. I switch between the two with ease, functioning appropriately depending on the cultural background of the people I interact with.

Rather, my unhappiness refers to complications in communicating and relating with other people that being bicultural can bring. I experience anguish when I wish others to fully understand me as a bicultural person.

David   You are expecting too much! Being so fully understood rarely happens, unless you are in the company of people who have been immersed in both cultures. Be prepared that, most of the time, you are going to be only half-understood. People from a Chinese background would have trouble comprehending your American side; likewise people from a Euro-American background would have trouble comprehending your Chinese side.

Moreover, you will find yourself often caught in reciprocal stereotypes and prejudices that people from one background have toward those from the other.

YF   A highly educated Chinese woman decided to terminate her brief acquaintance with me after I sent her some materials I had written on intercultural interaction. The reason: She found American culture alien to her and was apprehensive about the cultural distance between us.

This happens rarely; in fact, most people I know view my bicultural background favorably. Nonetheless, being bicultural can be a cursed predicament; and it is difficult to explain the anguish it may bring, especially to people without a bicultural background.

David   This accounts for why you want so much "to serve as an agent for intercultural understanding." You envision the day will come when bicultural or even multicultural persons are no longer viewed as marginal individuals but as models for advancing world citizenship.

In this connection, psychologists speak of multicultural competence. I don't think competence can be achieved without having a solid self-identity and self-esteem to begin with; at least, competence would be much more difficult to attain.

Self-esteem is as important as it is badly misunderstood. It's important because without it you would not dare to engage in dialogues (or play Ping-Pong) with your teachers or supervisors. Lacking in self-esteem, we would be misers in both giving and receiving: not knowing how to show or to respond to appreciation. Worse still, we might be lavish in belittling others.

It's misunderstood because educators and therapists often confuse the promotion of self-esteem with that of self-deception (e.g., saying to a child, "You can do whatever you set out to do," irrespective of the child's aptitudes).

YF   From this perspective, the self-esteem movement in America is largely misguided. There are cultural differences: People in the United States are more generous and direct in giving compliments than people in Chinese societies. In the United States, sometimes I take with a grain of salt compliments people give me. In Hong Kong, some former students tell me, rather unexpectedly, how they have been influenced by what I had done or said years before; that makes me very happy.

Self-esteem has not been much of a problem for me. Trouble comes with episodes of madness, during which my self-esteem becomes inflated.

David   More fundamental than self-esteem is the will to master. Self-esteem grows out of achieving a sense of mastery in life—not to be equated with the Confucian preoccupation over scholastic, occupational, or any other kind of achievement. It requires patience and hard work. Being appreciated by significant others for what one is and what one has done helps to foster its growth. But self-esteem based on empty slogans, "positive reinforcements" given mechanically or unconditionally, and other artificial means rests on a pile of loose sand.

Feelings of self-doubt and self-torment can no more be decreed out of consciousness than self-acceptance be decreed into existence. They do not necessarily imply an absence of self-esteem. They are an essential part of human experience; they may be restructured into a new, kinder concept of the self. If they activate the will to master and impel us to take constructive *actions*, then they too have positive value.

YF   I accept the generalization that Asians tend to lack self-esteem vis-à-vis Americans, just as Americans lack modesty vis-à-vis Asians. I therefore pray there will be more promotion of self-mastery and modesty, less of self-deception in the United States; more of self-esteem, less of shaming and self-debasement, in Chinese societies.

David   You have had plenty of unpleasant experiences, such as being rejected on account of prejudice or racism, on your path to world citizenry. In view of these experiences, how has the will to master developed in your personal journey?

YF   There are experiences for which the word "unpleasant" would make a gross understatement. My encounters with discrimination, racism, and rejection during my student days in North America were hurtful, but they did not damage my self-esteem or self-identity.

Observing self-rejection by members of my own group was harder to bear than rejection by an external group. Witnessing self-rejection by my own mother was the hardest of all. Embedded in her utterances were subtle, infiltrating messages that Chinese were inferior to Americans and that Chinese-Americans would always be second-class citizens. This was ultimate self-rejection that shook my self-identity to its core. I got really angry, enough to write to her (25 Dec 1965):

> Maybe you like Americans better than us poor Chinese.…
> Why bother with the backward Chinese? The hell with
> self-respect, as long as we are in America. We Orientals
> are inferior; but that is all right, as long as we … have a
> degree to make money.

David   In fairness to your mother, to be able to live in America by any means and to "have a degree to make money" were (and are still) preoccupations common to many Chinese people.

YF   But self-rejection is something else. I knew that nothing would change my mother's attitude or put an end to her messages of racial self-degradation. This did not prevent me from trying.

Predictably the result of trying to move an immovable object with an unstoppable force was more frustration and anger, sometimes reaching volcanic proportions. The unstoppable force for change inside me was simply no match for my mother's immovability. This was an engine that made my early adulthood more turbulent than it already was.

I was almost driven mad. Ironically, around that time I was working as a psychologist in a mental hospital. The thought of my being locked up there, with a change of roles from staff to patient, did arise.

David   Readers may rest assured that it was just an entertaining thought.

YF   Besides, if I were to become "insane," I would still know enough about insanity to conceal it from detection by psychiatrists—just as easily as to feign insanity to get myself locked up in insane places.

David   Admitting the need for change is a beginning, if not a battle half won. But as you have probably found after many costly lessons, changing yourself is difficult enough; changing another person may well be impossible when that person sees no need or doesn't want to be changed.

YF   At least changing myself is under my own control; changing another person is not. So eventually I abandoned my utterly futile, even counterproductive, attempts at changing my mother. Out of necessity, I redirected my "unstoppable force" to reconstruct my self-identity, onwards to self-mastery. Coming face-to-face with self-rejection strengthened my resolve to go through with cultural uprooting.

This was the most formidable task I had ever undertaken. It entails undoing the past, ridding myself of unwanted familial and cultural viruses in my mind. In particular, I performed a kind of psychological surgery, to identify and extirpate the pernicious *influences* of my mother's messages one by one from my mind and cleanse my soul.

David   Note that this does not involve an erasure of memories: Unlike computers, the human mind cannot rid itself of specific memories. The messages themselves will remain in your mind until the day you die; all you can do is to neutralize their effects.

YF   This realization helps me to formulate my ideas on forgiveness as a therapeutic strategy: To forgive is not only possible but also desirable; to forget *at will* is not only impossible but also undesirable.

One therapeutic weapon I used was to "cut the chain from rejection to self-rejection." Too often, rejection by others activates self-rejection, thus amplifying the damage caused. The chain of progressive self-rejection goes something like this:

> I am rejected by others. There must be something bad within me to cause people to reject me. I also reject myself because I am bad. I am a disgrace to my family, to my country, to humankind, and to myself. I am ashamed of myself.
> Moreover, there is nothing I can do about it. I am not only unloved but also unlovable, even to myself. I can't and I don't love myself. My shame comes with my birth, a mistake to begin with. It is intrinsic to my being and will accompany me until the day I die. Therefore, my self-rejection is total, unconditional, and unalterable.

David   Shame accompanies the rejected self; it aggravates self-rejection, resulting in yet more shame. It may penetrate into the core of one's being, and is much more difficult to deal with than guilt.

The possible conditions leading to shame are much broader than in the case of guilt: One can feel ashamed of not only one's thoughts and actions, but also one's body (e.g., lack of attractiveness), incompetence (despite having tried one's best), humble condition in life, heritage, and country. Shame may be experienced under conditions over which we have no control, and hence personal responsibility is not necessarily involved. Note that the "progressive self-rejection" above mentions nothing about what the person involved has done wrong.

The effects of shame can be pervasive and devastating. They may persist like a psychic scar, for which there is no easy prescription for healing. "Cutting the chain from rejection to self-rejection" would be a workable prescription, because putting an end to self-rejection destroys the underground factory in which shame is manufactured.

YF   It is not enough just to remove the negatives; I need to be pulled forward by positive visions. I reaffirm my belief in the dignity of each and every person, without exceptions. This augments my "unstoppable force." So, positive visions are essential to the will to master.

David   Going a step further, I would say that spirituality is based primarily on the pursuit of the most positive of goals, rather than on negating the negatives. It is the well-spring from which selfhood and identity grow into maturity; it guides the formation of worldviews; it confers meaning and adds color to life.

For psychohistory, a more significant question concerns how collective experiences figure in your personal identity and esteem. Chinese people have suffered repeated insults to their national and ethnic pride in modern history.

YF   "No dogs and Chinese allowed" was a sign erected in a park in one of the foreign concessions in Shanghai. It probably did more damage to the Chinese national psyche than anything else ever did. Similarly, recent media coverage of Chinese astronauts venturing into outer space shows clearly how they bear a heavy burden: Failure would result in a collective loss of face. As it turns out, their success, far from personal, brings pride to the Chinese people as a whole.

So, you see self-esteem is not entirely a personal matter. Individual identity is interwoven with collective identity. Each partakes in the pride of the collective and bears its humiliation. Even now, the collective Chinese identity still runs deep in my psyche. I am not totally a world citizen—at least not yet.

My Spiritual Journey Is Incomplete

David   I must not forget to ask: At what point in time did you begin to deliberately conceive of your life as a spiritual journey? From our interview, it would appear to be sometime in your golden age, during which you felt affirmed as a teacher-educator and your literary-artistic impulses found expression.

YF   I think so too. However, the more I dig into my past, the more I find that the germs of spirituality may be discerned much earlier. Going through my personal papers one day, I found a letter of recommendation (5 Oct 1959), written on my behalf by Professor Breen, the one who introduced me to psychology. In it he wrote, "It is nice to be able to add that his fine qualities are linked to an unusual sense of purpose in life. David genuinely wants to make a contribution to the spiritual well-being of his fellow man."

David   To contribute to the spiritual well-being of others is a recurrent theme of your spiritual journey. This is your karma, a Buddhist idea that we will explore further in chapter 5. It says that your journey is not an individual undertaking and must involve others.

The main ideas that appear recurrently in this interview are personal liberation, will to master, creative synthesis, intercultural fertilization, and psychohistory. That's a lot to digest.

YF   The strands of thought do weave into the overarching theme of self-transformation, by which I mean something more than growth. Transformation is quantum change. It is a dynamic process that entails not only quantitative, but also qualitative, change; and not only alterations of previously observed patterns, but also emergent patterns of thought and action that were previously dormant or unobserved.

Self-transformation goes a step further: It is self-initiated, self-directed quantum change.

David   You summarize and learn from firsthand experiences amassed from your family life, your education in Hong Kong and overseas, your career as a teacher-educator, and your intercultural encounters. Early on, you decided to embark on a course of personal liberation from the constraints of Chinese culture, particularly Confucianism.

The most drastic action you took was cultural uprooting. You then balanced this uprooting with the will to transform your marginal status into strength, and end up being a world citizen dedicated to the betterment of humankind. Creative synthesis of your two worlds, Eastern and Western, plays a crucial role in this process. This is self-transformation, self-initiated and self-directed.

Moreover, you are quite conscious of the parallels between your personal transformation and the historical transformation of the Chinese nation as a whole.

YF   It hasn't been a smooth process. A lot of fumbling along the way. What has helped *us* move forward is the dialogic action that you (David) and I (YF) have engaged in. Thus, our different selves can work together synergistically. This interview is, in itself, an illustration of how therapeutic dialogic action can be.

David   I must draw your attention to a perplexing question. There is hardly anything in your childhood or early adulthood to foretell, or even to suggest, that you would turn "mad" episodically in your later life.

YF   That's right. But I did mention obsessive-compulsive traits in passing. In actuality, I have been driven by the desire to resolve the contradiction between compulsivity and creativity virtually all my life. Creativity triumphs over compulsivity during episodes of madness, when artistic-literary impulses are unleashed, especially during my golden age. So the will to creativity is a cardinal force that drives self-transformation, and ultimately enlightenment.

David   More and more, you have come to conceptualize self-transformation as part and parcel of your journey of spiritual discoveries. But your journey is obviously incomplete. What kind of self-transformation is it, if you continue to alternate between creativity when you are mad and compulsivity when you are normal?

Enlightenment is holistic: It can be reached when, and only when, creative self-transformation is continually sustained. In the following chapters, we shall see how you confront the contradiction between madness and normality. Particularly in chapter 5, we shall see how being a world citizen dovetails and blossoms into the idea of spirituality-in-communion.

Chapter 2:
Episodes of Madness: All of Exuberance, None of Depression

If abnormality is so rich in its manifestations,
surely normality should be no less colorful.

This chapter presents a description of episodes of "madness" I have had. At first, I thought I had only a few. However, as I assembled my records, including diaries, it became clear that the number is significantly higher: ten altogether, from 1997 to 2010. I am sure there were no episodes prior to 1997, that is, before I turned fifty-eight.

Here, I should point out that I am using the term *madness* rather loosely. Madness is a nontechnical term that refers, in a broad sense, to mental disorders or abnormal conditions. It lacks specificity and does not refer to a specific disorder. Madness connotes insanity, frenzy, and severity: For instance, psychosis is madness, but we would not refer to a common anxiety disorder, which is mild in relative terms, as madness. In my case, at no point was there any threat of my losing contact with reality or of acting in ways that endangered myself or others. I was never destructive or violent. I remained intensely aware of what was happening in my mind and surroundings.

A hypomanic episode is a period of persistently and unusually elevated, expansive, or irritable mood. Common symptoms include inflated self-esteem or grandiosity, more talkative than usual or pressure to keep talking, subjective experience that thoughts are racing, decreased need for sleep, and excessive engagement in pleasurable activities that have a high risk of adverse consequences (e.g., engaging in unrestrained buying sprees). Social functioning during the episode is clearly uncharacteristic of the person. The mood disturbance and changed social functioning are observable by others.

You may find a person in a hypomanic state quite attractive in some ways, but you might also be driven crazy, if he stays hypomanic much longer. He feels unusually high, euphoric, and overly self-confident, coupled with a lack of self-doubt; he can be funny. Disinhibited, he can be forward or audacious. He talks a lot, at a fast pace, jumping from one topic to another. He's got a lot of energy. You can't catch up with him. Under the influence of inflated self-confidence, his judgment is compromised. In short, he is feeling and acting in ways that are uncharacteristic of his usual self.

Two episodes were the most severe, in some respects reaching mania. By definition, manic episodes are basically similar to but more severe than hypomanic episodes. Psychotic features, like delusions, may be present; there may be marked impairment in social, interpersonal, or occupational functioning. These features were absent in my case. Furthermore, it was during the most severe episodes that I gained the most dramatic of my extraordinary, mystical experiences: for instance, total access to the unconscious and what Dance Movement therapists speak of as authentic movements, so called because they come directly from the unconscious and are uncensored.

In Mania 1 (see table below), I experienced the empty, selfless self; self-healing of an injured knee; transforming myself into a woman; *willful* hallucination, in which I saw myself vividly on a cross and felt great pathos for the sufferings of humankind. In Mania 2, I performed a free association. Mania 2 was the most costly to me in occupational and social terms.

In the following, I record my struggles and lessons learned. Informed by these lessons, my personal journey continues in quest of spiritual discoveries. The episodes afford me opportunities to gain unhindered access to the unconscious, experience the extraordinary, and glimpse into the mystical-transcendental state of enlightenment.

The data on the episodes are drawn, in whole or in part, from diverse sources: epigrams, correspondence, email messages, poems, free associations, internal dialogues, and diaries by myself, most of which written during or around an episode (diaries and poems are dated whenever possible). Editorial changes are kept to a minimum.

I have the habit of inserting an epigram, from a list I have composed, at the end of my email messages. Since 2000 I have been sending out messages to friends, colleagues, and relatives to celebrate festive seasons or to express my thoughts on specific topics; in some cases, the messages included a poem I wrote or were written in the form of a poem. In this chapter I've reproduced some of these messages and epigrams, especially those written during an episode or illuminating its dynamics.

The following table presents a convenient summary of all ten episodes in a chronological order.

Although they share commonalities, the episodes varied greatly in intensity, duration, and social costs to me. Each has its own individuality. Mania 1, however, stands out particularly in terms of access to the unconscious, extraordinary experiencing, and glimpses into the mystical-transcendental. It is also the episode on which I have the most comprehensive and revealing information, which is now shared with the reader below.

Dates, Duration, and Salient Features of Ten Episodes

Episode	Date/ Duration	Salient features
Hypomania 1	Oct 1997/ 2 weeks	First encounter with hypomanic symptoms. Music figured prominently; I gave it the title "The Conductor Who Couldn't Count."
Hypomania 2	Oct–Nov 1998/ 1 month or longer	Prolonged insomnia. Pronounced changes in social behavior caused considerable anxiety in my family and among my friends and colleagues.
Hypomania 3	2-5 Nov 2003/ 4 days	Brief and mild. No adverse effect on occupational or social functioning.
Mania 1	18-30 June 2005/ 1 week or longer	Intensity exceeded previous episodes. Out-of-bound behaviors. Experienced selfless self; dramatic self-healing; androgyny; willful visual hallucinations.
Hypomania 4	About 17 June – middle of July 2006/ 1 month or shorter	Positive tenor; affirmation as a teacher-educator.

Mania 2	June–July 2007/ 1 month	Major problem was inability to fall asleep; brain fatigue. Recorded free association. Out-of-bound behaviors; heavy occupational and social costs.
Hypomania 5	Nov 2008/ 1 week or longer	Cognitive deficits and other scary symptoms. Immersed in dancing in public. Intercultural encounters. Recovery relatively fast and easy.
Hypomania 6	Feb 2009/ 1 month	Elated mood. Hypomanic symptoms were mild and kept under control. Holistic health and artistic self-expression were intertwined. No adverse social consequences.
Hypomania 7	June–July 2009/ 1 month	Elated mood. Imbalance: dramatic fluctuations in energy level. Managed to keep episode under control; no adverse social consequences. Engaged in demanding physical activities, such as qigong and taiji push-hands.
Hypomania 8	March–April 2010/ 3 weeks	Shaking chills; mental fatigue and confusion, severe enough to require emergency admission to hospital. Outward manifestations of hypomania kept under control.

Glimpses into the Mystical-Transcendental

Though lasting no more than two weeks, Mania 1 was probably the most dramatic. Exceeding the hypomanic episodes, this one was serious in terms of social costs. My behavior exceeded what most other people regarded as the bounds of normality. During a staff retreat, I played tricks or antics that annoyed others; I shouted at the top of my voice to demonstrate my qi (air, breath), in locations where few people were around but where I could still be heard; I had a quarrel with a friend in the middle of night, loud enough to be heard by others.

My colleagues at work, with whom I had formed the most congenial of relationships, became very concerned about me. They knew I had difficulty sleeping during this episode. Afterwards, they would become nervous whenever I mentioned sleep disturbances. They had become sensitized to the trigger of my manic-like behaviors.

Here is an imaginary dialogue between two of my different selves, David and YF, I wrote around the end of the episode. In some cases I have added comments or explanations in square brackets.

* * *

David   You often refer to your personal experiences. The most private portion of these is a precious resource for gaining insight into the inner workings of the human psyche. What can you share with the reader?

YF   I have had the good fortune of gaining the most extraordinary, mystical experiences, each time during a period of about several weeks. My inner-private and outer-social selves merged.

The child inside came out. I became unusually playful, spontaneous, disinhibited—in a sense, more genuine.

David   To be disinhibited is not valued in Confucian societies, given their emphasis on impulse control and social order. I sensed a willful disregard of social convention when you speak of "good fortune." Rather self-indulgent, you didn't want to bow down to how others viewed your behavior. Perhaps your "mania" represented a rebellion against Confucian control, under which you felt you had suffocated long enough.

YF   Here is an excerpt of what one of my close friends wrote down (translated from Chinese) about my condition during the latest episode [Mania 1].

> You couldn't sleep. You talked a lot, often with yourself…. From your words, I felt at times you were exceedingly mature; at times innocent, like a child. No matter, whether you were adult or child, your thinking was always so genuine; everything utterance came from your heart, expressing your true thoughts…. self-confident, praising yourself…. Your blood pressure was high. Your face was radiant, flushed. [On special occasions] you were in a state of complete intoxication, as if you were not in this world, uttering a lot of words of enchantment, like in a nightmare…. Listening to music every day, you let your thoughts and emotions run unbridled, nonstop. You took a pen and wrote [Chinese characters] on paper without stopping, telling me that [different writing styles represented different emotional states]. Sometimes, when you got excited, you would close your eyes, move both hands beating to the music. Or, you might suddenly cry out aloud for a while…. When going out to eat, walk in the street, travel, you were invariably different from the crowd.

I was indeed talkative. I phoned my friends, old and new. Actually, the talkativeness, interspersed with periods of contemplation, was impelled by an intense desire to communicate, to be understood, and to share my newfound self.

David   Your professional colleagues thought that your condition met the criteria for hypomania, if not mania: difficulty in falling asleep, emotional lability and intense reactivity, and so forth. They were simply following the psychiatric bible on diagnosis, the DSM-IV (*Diagnostic and Statistical Manual of Mental Disorders*, 4th edition).

YF   In retrospect, I did cross the boundary of social and cultural acceptability. But I retained the master switch: metacognitive awareness and control of my actions. Critical reflectiveness and scientific doubt were fully operative. I was aware that other people viewed my behavior as weird. However, I caused no harm, to myself or to others—only a great deal of worry to bewildered people close to my life. My impulse control was intact. At no point would I do anything that I considered morally wrong or reckless.

David   What was your physical condition?

YF   Imbalance: My body was near exhaustion, yet my mind remained active, running on fast time. I was mentally hyperactive. I was thirsty most of the time. I felt hot where others would feel cold. Aware that my energy reserve might be depleted, I moved around slowly. Sometimes, I would half-close my eyes, a conservation technique that I had learned from a yoga master.

David   Your brain's consumption of energy must have been extraordinarily high. Coupled with prolonged sleeplessness, this led to disturbances of cognitive functioning.

YF   At worst, I found it difficult to perform even simple arithmetic. I got confused easily. I could perform only one task at a time. I could be extremely forgetful, like forgetting what I had done or where I had put something just a few seconds ago.

At times, I could focus on just one thought at a time. While I was staying focused, I would make myriad associations. The next moment, no trace of what I had just been thinking about could be found. The thought was gone. I became obsessive about lost memories—lost in the cosmos forever. I tried to record some of my thoughts on paper or in a computer file before they got lost. At some point, I said to myself, "Let go of lost memories. They will come back. Let my mind rest." That helped to put an end to the obsession.

When my energy level improved, I was unusually focused and efficient. At home, I performed different household tasks very efficiently. Often my hands and legs maneuvered and performed complex tasks without conscious direction, as if the "wisdom of the body" had extended to the executive ego: They accomplished what my mind had intended, without deliberation or being aware of its own intention.

Freed from obsessive-compulsive tendencies, I read rapidly, without worrying that I might have missed something; unencumbered by perfectionism, I wrote fluently.

David　Perhaps your retrospective account may throw fresh insights into brain functioning. With regard to memory, your forgetfulness probably reflected a disturbance of registration (encoding) and/or storage of information. At the same time, however, retrieval of information already stored in your long-term memory was amazingly efficient.

YF　I enjoyed doing even "tedious" tasks, such as throwing the garbage out. Every second of life was enjoyable. When I was a schoolboy, a Jesuit teacher once said, "You can pray twenty-four hours a day, even when you are brushing your teeth." Finally, I really know what he meant, for I have experienced it.

Better still, I felt a sense of tranquility, at peace with myself, at home in the cosmos. I have had my share of self-torment, overattachment, compulsivity, embitterment, which I had tried to overcome for decades. All vanished. I achieved shamelessness. I became more tolerant and compassionate. I cherished the simple joys of just being alive. Walking around in the streets, I would say to myself, "Life is wonderful. The world is so beautiful."

I felt humbled by the commanding heights of human achievement, the vastness of the cosmos. I wrote, in the midst of this period, "Nothing in the cosmos is alien to humans. Therefore, speak not of what is alien." (In response to Terentius, Latin playwright, who wrote "I am human, therefore nothing human is alien to me.")

David   Clearly, your manic period was marked by extraordinary creativity, heightened aesthetic sensitivity, depth of feelings, and deep humility. These positive, delightful features are significant: They define the nature of your mania.

YF   The more I knew, the more I became aware of my profound ignorance. Knowledge and humility were like twins. I experienced the near-despair of trying to fathom the infinite with a finite mind.

Around 2003, I wrote the following poem:

Sea of Learning

The sea of learning
Knows no bounds.
No shore in sight
To return to land,
I drift on, lost
In her bosom—
Only to lift
From the depths of the deep,
To receive the love that moves
Upon the face of the waters.

The poem gives a new twist to the Chinese idiom:

The sea of learning knows no bounds,
No shore, save diligence.

David   Interesting, you invoke biblical imageries in the Genesis. But love, rather than the Spirit of God?

YF   They should be identical.

David   "Lost in her bosom" brings to mind the immortal lines of Tennyson:

> Now folds the lily all her sweetness up,
> And slips into the bosom of the lake:
> So fold thyself, my dearest, thou, and slip
> Into my bosom and be lost in me.

The difference is that you long to slip into "her bosom," rather than inviting her to slip into yours. The deeper meaning I read: Ultimately, salvation comes from love, not knowledge.

Along with creativity, you probably experienced what psychiatry calls "flight of ideas," or rapid succession of ideas or verbalizations with abrupt shifting from one idea or topic to another.

YF   Definitely, racing thoughts, faster than usual, appeared. Sometimes I was obsessed with losing these thoughts, which I couldn't utter fast enough, let alone put down in writing.

Speed was also manifest in an extraordinary sensitivity to cues in social interaction. Watching films or TV shows provided delightful occasions for predicting the next scene, what the actors would say and do. My predictions showed uncanny accuracy, as if I had overtaken the role of the director. That was empathy: I and the director became one. Probably I conducted some of my best psychotherapy sessions or workshops, during which my empathy joined forces with the courage to be myself.

Things of beauty appeared in plentiful ways. More precisely, I keenly perceived many things as never before—ordinary things, like people's faces; the sound of running water; tree leaves, through which the rays of the setting sun penetrated.

My friends once showed me a Japanese painting, which instantaneously absorbed my attention. In my early days as a graduate student in clinical psychology, I developed an interest in the clinical use of drawings. Now, that interest was elevated to aesthetic appreciation.

I talked with my friends about the aesthetic features of the painting, and in so doing also about the artist endowed with the faculty to create it. I surprised myself, because I never thought I had much capacity for appreciating visual art.

Music evoked strong emotions. Reactions to J. S. Bach were total and could not be described as anything short of spirituality. Tears would flow profusely from my eyes whenever I listened to the Largo from his Violin Concerto in E Minor. Such emotional response was specific to this piece of music and to none other. I was in touch with the deepest pathos—without despair. Real catharsis! Listening to music induced spontaneous movements, involving my head (inside and outside), my limbs, my whole body and being.

My artistic impulses, long subdued, demanded expression. I rebuked myself:

> You coward, where is your courage-to-be?
> The artist that you are,
> To fulfill your potential
> In working, living, and relating?

David   As a Chinese saying puts it: "There is no greater grief than the death of one's heart." The capacity for depth of feelings, both positive and negative, versus psychic numbing, is the watershed that separates emotional health from sickness. Dysphoric feelings do not necessarily incapacitate.

I have long wondered if prolonged inhibition of artistic or creative impulses can lead to neurosis. Dance Movement therapists speak of authentic movements, so called because they come directly from the unconscious, uncensored. Did you experience anything like that?

YF   There were times when the body moved involuntarily. The movements differed from aimless automatism described in neuro-psychiatry. They were clearly meaningful, albeit raw, expressions. I liberated myself. I danced. I entered into a state of dynamic meditation.

In that state were incorporated elements of hypnotherapy, martial arts, music, dance, meditation, yoga, and qigong, which I had learned imperfectly in past years. I experimented with different forms and techniques. For instance, independently one arm might move slowly and softly, draw an imaginary circle of varying size, and so forth, while the other was doing something different.

Recently I engaged a personal instructor to teach me expressive dance. She did not instruct, but taught through a classic master-disciple relationship, mostly nonverbally. I learned to express myself in ways I had not known before. My body was transformed.

David   My psychologist friend Bruce Bain says that the self-conscious mind is formed through acts of speaking with others and with oneself. This assertion resonates with your ideas about the dialogic self: The self engages in both internal and external dialogues, in the process of which it may participate in its own transformation. Thus, the self has immense potentiality for creative self-transformation, even self-creation. What do your experiences tell us about the dialogic self?

YF   During meditation, at times the self seemed to have vanished. I experienced the no-mind state of emptiness. I felt energy flowing within my body. So I thought of taking advantage of it.

Several days before, I injured my left knee; the pain was so bad that I was walking with a limp. I absorbed sunlight outside to magnify the energy flow and directed it to my injured knee. There was a growing sensation of warmth around the injured area. I visualized a volcano around this area, which magnified the sensation further. Finally, there was only light: The body, together with the self, had dissolved. When I came out of this transcendental state, I found the pain gone. I had healed myself—a tangible benefit that was verifiable to several people who knew about my injury.

On other occasions, vivid images appeared, spontaneously or directed at will. The virtual was experienced as the real. I came as close to willful hallucination as I had ever.

One unforgettable sequence was seeing myself being nailed on a cross, which was lying on the ground. I wanted it to be raised, so I could see things from a vertical perspective. I felt no physical pain, but intense feelings of pathos for the sufferings of humankind. I felt what Jesus must have felt. (Please don't read this as "I believed I was Jesus.") All these came as close to a transformative, religious experience I have had in my life—up to now, that is.

Another sequence was a transgender experience: turning myself into a woman, feeling and acting like one. It was educational, more powerful than any role-reversal game in psychotherapy. I also experienced androgyny, the yin and the yang, united in one body.

David   Your phenomenological report serves as a means to glimpse into the mystical-transcendental. One concern I have is that the combined forces of heightened sensibility and intensified emotionality can be hazardous. You may be too easily fired up by ephemeral ideals and thus act impulsively. Or you may be overly attached to, and hence enslaved by, objects of pleasure or beauty.

The Buddhist attitude of nonattachment, however, may keep overattachment at bay: engaged and involved with worldly objects, without being possessive; letting go of fixations. It differs from detachment, which refers to emotional noninvolvement with and disengagement from the world.

When and where were all these experienced? Were others aware of how unusual they were? Were there differences among the episodes you have had? How did you come out of mania?

YF   All of the episodes thus far occurred within the last eight years. My unusual experiences occurred mostly at home, in private. Only a few people had intimate knowledge of them. So I didn't appear stranger than what I was already perceived to be.

By the present episode, I had learned enough to anticipate what was coming and tried, though unsuccessfully, to avoid behaving publicly in ways that would cause unease in others.

The present episode surpassed previous episodes in intensity. But it also pushed me to new heights of artistic expression.

Sleep held the key to recovery: I knew I would come out of it if only I could get enough sleep for a few days consecutively. Alas, I also feared that, having succeeded, self-torment and other negatives would return, along with normality.

David   A psychoanalyst would say that in your case repression vanished. The unconscious became accessible. Nothing was unthinkable. Your mind functioned with holistic oneness, interconnected. This had the effect of enhancing your aesthetic, empathic, and cognitive capabilities.

Retrieval of information and association of ideas were super-efficient, so much so that you were overwhelmed by your own outpouring of creativity. You became obsessively attached to ideas and objects, including the self. You had no physically aggressive or destructive tendencies, although direct expressions of verbal aggressiveness sometimes exceeded your normal level.

YF   I have now greater insight into what mystical experiences are like. Here is a question to absorb the interest of those in search of enlightenment. How does one maintain optimal balance for extended periods between creative expressiveness and control? That is, exercise adequate control over impulses without the need for repression; get in and out of manic-like states at will.

David   The person who attains such balance would be sage like, united in body, mind, and spirit; he lives his daily life in accordance with his inner wishes, and acts without transgression. Destructive forces having been harnessed to serve creative purposes, genuine harmony within the self is achieved. Mastery indeed!

* * *

I have not been able to duplicate the feats achieved during Mania 1, at least not as dramatically: self-healing, the completeness of the no-mind state of emptiness, or the willful visual hallucinations. The depth into which I had gone was proportional to the extent to which my social relations suffered. The greater the pain, the greater the gain? Can rare and precious experiences be gained without social and emotional costs? This is but one of the themes discernible recurrently in other episodes, to which I now turn.

Loneliness and Anguish amid Exuberance

Social costs are incurred when we get carried away by our own intentions and desires, without sufficient regard for the feelings and reactions of others. So even an eccentric has to be mindful of how he is perceived by others. This point was made painfully clear to me in Mania 2. Early in the episode, I wrote in my diary (30 June 2007):

> I must preempt the extreme condition, sleep before I fall into the manic phase, keep the hyperactive sympathetic autonomic nervous system under control, learn to keep my behavior within the bounds of social acceptability.... Eros without thanatos, safe.

Clearly I was apprehensive about falling into "the manic phase"; the "hyperactive sympathetic autonomic nervous system" was the culprit; I thought there was safety in "eros without thanatos," that is, loving without destructiveness or aggressiveness. But I did not succeed in keeping my behavior "within the bounds of social acceptability." I sent out email messages that offended some people, and acted in ways that cost me dearly in occupational and interpersonal terms.

Disinhibition surpassed Mania 1. My words and deeds were expressed more directly, sometimes pointedly or aggressively, than I had before. I probably offended or alarmed quite a few people. However, there was at no point any violence, loss of impulse control, or disregard for the safety or well-being of others.

From a positive perspective, I exhibited what Dance Movement therapists call "authentic movement," which I gather means unbridled movement stemming directly from the id without censorship. For the first time in my life, I danced (in private) as a totally uninhibited person, liberated from *all* feelings of shame.

My judgment was compromised: I failed to consider adverse consequences that might follow my actions. For instance, I sent an email to my colleagues at work. The following is an excerpt:

> During the few days, I have been in hiding…. For a good reason. I have achieved a quantum leap, self-transformation, at home….
>
> Quality must be restored to qualitative research. (Remember, academic glory should not be measured in catties.)
>
> Unproductive, random activities are unproductive.
>
> Consistently predictable chaos is incurable.
>
> Boundaries, professional/organizational, if not maintained, is anathema to organizational psychology.
>
> Unethical practices, here, as in the rest of HKU, must stop.

That was a dumb move. I miscalculated how the staff would react. "Self-transformation"? To them, it was more likely just another descent into madness. I minced no words in my criticisms of the research and professional work done in the center at the University of Hong Kong where I was working. Most of my colleagues shared my views, which they dared not express openly. My boss was miffed, and terminated my employment. This greatly upset the students I had been teaching.

The social cost to me was the highest among all my episodes. A few of my friends terminated their relationships with me. But what kind of friends were they, considering the fact that none suffered any harm other than embarrassment or apprehension consequential to my actions? They ended our friendship simply because they were bewildered by behaviors they could not, and did not, comprehend. Of course, that's my fault. An eccentric to begin with, I turned myself into an even odder person and in doing so invited others to perceive me in psychopathological terms.

I was humbled by my failure to keep this episode under control. I have yet to learn to modulate my actions to avoid damages to my social image, without dampening creativity and heightened sensibilities. After recovery, a friend sent me a message, an excerpt of which (translated from Chinese) is reproduced below.

> Dear Professor Ho:
> In your eyes, many people like us all think slow. You always say that your demands are not high; but even these not-so-high demands of yours make people feel they can't meet them. This perplexes you…. You lament that people are foolish, selfish; that you are always helping others, but others can't ever help you….
> You want all academics to excel. So you get really put off when you see some academics you regard as basically incompetent proclaiming they are doing so-called research….
> Because you are a person who has an extreme passion for living, your taste and demands are extremely high…. You are an extremely kind-hearted person; moreover, you treat people with extreme sincerity. That's why often you don't know how to protect yourself; you don't quite understand that sometimes you need to keep your inner thoughts private. Precisely because your sincerity and trust toward people, you have brought forth a lot of unnecessary troubles…. As I said before, better to be your friend than to be your intimate companion by your side….
> Your thinking is quick, with leaps and bounds. Your voice is sonorous. You talk primarily about things that you are interested in, not listening or unwilling to listen

to others…. Regardless of whatever you say, I can feel that your mind is lucid, your thinking is normal. The way you deal with problems during the whole process is logical; however, your thinking is indeed too fast, making it difficult for people to accept you. You've got to know, because of this, you may have indeed given those jealous of you an excuse to make people who don't understand you to be awfully fearful of you…. Besides, you have such an unusual, distinct period annually, like a woman's menstrual periods…. I hope that you will learn to self-control your "cyclical periods of excessively quick, leaping thinking"…. You mind is extremely lucid from beginning to end. By your strength of how to conduct your life, you are completely capable of mastering your own behavior, so other people wouldn't find your quick thinking unacceptable. You are completely capable of going up and down, left and right, really "acting according to your wishes." I pray that such a day will soon arrive.

I am amused by the analogy of "menstrual periods"; at least menopause is predictable, which is a comforting thought. It is reassuring to hear that my mind was lucid and that I was logical in the way I dealt with problems during the whole episode. But I must also mend some of my ways, such as "not listening or unwilling to listen to others."

My self-perceptions differ from others' perceptions of my mania: I find the experiences inspirational; people around me are worried, perhaps even petrified. This remains a contradiction I have to face. Attending to perceptions by other people about my behavior is no less important to effective social functioning than self-perceptions. The art of persuading without offending *unnecessarily* is what I have to acquire and perfect. Above all, I must learn to master myself, to "act according to my wishes," without arousing fear and inviting rejection from other. When will such a day arrive?

All my life, separations from or departures of friends often evoke transitory feelings of depression in me. I don't like saying good-bye. As I once wrote, "No beginning and no end; so whence the need to say good-bye?"

Mania 2 magnified those depressive feelings, adding to the high emotional costs I had to bear. Devoting most my time to academic and professional pursuits, I seldom engaged in social activities, other than those involving my colleagues and friends at work. So being cut off from work was a great loss, in terms of not only occupation but also human contact. Living alone at the time rendered me even more socially isolated. My response was to spend a lot of time on telephone conversations, something I would normally not do. The episode was, in large measure, "mania via telephone."

It was time for emotional healing. Out of nostalgia, at the height of the episode, I went back to the Jesuit school for boys that I attended as a child. That visit was a watershed experience in my life. It evoked a lot of memories. One sadistic physical education teacher made me crawl between the legs of the entire class standing in line. I couldn't remember what I had done to deserve such humiliation, but I didn't feel at the time that I suffered any psychological damage, other than embarrassment.

But walking again, in my adulthood, on the sports ground where the incident took place brought forth strong emotions. Seeing that nobody was around, I took off my shoes, feeling the pain from walking on gravel. I cried like I had never cried before: total catharsis. I said to myself: "I have arrived."

This was also a time that I extended personal healing to loving thoughts and actions for humanity. I wrote in my diary (30 June 2007): "Return to my original face [nature], love." This theme stands out and reverberates in other episodes. It affirms two core values of spirituality, love and authenticity.

Ironically, I am more ready in states of madness than of normality to taking concrete actions of caring and generosity. Some examples are offering to pay for the dental expenses of a taxi driver, whose wife is a friend of mine; helping friends in financial need with large sums of money, without expecting repayment.

For a number of years, I had been contemplating the foundation of a philanthropic organization. I finally took action after Mania 2 ended. The organization, named Chizi Institute, was established. The name comes from the *Book of Mencius*, which refers to "the heart of a *chizi* (newborn babe)." The word *chi* means many things: red, bare, loyal, empty. So the ancients of China used *chizi* to refer to the modern concept of authenticity. "Newborn" or "nascent" are the closest English translations of *chizi* I can think of. What better name could there be? It resonates with "return to my original face."

The Institute is devoted primarily to advancing civic-environmental-health education. It supports projects and educational activities aimed at promoting civic values, environmental conservation, and holistic health.

Finally, I made good on the claim of being a world citizen. This is a milestone in my journey of spiritual discoveries. Why focus on civic virtues? Because spirituality is to be realized not just individually but also collectively, by being-in-the-world, no less than in the wilderness. Why environmental conservation? Because an aesthetic environment beautifies the spirit, and a beautified spirit will not pollute the environment. Why holistic health? Because health is holistic in nature, an integration of body-mind-spirit; it is not just the absence of illness or disease.

Aesthetic Sensibilities: Music, Art, Creative Writing

Hypomania 1 had everything to do with music. In this respect, J. S. Bach was special. I listened to his music in a way I had never listened before. The music came to life for me, evoking emotions that brought me to the lofty realm of spirituality. I wrote in my diary (12 Oct 1997):

> Great are the creators of music for all time. Second best are the creators for the moment. The third are the simulators, imitators who partake in the creation. The fourth are the audience. The last are the creators of nonmusic.

I named the episode "The Conductor Who Couldn't Count." As I listened to music, I began to move—first my arms, then my whole body. I pretended to be a conductor. Conducting for the first time, I surprised myself. "Ah, I can do it. I can count!"

This was a moment of rational exuberance. You see, I began taking violin lessons at age sixteen. I loved playing the violin, excited by the dream of being a performer. But I had trouble tuning it, and I couldn't count. I used a metronome. I practiced hard. But it didn't work. Finally, I gave up.

During Hypomania 1 my music appreciation took a quantum leap, even for pieces that I had listened to countless times. I noticed the sounds of different instruments; I sensed the beat, rhythm, tempo, intonation, and dynamics. I discovered that I have previously unknown capabilities. As I practiced more, I become more proficient, on the beat. Instead of following the music, I felt as if I were creating it. The more I immersed myself in the process, the less self-conscious I became and the more I enjoyed doing it.

Unlike passive listening, conducting is strenuous to an extreme. One can get exhausted after doing it for some ten minutes. The conductors Arturo Toscanini, Bruno Waldheim, and Herbert Von Karajan lived long lives. Aside from the regular exercise, they benefited from the intense love of their work. I strongly suspect, too, that music has intrinsic qualities (like rhythm) that are associated with longevity. Therefore, you don't need to look beyond conducting music for the elixir of leading a long and healthy life.

In retrospect, I might not have been as hopeless as I thought. Perhaps my approach was flawed: too methodical and overly cognitive, not spontaneous. Now, immersing myself in the music and entering into a state of selfless-oblivion, I no longer have trouble. It is like entering into trance.

Actually, such altered states of consciousness are not that unusual, and may require no special training for experiencing them. (Witness how two lovers become totally absorbed in and by each other, oblivious to everything around them.) However, cultivating a habit of mind freed from overcontrol through some activity, such as simulated conducting, certainly helps.

Music figured prominently in other episodes as well. I would turn on my high-fidelity system, on which I have spent an extraordinary fortune, and listen to music all day and night—literally, I lived by music. Listening to Wagner evoked imageries of bedroom acrobatics; J. S. Bach invariably spiritual feelings. In Hypomania 3, I wrote in my diary (2 Nov 2003):

> Listened to *Rigaletto* [*Rigoletto*]. I never knew it's so beautiful. The story too. *Rigaletto*, loud, occupies my right brain, so I don't have to think, [would be interesting to have an] fMRI.... cried, brief but extremely intense, father-daughter [evoked thoughts of relationships with my own daughters].

The aesthetic-spiritual dimension cried out to be heard during Mania 2. I wrote in my diary (July 2007), "I have rediscovered everything (not quite everything) that the mystics of old knew." I was referring to aesthetic-spiritual experiences (e.g., heightened aesthetic sensibilities, depth of feelings, complete spontaneity). I told a friend, "I have never felt so good in my life."

I recited poems repeatedly. Not only that—I moved my head and upper body in a circular motion, like the Chinese poets of old did. Poetry has to be not just read out loud, but read in unison with movement of the body. Try it, and you will see what I mean.

I also did a free association. It was my first and, thus far, only attempt. It was written rather than uttered. Using my computer, I simply typed as fast as I could what came to mind, without attempting to make any corrections. The free association numbers 1,620 words. Here is an excerpt:

> **not** allowed to change a word anticompulsive training use this as illustration finally i know how to treat read on, all ye who suffer from sleepless nights cunning [not cunt please] go with the folw do not resist and you will fall asleep try it…. Now laugh those of you who are informed if you are indeed informed rm donald ? rumsfel you don't know what you don't know the most brillian man who ever lived now you are really offended right? Go with the flow don not resist and every vally shall be exalted meaning that in case you don't know what i am talking about this treasure trove … enough is enough you have suffered long enough please suffer no more if you would only listen to you inner voice….
>
> i am really tired can't go on i am going to sleep my apology … but you see you have been tricked, i am not going to slppe because i don't whqt you to suffer sleepless not anymore read on because you get this opportunioty only one in your life time the see that falls on bareen soil will not grow be kind to yourself after you have been so creel to all your life read on i beg you sat guanranteed … not i am not sure i am SURE you have been tricked again and again i guarantee you innumberable time….
>
> i became enlightened have you ever been enlighted i bet you have ? i am not going to insult you yes i am goint o insult you to wak y up from you rslumber ylou have3 ben sleepijg long enough

The excerpt makes clear that I was "**not** allowed to change a single word," as "anticompulsive training." I was "really tired" but could not fall asleep; my strategy was to "go with the folw [flow]" and not to resist. I seemed to enjoy playing tricks on the imaginary reader with opposites, such as "i am not sure i am SURE you have been tricked again and again." Significantly, I told myself to "be kind to yourself after you have been so creel [cruel] to [yourself] all your life"; and I felt "i became enlightened."

Freud devised two avenues to the unconscious. The first, which he called "the royal road to the unconscious," was the interpretation of dreams. The second was free association, the fundamental rule of which is to say whatever comes to mind, regardless of how trivial, irrelevant, irrational, embarrassing, or painful it might be. Unfortunately, I have not been able to locate actual transcripts of free association by clients undergoing classical psychoanalysis. Free association is difficult to do; try it to discover how difficult it can be.

As I look at the entire free association later, it is perhaps more like an outpouring of a stream of consciousness than totally free association. Progressing from the beginning to the end, it becomes increasingly free; the outpouring became increasingly uncensored. Discursive thoughts, including flight of ideas, are rampant, and features characteristic of mania may be discerned. Still, the passages are intelligible, arguably more so than some of *Ulysses* by James Joyce (whom I alluded to). There is fragmentation and incoherence, but no confabulation or loss of contact with reality.

On the contrary, in the last sentence I wrote at that time, I showed a capacity to anticipate the reader's reaction: "NOW you must be really *confused* good for you i know it." I also had a playful attitude while reflecting on my writing style in this passage: "Let see who has the last aaugh notice why how already my stuyle changes no english professor can write like i do they will regret it you see highly competive people they don like to see others game of oneupmanship they jealos of their competitors no? i have offended you enough just kidding [i laughing this very moment]."

I showed low regard for professors, but held students responsible for allowing their instructors to remain boring:

> Funny professor have been teaching all their life then were
> students once how come they have never learned to less
> boring just a little but you think i am curing professuions
> i was once a PROFESSOR a dime a dozen no i am cursing
> you the students who allo it to happen respoonsibility.

This is coupled with disdain for the counseling profession (not to be confused with disdain for counseling itself): Therapists "are a hopeless bunch." I confessed that I never read a book in counseling "from cover to cover," implicating counseling texts as boring, intellectually bankrupt.

I mentioned some negative aspects of American society: "Salesmen in the United States those blasted psychopaths who sell their mothers for a dime." George Bush is singled out for attack:

> He will come down a the worst p in US history asndnow
> the rest of the world is very very angry with you why
> becase you had the aufacity to elect an idiot you have
> only yours to bl American have short mem.

Animosity, however, was reserved for arrogant Brits: "Damn the brits arrogant SABs [SOBs] who not that long ago felt so superiot to americans."

In all, I had critical-aggressive-hostile as well as lewd impulses: "cunt," "fucking shit [first time in my life, deep apoloty if i have offended you but i don't mind if i had indeed offended you."

I was aware of megalomania and acknowledged the explosion of creativity as I free associated: "Megalomanic this is what i m racing thoughts pass through my head a explosion of creativty."

Toward the end, positive themes of struggle with compulsivity, self-transformation, and benefiting mankind appear: "Breakthoughtsd self-transformation … i really have struglle hard resis compulsity all my life 'i am dead tired but i can't let this these thoughts be lost forever without their benef mankind.'"

What have I learned about my unconscious? Not much, if anything, that I don't already know. I am not negating the value of free association. After years of self-analysis, and especially having gone through previous episodes, I have already gained ready access to my unconscious. Nonetheless, to me the free association is quite an achievement; in particular, never before have I expressed my lewd or hostile impulses so blatantly (in words, not deeds).

Increasingly, my literary impulses found expression during the episodes. In Hypomania 7, I wrote a "Chinese" poem in English. It began with going to Victoria Park in Hong Kong, an interesting place where one can find people doing all kinds of exercise or practicing wushu (martial arts). I had been spending too much time in isolation; going to the park opened my eyes to a new world. Walking around, I was inspired to write a poem (3 July 2009).

Walk Like a Buddha

The taiji circles go round and round,
Small, yet boundless,
Surrounded by wooded enclaves,
Themselves surrounded by concrete jungles
That threaten to engulf their existence.

Now walk like a Buddha in the circles,
Listen to the droning sound of cicadas,
Look up, see the rays that penetrate
The green leaves in ceaseless motion, and proclaim
That Heaven, Earth, and Man are One.

This was my first attempt to write a Chinese poem in English. In this connection, I am reminded of the evangelist John's extraordinary language in the Book of Revelation. Biblical scholars have noted that John breaks all sorts of grammatical rules. This is not due to incompetence, for he is capable of writing correct and powerful Greek. He seems to be echoing Hebrew constructions, perhaps to give a biblical feel to Revelation.

I could not have written the poem had I not actually walked around the taiji circles, listened to the sounds, and saw the light in their midst. The idea of walking like a Buddha came from a Buddhist retreat, where I followed the Vietnamese monk Thich Nhat Hanh and walked "like a Buddha" for days. It also came from the conquest of my poor posture several months earlier. Walk like a Buddha, stand like a Buddha, and sit like a Buddha: That's dignity. So, experience and knowledge are required for writing poetry, no less than for writing scholarly works. That much I understand.

Extraordinary Experiences: Audacity or the Courage-to-Be?

This theme underlies two episodes, Hypomania 2 and Hypomania 4. In terms of duration, intensity, and extensiveness, Hypomania 2 exceeded the previous episode (Hypomania 1). Characteristically, I had trouble sleeping; toward the end of the episode, I was physically exhausted.

However, I felt that my motility was efficient, "with not a single movement wasted," as I wrote in my diary. Even my handwriting changed. The association of ideas was fast and rich. In my diary I also wrote, "The density and intensity of creative, new discoveries surprised even myself." Intense feelings, fluctuating between negative (loneliness, anguish) and positive (liberation, enlightenment), were constant companions.

Changes in my social behavior were pronounced and sometimes publicly noticed. I called friends and talked with them for hours. My behavioral changes caused great anxiety in my family and among my friends and colleagues. Some thought I was acting more strangely than expected even from an eccentric person like myself. Others undoubtedly thought I was mentally disturbed. Some of my colleagues in psychology pointed to their bible, the DSM-IV, and made their diagnosis of mania.

What was the most outrageous thing I did or manifest? On one occasion, standing in front of a large class of undergraduates, I talked about the June Fourth massacre in Beijing. Suddenly, uncontrolled (not the same as uncontrollable) emotions took hold of me. Tears flowed from my eyes, visible to all. This was the first time I had displayed such emotions in public. Some students were disturbed, because my public display was incompatible with their image of a professor. I thought to myself, "This just goes to show that the Chinese are a people whose capacity for emotional expression has been truncated."

I felt no shame. More fundamentally, self-acceptance came at last. I saw myself as indeed an unusual person, kinder, more sensitive, perhaps even wiser than most other people. This gave me comfort that my self-perception had become more accurate and adaptive.

Self-acceptance did not result in arrogance. The thought of just being different calmed me. Still, could I ignore other people's perceptions of me for long? Being different has been an issue in my life, regardless of cultural context. It has haunted me from my student days in North America to my life back in East Asia. It underlies my loneliness, stemming largely from feelings of not being understood or accepted.

The overall tenor of Hypomania 4 was remarkably positive, despite my physical and mental exhaustion. Significantly, it occurred during my golden age. I wrote in my diary (23 June 2006), "Suppression of artistic impulses can be hazardous to your health." This realization would evolve into a cardinal drive in subsequent episodes.

I felt more positive of my role as teacher-educator than I had ever felt before. For decades, my professional superego had been weighing on me heavily, haunted by the feeling that I was failing to live up to my ideals. I learned to treat myself more generously:

> I have been liberated from self-doubts. Now, I have the courage to be myself, an inspiring teacher, loved by students. Every class I conduct is an enjoyable experience, full of laughter. I have succeeded in touching the lives of many students in a positive way. I can now rightfully regard myself as an educator.

In the midst of this episode, I attended the graduation ceremony of a youngster in mainland China, whose education I had sponsored for a number of years. The location was the international secondary school he had been attending. It was an expensive school, attended mostly by children from families of China's privileged class, the rich and the powerful. Several on-site visits I made to the school, however, raised many disturbing questions about the school's educational philosophy, policies, and practices. In a nutshell, the school conformed to examination superstition: Examination results are everything.

During the ceremony, the school boasted of its achievements, such as the number of its graduates admitted into first-rate Chinese universities. One by one, dignitaries, teachers, and student representatives came onto the stage to read out prearranged scripts in a soulless manner. After a while, I couldn't stand it anymore. I went up on the stage and addressed the audience. Here is a translation of what I said:

> [Preliminary niceties….] As the sponsor of one of your students and hence an honored guest, I feel obliged to share some of my thoughts with you. Weeks ago, during the time of the university entrance examination, parents

could be seen near the examination sites, staying in hotels and giving support to their children. Today, hardly a parent has come to attend the graduation ceremony. What does this say about our educational priorities?

The school has listed many of its achievements. Student representatives come onto the stage and read out their scripts. I would have appreciated much more their display of creativity. Why not let them speak their own minds?

This ceremony is prepared for only those who have done well in the examination. The higher the marks, the greater the glory. What about those who have not done so well? They can't hold their heads up high. Right now, they need the understanding and support of educators more than ever. Why, then, not a word for them has been uttered? We teach by setting personal examples. The State Council of the Chinese government has urged the people to practice conservation. Yet, today, I see the doors of this assembly hall are open while air conditioning is running. Are educators concerned about wastage and damage to our environment?

[At this point, the school principal stood up and spoke.] Are you here to stir up a fight?

[I replied.] No, that's not my intention. I am responsible only for what I say. You have to be responsible for how you hear it.

At this point, several people approached me, with the intention of grabbing the microphone from me. I surrendered it, walked down the stage, and left the assembly hall. After the ceremony, some teachers and students approached me stealthily and told me how much they appreciated my remarks.

The speech was impolite, even inappropriate, given the occasion. Lest misunderstanding may arise, I hasten to add that I had never done anything like that before. I wouldn't normally have the audacity.

Hypomania gave me the courage to speak my mind publicly, on the ills of education in China I had been feeling very strongly for decades. Having done it, I am proud of it. For at least once in my life, I have spoken, with conviction and fortitude, if inappropriately. So be it, if my inappropriate speech served the purpose of making a point for the good of education. Would my life be lesser lived, if I had not done the inappropriate?

My evolution from audacity to courage-to-be, if punctuated by madness, is an essential part of my spiritual journey.

The Empty Mind: Gone with Repression and Overcontrol

In Mania 1, I experienced the selfless self, self-healing, and vanished repression. This theme is developed further here. I learned from Hypomania 1 more about how the mind is capable of performing amazing feats (e.g., simulating music conductors) when it is freed from conscious overcontrol.

In this connection, I recalled in the midst of the episode that I was once asked to be a simultaneous interpreter between Chinese and English at a technical conference. Not having performed simultaneous interpretation ever before, I had no clue about how it could be done. Not surprisingly, I made a mess of it in the beginning. I waited for the completion of a sentence in one language before translating it into another. That, of course, was a fatally flawed technique. The result was that I found myself hopelessly behind, not "simultaneous." I resigned myself to disastrous failure. I didn't care anymore. Suddenly I found that I could do it. I simply kept on translating continually. Utterances flowed from my lips with the ease of water flowing out of a tap. I called this *automatization*, a fundamental attribute of language performance.

Compulsivity and fear of losing specific thoughts are manifestations of overcontrol by the mind. These reemerged in two subsequent episodes, Hypomania 3 and Hypomania 4.

Hypomania 3 was marked by its brief duration of only a few days. I recorded that I "slept for 12 hours [and] completely recovered." So sleep held the key to recovery.

There were no adverse effects on my occupational or social functioning in the least. For instance, I conducted a two-day workshop on depression and suicide prevention just before the onset (ironic, isn't it?). I attended court as an expert witness on the following day. However, at home I was struggling with fatigue, compulsivity, and disturbance of short-term memory. The following is an excerpt from my diary (2 November 2003):

> Physical fatigue, but tremendous energy, mentally active, auto racing … very alert, but the body needs rest and sleep…. Feels wonderful…. Compulsive about recalling tidbits of specific information…. perfectly OK if I am just doing one thing at a time, like if I don't look at the screen, just type….
>
> Battle between the sexes (thinking about Workshop, "Love Sex, and Marriage," I had conducted)…. Men talk, but it is the women who perceive. Started to write things on paper, amused, good ideas….
>
> Takes 20 minutes to find my underwear, distractible, how annoying….
>
> Trying to recall now what I said afraid I might branch off, loss of central control mechanism to block off thought Ah no unconscious anymore no repression anymore I have a theory about intelligence the brain is the same but after removal of repression the whole bloody unconscious is available the raw emotions like when I cried I am now concentrating so much that I don't hear Paganini play it louder no repression = greater intelligence, creativity =

intelligence infinite association of ideas all at once now the theory in a talk trying to recollect something I wanted to say a while ago, annoyed not to be able to theory, no what I said in response to the question in real life I sometimes do several things all at the same time going back and forth "?????" Trying to recall, now able to walk away Amadeus Living = not dead thing and vice versa, [experienced] difficulty processing [this equation], no, I mean which is which, who is living/dead (I was referring to in an imaginary conversation with Orchid, joke, on living or dead) Imaginary? Really imaginary? Branches and branches of thought joke perfectly OK, but can't recall the exact ending of the joke in just a split of a second, it's gone, can't recall, and lost memory, forever [like] Korsakoff syndrome? Keep trying to reconstruct the past when immediate memory cannot be transferred to long term memory like a funnel, can't hold water

Use logic, make distinctions, fear, now I know what ob-compulsive is!? (joy and delight) save this file before it's lost, but I dare not!!!

No longer able to process thoughts, recollect, obsessive, like the brain is no longer able to function properly (the night before, difficulty in computing simple arithmetic, keep on making mistakes)

[Listened to] Paganini Decided to record thoughts, music not able to distract myself, thoughts continue I don't want to think, I want to sleep

Stupid, can do only one thing at a time, keep on forgetting what I had been doing a minute ago, start looking the things ("I spend most of my life looking for things", in the past, previously, no, in the past, previously, ... compulsive!!!!!) keep on forgetting thoughts I had just a while ago

> [Listened to] Amadeus Can't keep track of things (while I
> am typing now), can do several things all at once, brilliant
> flashes of insight mingles with random thoughts
> (where's "fMRI" on this screen, cannot find it) pulled in all
> directions afraid (afraind, made type correction, annoyed
> by the Microsoft) to go away and be lost spend more time
> trying to recollect, start all over again I want to stop lose
> the place concentrate to avoid compulsion
> (Nov 4) opposite pattern, cerebral activity associations
> become automatic, executive functioning is disrupted
> (e.g., getting a drink, forgetfulness, clumsiness)

These passages illustrate my intense struggle with brain fatigue, an inability to recall, and disturbances of executive functioning. Flight of ideas (one idea rapidly associated with another, leading to another, and another) and distractibility, two classic symptoms of mania, were loud and clear. The thought that my memory was "like a funnel, can't hold water" was scary. It was as if I were suffering from Korsakoff's syndrome, which is found among older alcoholics after many years of excessive drinking.

There were also lucid moments of reflectiveness, during which I brought my inflated self-confidence down to size. I mused that "I spend most of my life looking for things." Of my thinking output, I wrote: "It's nonsense, from a science point of view; uninspiring from a literary point of view." (But today I would say that wasn't true of all of my thoughts.) I thought of the potential of brain alteration through self-reprocessing: "same brain → self-reprocessing → different brain, self-creation potential!"

The most interesting idea was that I had "no repression anymore." What does this mean? The consequences must be profound: Truly "no repression = greater intelligence, creativity = ... infinite association of ideas all at once."

The writing is clearly different from my normal writing. It resembles the free association I did in Mania 2, but it isn't really free. One particular obsessive fixation deserves elaboration: "In the past, previously, no, in the past, previously, … compulsive!!!!!" I tend to become perfectionistic when I write, fixated on finding the exact, right words. As a lexicophiliac, I could be immersed in dictionaries for hours. (An inner voice now says: "You've got to liberate yourself.")

Also salient was the obsessive-compulsivity I struggled to rid myself of. I experienced "joy and delight" when I felt freed from its grip. However, "ob-com and creativity can co-exist," as I wrote in my diary (4 Nov 2003). I also theorized that the obsessive-compulsivity was "not the same ob-compulsive [symptoms, better understood in psychoanalytic terms, I had in my] youth, [but was due to] excitation beyond the ability of the central nervous system to cope…. nothing to do with forbidden/sexual (Freud doesn't apply)." The question now is how to be creative and experience "joy and delight" in normality, no less than in madness.

Hypomania 4, sandwiched between two manic episodes, was quite mild. It lasted less than a month. Here is an excerpt from my diary (23 June 2006) about my physical and psychological condition.

> My physical condition was one of great imbalance. The body was near exhaustion. The mind remains active, running on fast time. I felt thirsty all the time. I felt hot, where others may feel cold. Aware that my energy reserve might be depleted, I moved around slowly to conserve energy….
>
> Recollections or remembrances may throw fresh insights informative on brain functioning. The positive side was the creativity. Like boundaries between the conscious and the unconscious had vanished. The unconscious became accessible. Retrieval of information was superefficient. In addition, association of ideas was facilitated, fast, but I also felt overwhelmed by these endless associations. In the psychiatric literature, these are called flight of ideas.

Consumption of energy by the brain must have been extraordinarily high. The normal level of consumption is about 20 Watts. This led to some very disturbing states of brain functioning. I could not perform simple operations, such as simple arithmetic. I was completely forgetful. Immediately forgot where I had laid something down a moment ago. I had to walk around for some 20 minutes before I located the "lost" object.

Similarly, I had to try to focus on one thought. While staying focused, a myriad associations. The next moment, the memory of what I had just been thinking about was gone. Attempts to recall were usually futile. I became obsessive about keeping memories from being lost. So I tried to record my thoughts on paper or in a computer file. Thus, brain fatigue may well be the mechanism for obsessive symptoms. I have also experienced this when the air con is turned off. Mild cerebral anoxia. I don't want to say that this applies to all forms of obsessive phenomena. These obsessive phenomena I have described are qualitatively different from the psychoneurotic varieties described in the psychiatric literature.

Cumulative experiences eventually lead to insight. I have come to think of obsessive-compulsive overcontrol as "cerebral constipation." My antidote is No-Mind Therapy. It began during Hypomania 4 with my attempt to help a student who was cerebral to a fault. He sent a message to me that raised all kinds of questions about therapy. Here is my reply to him and his classmates.

Your diligence is impressive. It could also be an impediment to enlightenment. Do nothing, no-think, for a while, and see what happens.

DAT [Dialogic Action Therapy] can be hazardous to those who use their brains too much. To treat the patient with the right kind of medicine, I use No-Mind Therapy (invented/created at this very moment; see, therapies can be a dime a dozen).

Mindfulness is a misleading word that may lead many into tortured paths. It does not allow for the full strength of no-mind to run its course. If people from the West don't understand, they may be forgiven; it would be tragic if we don't.

The adult is full of thoughts pure and impure. Therefore, to return to his natural state, he must focus his attention to reexperience the emptiness of mind.

Focus, alas, implies conscious effort. For some, heroic effort, too much for a lazy person like myself. My path to the no-thought, selfless self is one of least resistance. Sorry, I can't tell you what it is. Each will have to discover it for himself. (Hint: music and poetry help.) You must read a poem aloud. Hear its beauty. Let your head, your whole body, move, like the bygone poets of China.

Now, empty yourself of even the *idea* of emptiness. Simply embrace it, experience it.

Therapy is poetry. Poetry is beauty. Therefore, mind and no-mind. Get it?

Mindfulness-based therapies are in vogue these days. I prefer the term *selfless mind* or *empty mind*, which comes closer to the Buddhist notions of selflessness and emptiness. A mind empty of ideas, cravings, even a sense of itself is the antithesis of overattachment, fixations, or rigidities. No-Mind Therapy accommodates much better the notion of vanished repression. What is there to repress in a mindless, empty mind? Two poems capture my thinking on what a true selfless self can do.

The Mindless Mind (20 Dec 2009)

A mindful mind is mindful of dust.
A mindless mind, mindless of the dust,
Minds nothing and everything all at once.
Full and empty, empty and full at will,
The selfless self acts without effort,
On target every time.

The Selfless Self (25 July 2010)

Without the self in the heart,
With feelings then reason flies.
Now ask the heavens,
Now ask the heavens, search
The earth, and penetrate
The cosmos's mysteries.

Now Get Physical: I Could Have Danced All Night

The idea that repression of artistic impulses can be hazardous to one's health evolved into a cardinal drive. Here, my body could be tired but still driven to perform. Music and dance figure prominently, especially during sleepless nights. I fall into an enchanted state, in which pieces of music I love have the power to grip my being and keep my body in motion. The lyrics in My Fair Lady, "I could have danced all night and could have begged for more," come to life, literally.

Recall in this context that in my youth I once went to a folk dance camp and danced for three days and nights, almost nonstop. But I know full well that the fountain of youth is not eternal. Be that as it may, music and dance in madness has informed me to grow professionally. Later, I created Dynamic Relaxation and Meditation, with music and dance as key components, as an avenue to enhance holistic health (see chapter 3).

In view of these, liberation from stagnation beginning from the body provides a natural thread that weaves the following episodes into a coherent story.

Hypomania 5 took place on board the *Queen Victoria* cruising around the Mediterranean. A confluence of circumstances and mishaps made joining the cruise physically and psychological exhausting.

Being traumatized in Heathrow Airport in London deserves special mention. Its Terminal 5 can only be described as a Terminal of Terror. The staff is positively unhelpful and rude. Understandably, security has to be tight, in view of the terrorist threats that Britain has been under. There is little excuse, however, for the security staff to yell "Take off your shoes," and scare the daylights out of passengers, including me, on transit.

By the time I saw the *Queen Victoria*, it was getting ready to set sail. The last gangway was about to be closed. I made it just in the nick of time. By then, having been deprived of a good rest for several days, I was in a state of exhaustion. What followed was a clinical tale of scary symptoms.

On board the *Queen Victoria*, I had a hard time recovering. There were lots of activities, and I could not fall asleep. Hypomania 5 differed from previous episodes in that the salient symptom was mental and physical depletion, rather than racing thoughts; however, elation of mood remained an important feature.

On the fifth day, I finally went to consult the physician on board. This was the list of symptoms I described to him: constipation, insomnia, extreme fatigue, disturbance of executive functions; in addition, I had cognitive deficits and spells of shaking chills, which I had not experienced before.

My body, impervious to signs of exhaustion, was pushed to its limit. In fact, I was dancing almost nightly, which I enjoyed immensely. I surprised myself with how good I was. I entered into a state of selfless-oblivion with ease. That was the secret. For the first time, I was able to be spontaneous, to move without any inhibition, to enjoy myself, *in public*. Sometimes, when I danced alone, people on the dance floor would stop dancing and watch me.

My sociability, love of adventure, and aesthetic capacity were undiminished. I took the initiative to interact with passengers as well as staff on board. One night, I ventured into the grand theatre inside the *Queen Victoria*. No one was there. I took advantage of the occasion, walked onto the empty stage and danced as if the theatre was full of people—thus to satisfy my aspiration, long frustrated, to be an artistic performer, at least for a while.

Unable to fall asleep, I went up to the upper decks of the ship early one morning to watch the sunrise. I discovered what "the majesty of the heavens" really meant. Above the horizon, brilliant golden rays penetrated a dark cloud, making a colossal sandwich of lights in the sky.

The cardinal symptom of Hypomania 6, as in Hypomania 5, was a prolonged low level of energy, punctuated with frequent bouts of depletion; racing thoughts or excessive talkativeness was secondary. I remember I had a three-hour therapy session with a family, which involved nonverbal techniques demanding an enormous expenditure of energy. At the end of the session, I was so tired that I simply collapsed. Afterwards, when I went to a restaurant for lunch, I had to conserve my energy with extreme measures, such as half shutting my eyes, avoiding all unnecessary talking or movements; I ate at the slowest pace ever. These I had not experienced before, not even in Hypomania 5.

The quest for holistic health and artistic self-expression marked this episode. It began in the physical realm. One of my blessings is good health, at least in relative terms, which I have enjoyed all my life. I've never had a major illness or been hospitalized, except for a nasal operation I had in my youth.

However, posture had been a problem for decades: Spending hours in front of a computer monitor was an occupational hazard. My upper back had been slightly hunched, and my head used to stick out. I was not aware of how bad it looked until I saw some photographs in which I appeared with a "turtle neck." My massage chair was not a luxury, but a necessity to relieve the tightness around my neck and shoulders.

I had to do something: Fight back; exercise. While using the massage chair, I would move around in order to reach different parts of my body. This I did a lot, until finally my body was more relaxed than it had been for a long time. One day, while walking along, I noticed that my posture was completely upright. The hunchback had gone!

This physical breakthrough ignited a chain reaction in the psychological and spiritual realms. With heightened artistic-aesthetic sensibilities, I experimented with Chinese character writing for weeks. Deviating from standard writing, I used curved strokes to construct rounded characters, which suggest femininity, softness, and smoothness of emotions.

I also took up singing in German. This I informed a German-American friend of mine in a message. An excerpt:

> Two days ago, I was listening to some German opera arias, which I normally don't do. But the beauty of *O du, mein holder Abendstern* in Wagner's Tannhäuser gripped my being, and I started to sing. Now, I have never sung anything properly, least of all in German. After a lot of repeated practice, I finally succeeded in making myself a semblance of a baritone. I taught myself. Lacking in technicality, strength, *usw* [etc.], I made up with expression. I then went onto Schiller's ode *An die Freude* in Beethoven's

choral symphony and Louis Spohr's Faust, immersing myself in these beauties.

It seems that working with the physical domain is easier and hence may be a recommended first step. In this episode, I gained health first through conquering poor posture and second through allowing myself full artistic self-expression, *without regard for how well or how poorly I performed*. Thus, art and health are intertwined. Isn't this a vindication of the claim that repression of artistic impulses can be hazardous to one's health?

Hypomania 7 was basically a continuation of the preceding episode. My level of physical activity was very high, spending a lot of time singing and performing qigong and wushu. But I was low on reserves, frequently overcome by both mental and physical fatigue. My energy level fluctuated dramatically; my condition was one of severe imbalance.

On one occasion, I suffered from acute cognitive dysfunction for about an hour. It was like a sudden attack of mental depletion (rather than confusion). I was simply mentally exhausted. I could not perform even simple tasks, such as making a telephone call. I also suffered from ejaculation retardation and even ejaculation incompetence for several weeks, something I had not experienced before.

Despite the physical imbalance, however, my mood was elated. I felt confident and self-assured. I felt a sense of mastery. Perhaps, finally, I have learned to reap the benefits of explosive creativity without incurring social costs. There was little or no indication that people with whom I interacted found my behavior out of bounds. To them, I was eager to learn, friendly, and jovial.

Years ago, when I was about to receive my Ph.D. and then depart from the United States to return to Asia, I wanted to learn as much as possible about how to do hypnotherapy in the remaining months. I had private sessions lasting two hours every day, seven times a week, with a former professor of mine. Now, I was busy preparing for relocation to the United States in the midst of this episode. I became an apprentice again.

This time, I wanted to learn qigong and taiji push-hands, an advanced taiji exercise involving two persons "pushing hands" against each other. I took private lessons from two taiji masters. Taiji is one of the "inner" schools of Chinese wushu (as distinct from the "outer" schools, e.g., Shaolin gungfu).

It is difficult to learn, far more than I had imagined. It demands strict adherence to an attitude in conformity with the Daoist idea of *wuwei* (nonaction, not inaction). The principle is to use your opponent's own forces to defeat him. This means suppressing common, instinctive tendencies and waiting for and capitalizing on the opponent's mistaken moves.

For months I had to learn, and relearn, the fundamental technique of moving my arms in "perfect" circles. My taiji masters were impressive and convincing, capable of doing things to which verbal description can hardly do justice. Their forearms felt like rods of steel; they could push and move me off my feet at will, but I couldn't move them an inch. So immersed I was in the push-hands that when I awoke in the middle of the night, I would find my arms moving in circles.

Hypomania 8 took place in Southern California, after my relocation from Hong Kong in July 2009. It occurred just shortly after I thought I had finished writing this book. It lasted for about three weeks. Familiar symptoms appeared, such as mental hyperactivity, mood elation, enhanced artistic sensibility, and aesthetic appreciation of ordinary objects (e.g., the root of a tree).

I craved physical activity. I yearned to listen to music. Unfortunately, I noticed that my tolerance for volume diminished dramatically, and somehow the music didn't sound right; reminded of how brain trauma (e.g., concussion) may result in oversensitivity to noise, I thought that these were signs of a tired brain. There was, as usual, insomnia, but having severe, frequent shaking chills was a new experience.

What followed was a descent into a scary state of severe mental fatigue and confusion. It was so bad that I would get lost while taking a walk around my neighborhood. I dared not drive. However, even in this state the wisdom of the body could be discerned: I moved around and performed tasks without conscious deliberation, as if my movements were to a large extent automatized.

I consulted a physician. He ordered laboratory tests, none resulting in positive findings. Unable to sleep, my condition got worse. I took sleeping pills for a few nights and slept better, but that did nothing to stop the mental hyperactivity and fatigue.

I was then desperate enough to go to a hospital on an emergency basis. All sorts of tests were done, again none resulting in positive findings. The attending doctor decided that hospitalization was not necessary. He prescribed risperidone, an antipsychotic drug, after I told him about how previously taking Risperdal (trade name for risperidone) helped to clear my mania. Taking the drug put me on the track of recovery. Predictably, as my mood elation disappeared, my mundane life resumed again.

Body-Mind-Spirit Health: Interconnectedness

What have the episodes of madness informed us about how the mind, body, and spirit are interconnected? An internal dialogue ensues.

David Manic or hypomanic states are thought of as disturbances of mood. So I am particularly intrigued by the physical, flesh and blood changes you have described, such as fatigue, oversensitivity to noise, and energy flow within the body. Clearly, physical changes are concomitant, even integral, to changes in mind and spirit. What are some of the more dramatic changes?

YF   On several occasions, I had hiccups that lasted on and off for some five hours in the middle of the night. Bewildered, I consulted a taiji master about what happened. She congratulated me, saying "It's a good thing." True enough, although the process was unpleasant, the end result was beneficial to my health. After the hiccups subsided, I felt a sense of extraordinary well-being; whatever gastrointestinal imbalances or disturbances I had previously were gone.

One particular feat I achieved stands out in my memory. In a chilly morning, I practiced Taiji in a park. I did not follow a set sequence of movements, as most practitioners do; instead, I moved spontaneously, without constraints. I entered into a state of selfless-oblivion. Soon I felt a powerful flow of energy or qi within my body. I felt warm throughout, even though I was wearing little. My hands turned red, radiating heat that another person could feel at a distance of several inches.

David   This brings to mind Tibetan monks who are able, in a state of deep meditation, to generate enough bodily heat to produce steam effusing from blankets put over their bodies. Incidentally, your body must have been burning up calories at an explosive pace, depleting reserves. This may explain why you have shaking chills during your episodes.

YF   Additionally, I could just feel a magnification of physical strength, in proportion to my increase in self-confidence.

David   A measure of "megalomania" may be essential to creative adventures and is, to that extent, healthy.

YF   Afterwards, I joined a couple of advanced taiji practitioners and followed them in performing a set sequence which I had learned only as a beginner some year ago. To my surprise, I had no trouble at all. So it seems that my kinesthetic sense may be enhanced, in dancing as in practicing wushu, when I am loosened from being self-conscious.

There were also perceptual changes as well. Most dramatic of these was a supersensitive sense of smell. On one occasion, I was walking along the bank of an inland swamp. Incredibly, I was able to smell the unpleasant odors from the swamp more than a hundred feet away, even though there was a steady breeze blowing. I am positive that normally I would not have been able to do so. Was my sense of smell really enhanced? I don't think so. It was my mind made quiet that enabled me to read the odorous signals with my normal nose.

My time perception also changed. Eating a meal, for instance, might take hours—to my surprise when I looked at my watch. Simply, I had no awareness of how much time had passed. On one occasion, it took me some two hours to adjust a pair of new goggles, fumbling clumsily along. This exceeded by far the time I took to learn how to do it for the first time (an embarrassing thirty minutes or so), bearing testimony to my extraordinary inability to perform even simple tasks during episodes. I didn't know how long it took until I asked someone what time it was. Then it dawned on me that my time perception had altered.

In all, I am grateful that I have learned so much from the episodes of madness through groping and self-discovery, without the benefit of guidance from a master. But I don't think that I have really discovered anything new. I am only fortunate to have *experienced* what is already known to luminary masters of wushu, qigong, or yoga, and thus to marvel at the hidden potentialities of the human body.

David   There is an irony. In Hypomania 8, you said that even in a state of severe mental fatigue and confusion, "The wisdom of the body could be discerned: I moved around and performed tasks without conscious deliberation, as if my movements were to a large extent automatized." This recapitulates what happened in Hypomania 2: "I was physically exhausted. However, I felt that my motility was efficient, 'with not a single movement wasted.' Even my handwriting changed."

Wouldn't it be great if "the wisdom of the body" were to take its course in your normal life as well?

YF   The wisdom of the body reaches its pinnacle in what I would call Body-Mind-Spirit (BMS) Interconnectedness. BMS Health presupposes interconnectedness among the body, mind, and spirit.

It is, above all, holistic: Changes in one domain lead to changes in other domains. A disconnect spells trouble, resulting in imbalances. Hence, balance is the hallmark of holistic health.

My episodes are a goldmine of imbalances: inability to fall asleep; physical and mental fatigue and even depletion of reserves, coexisting with mental hyperactivity; cognitive disturbances, such as extreme forgetfulness; alterations between compulsivity and bursts of creativity. Running through the episodes are recapitulations of what happened in Mania 1: "The body was near exhaustion, yet the mind remained active, running on fast time."

David   You focus too much on the negatives. You have experienced remarkable realizations of the human body's potentialities, particularly when you enter into the state of selfless-oblivion.

I have been pondering another question in connection with BMS interconnectedness. Earlier, you thought that a hyperactive sympathetic autonomic nervous system (SANS) characterized the underlying physiology of Mania 2. So the physical underlies the mental: Underlying mental hyperactivity is probably a hyperactive SANS.

Two implications follow. One, physiological causation should be given more weight. Two, controlling or reducing SANS hyperactivity may hold a key to treatment; medication may be indicated. Of course, the mental also underlies the physical: Mental hyperactivity contributes to fatigue and is prodromal to mania.

YF   My libidinal drive tends to be stronger than usual during episodic spells. I strongly suspect that a hyperactive SANS has much to do with it.

David   Also your unbridled imagination and capacity to appreciate beauty! SANS is not the only culprit.

"Pleasures of cloud and rain," a Chinese euphemism for sexual congress, sounds more abstract than "the birds and the bees." Both euphemisms are rooted in poetry. Samuel Coleridge wrote: "All nature seems at work.... The bees are stirring—birds are on the wing."

Also, in English the term "cloud nine" refers to a state of blissful oblivion.

YF   In contrast, the Chinese idiom "whirling clouds, a blanket of rain" suggests the workings of considerable natural forces.

Apparently, clouds in the sky evoke all kinds of fantasy on earth in different cultures.

David   To poetic minds, anything can.

Revisiting Hypomania 5, you saw "a colossal sandwich of lights in the sky" on sunrise in the Mediterranean—brilliant sun rays penetrating a dark cloud. You felt overwhelmed by the majesty of the heavens. Now I read a deeper meaning into what you saw: the triumph of light over darkness. I bet you must have come close to a religious experience facilitated by madness.

YF   But I also see beauty in dark clouds. I would like to have nothing more than to remain in cloud nine in the midst of a cumulonimbus, a cumulus with a low dark base and fluffy towers that rise to great heights, portending the arrival of thunderstorms—and proclaiming the awesome power of the heavens.

David   Finally, we must spell out a major lesion learned from your experiences: Don't forget the body in any spiritual journey. Strategically, getting the body in shape is a good first step to take.

The body suffused with libido produces a mind that sees beauty everywhere, sublimating the spirit. That's BMS Interconnectedness.

Unanswered Questions

YF   At rock bottom, what is the nature of the conditions I "suffered" from? I was perplexed about my episodic experiences, especially in the beginning. They appeared alien to me, for I had not yet gotten used to them. So after Hypomania 1, I wrote a message to a psychologist, renowned for his studies of intelligence, hoping that he would provide me with some answer:

Recently I experienced something extremely unusual, which I would like to share with you. It relates to intelligence and creativity, I think; but I don't know if it has been intensively studied as a phenomenon.

For about a couple of weeks, my mind "exploded." All kinds of ideas came so fast that I could not put them down on paper, or into a computer, fast enough. Thoughts, ranging from cosmology to psychology, raced through my mind. They were entertaining thoughts, at least to me, so much so that I had difficulty sleeping (unusual for me). What I experienced may be called mental hyperactivity, but it might be more than that…. The ideas were creative ideas: enough for a book that I would love to write.

I also experienced flashes of insight. Somewhat like enlightenment! I noticed many things more sharply than before. For instance, I listened to music, and heard sounds in a way that I did not before. And I did many things for the first time in my life, such as dancing, entering into a trance, and so forth.

People around me say that I have become "strange"—or, more precisely, stranger. More expressive, for instance.

I am not sure how these fit into current understanding of intelligence. Because of your research in human intelligence, you might be able to provide me with some answer.

Unfortunately, I did not receive a reply. My perplexity continued.

David　Physical symptoms (e.g., insomnia, fatigue) were prominent during all episodes. Shaking chills appeared for the first time on board the *Queen Victoria* in Hypomania 5 and became severe in Hypomania 8. Experiencing cognitive deficits (e.g., extreme forgetfulness) and mental confusion (e.g., getting lost easily) really scared me in both of these episodes. No physician has yet proffered a medical explanation for these symptoms.

Are the physical symptoms a part of your madness? And what is the nature of this madness? What is the dynamics of positives (e.g., exuberance) coexisting with negatives (e.g., anguish) in terms of spirituality? These are crucial questions to be addressed in the next chapter.

YF   I have learned to identify telltale prodromal signs that forebode the onset of an episode and to prevent it from developing into full-blown hypomania or mania. Preceding onset, there are times when I easily get tired and absent-minded, so much so that I can do hardly any work at all for weeks. At the same time, I become more emotional and sensitive. Tears would flow from my eyes when I hear music I love or contemplate about my life condition. I can just sense that something is brewing. Sure enough, an episode would follow.

David   But I admit to an unsettling thought: Since 2005, at least one episode has occurred each year. How long will your madness last?

YF   I have a premonition that it will last for a long time to come.

David   Your parents had a long life. Physically you can do things that most other people of your age cannot do. You have discovered the elixir of longevity in your passion for music and dance. All these point to a long life. As you say, "I want to die young, but to delay it as long as possible." I look forward to seeing more madness in a man at age 100 or beyond! That would be legendary.

YF   Again, the benefits give me consolation if I am indeed condemned to be mad unto the end of my days. The greatest benefit of all, which occurred in Hypomania 8, was nothing short of a transformative religious experience on an Easter Sunday. Unlike previous religious experiences, which were experienced in private, this one took place in public, in front of an assembly. This experience we shall describe at the end of chapter 4.

David   In Hypomania 7, you were in a state of imbalance, yet you felt a sense of mastery, as you did in Mania 2: "I have arrived" (to enlightenment). (This may be one of the rare instances where *arrive to* is acceptable.) Now I know better what Confucius meant when he said that, at age seventy, he acted according to his heart's wishes.

But what happens to you when balance is restored?

YF   Life becomes mundane again. Inertia sets in: I become physically lazy. I succumb to one of the Seven Deadly Sins, sloth. Moreover, I do many things better when I'm "imbalanced." I dance without being self-conscious; I don't question myself about accepting new challenges, like learning taiji push-hands or writing Chinese poetry in English. Now that I'm "balanced," I've become more self-conscious, and I question myself. Damnation!

Clearly, I fall short of the ideal of BMS interconnectedness. Otherwise, the episodes would not have occurred. The greatest irony is that my transformation is characterized by sequential alterations between creativity and stagnation.

David   You are being harsh on yourself. I've caught you again.

YF   Nevertheless, I do recognize that I owe much to the episodes of madness for the creative ideas I have gained, "enough for a book that I would love to write."

CHAPTER 3:
FROM PSYCHIATRY TO SPIRITUALITY

To your own self be kind.

*A body in motion invigorates the mind and uplifts the spirit;
an invigorated mind makes the body healthier and pushes the
spirit forward; an uplifted spirit gives the body calm and the
mind serenity.*

What is the nature of my episodes of madness? Many perplexities
remain unresolved. For instance, reflecting on Hypomania 5 in
the preceding chapter, I raised the question: What condition was I
suffering from? My answer was: "To this day, I am not sure"; brain
fatigue appeared to be the salient feature. I now turn to the larger
picture of my case as a whole. More questions are raised. What
mental disorder, if any, did I suffer from? What is the diagnosis?

Actually, I have already made a thorough self-diagnosis once
before. As a graduate student in clinical psychology, I went through
intensive training in psychodiagnostics. Back in the 1960s, students
spent a great deal of time in psychological testing, probably more
than present-day students do. I was required to submit case studies,
each involving a case history and a battery of psychological tests,
as assignments. I used myself as a subject for one assignment: I
wrote reports on my functioning and diagnosed myself. So it was a
self case study. Little could I foresee that I would do it for a second
time years later.

Later, I engaged my former professor for didactic psychoanalytic therapy for several months, as intensive as having two-hour
sessions daily for seven days a week. The most memorable experi-

ence was having my Rorschach protocol interpreted while I was under hypnosis. Thus, I may claim to have a fair degree of self-understanding.

A diagnosis should be based on adequate evidence. Already I have amassed considerable material on my case. In chapter 1, I presented my life history. Clinical descriptions of my episodes are given in chapter 2. In the present chapter, I add excerpts of self-reports submitted as assignments. Together, these materials cover diverse areas of my life history and psychological functioning; they provide the evidence for making a diagnosis.

An Early Self Case Study

Digging out my old reports turned out to be a revealing search for the early stages of my spiritual development. Decades later, I can see my former self containing the buds of my present self clearly in the responses to various psychological tests.

A number of themes were already present in responses to the Incomplete Sentence Blank.

> I want to know: sufficiently about the universe and man's part in it.
> I can't: fight against the entire historic background under which I grew.
> My mind: is a complex phenomenon which reflects the cultures of the East and the West today.
> When I was a child: I became aware of things that other children were not aware of.
> My nerves: are sometimes extremely excited.
> Sometimes: I feel the ecstasy of life, sometimes its sorrow.

I secretly: cherish thoughts that society does not accept in general.

I: am a being—unique in own ways.

Here we find themes like being caught in history and between cultures, being different, nonconformity, struggle, wanting to know man's part in the universe, extremely excited nerves, ecstasy and sorrow.

The Thematic Apperception Test is a well-known projective technique, in the sense that the subject projects his inner drives, emotions, and complexes onto outer stimuli of varying degrees of ambiguity; the more ambiguous the stimuli, the more projective the test. The subject is asked to tell a story in response to each of a series of pictures presented. The test manual claims that "as a rule the subject leaves the test happily unaware that he has presented to the psychologist with what amounts to an X-Ray picture of his inner self." An exaggeration?

No matter. Here are excerpts (with key words appearing in italics) from some of the stories I gave and, where suitable, from my TAT report submitted as an assignment (following the word *Interpretation*—in other words, my own interpretation of the stories I told about the pictures). The serial number of the picture is given within parentheses (B for young boys, G for young girls, M for men over age fourteen; F for women over age fourteen).

(3 BM) ... This picture seems to be symbolic of the misery many boys in the world face, and of the hardships they have to overcome to realize a bright future. The last picture was also symbolic: of *artistry*; but this one is symbolic of *pathos*, which is *universal*.

(7 BM) A father is talking to his son.... [who] has lost *faith* in goodness.... the young man will regain some of

his faith in man. [Pause] Gradually and surely. It looks like they are both philosophers.

(12 M) Here is a boy lying in bed. He is asleep. He has been sick. Now this man is putting his hand on his forehead, and is lifting it. He has great *spiritual* powers. Symbolically, it is like faith. With faith, the boy will get well again. Perhaps this is what the artist is trying to depict in this picture. (*Interpretation.* The Subject qualifies his acceptance of spiritual healing at two levels: it is symbolic, and it is only a picture of an artist.... By being impersonal (using qualifications), the Subject in essence says that he has not abandoned his faith in logic or reason either.)

(12 F) This is a picture of two women, one young and beautiful, the other old and ugly—a striking contrast. The artist illustrates the inevitable course of human development; nothing human is *everlasting.* There is an end to everything, including beauty and youth. Also the young woman is calm, but the old woman seems to be afraid and worried, perhaps of approaching death. What is lasting? The art of capturing fate in a painting. That is everlasting. (*Interpretation.* Actually there is no story told to this card, but an interpretation of a painting perceived by the Subject.... The response is rich in description, both in relation to the stimulus and its symbolic significance as the Subject defines it. The subject's interpretation shows that he tends to think in terms of generalities.... As in [a previous story], there is an intense awareness of the natural forces beyond man's power, and to which man must submit and accept. But it is not true that man can do nothing about his fate: At least he can capture it in art....)

(14) A young man is looking from his window in his room.... His head is help up high, as if he is full of *hope*. Here he is surveying the town from his window. He can see many things other people cannot see. With hope and conviction, he will go out and make his hopes and aspirations come true.

(17 BM) This is a man climbing a rope. He looks very strong, but how can he measure against infinity! Half way in between heaven and earth, what can he do? ... Man against *infinity*; it's impossible. (*Interpretation.* The mode of response is much like that to 12 F. The card is only a painting by some artist, conveying symbolically the impossibility of measuring against the infinite. This is therefore a concept-driven response. Again, the Subject shows his intense awareness of man's helplessness against nature, insofar as his ability of completely transcending it [is concerned]. He readily resigns himself to this fate and accepts his *limitations* as a human being.)

In these stories, even in fragments, I cannot help noticing the words *artistry, pathos, universal, faith, spiritual, everlasting, hope, infinity*. These words would be found in a book on spirituality. Thus they presage the present undertaking. The idea that nothing is everlasting, in particular, is akin to the Buddhist notion of impermanence—nothing is, everything becomes—although I knew next to nothing about Buddhism in my student days.

Thinking in abstractions or symbolic terms is clearly characteristic of my cognitive style. The feeling of distinction ("seeing things other people cannot see") reverberates with another response in the Incomplete Sentence Blank ("When I was a child: I became aware of things that other children were not aware of"). Optimism, backed by conviction, comes through clearly. Yet, human limitations and acceptance of the inevitable are recurrent themes.

What began as an intellectual attitude in my youth has evolved into spiritual experiences of humility and acceptance later in my life. In the midst of Mania 1, I felt a deep sense of humility: "The more I knew, the more I became aware of my profound ignorance. Knowledge and humility were like twins."

Themes of human limitation and humility reemerge in epigrams I have written in the last decade or so. Some of these echo the theme of not knowing what one does not know and the dangers of absolutistic self-conviction; others wonder about the nature of knowledge itself. Reading these epigrams again, I note that self-reflective thought and the sense of humility in the face of human limitation come through loud and clear, amounting to what has prevented me from descent into greater despair.

> To know what one does not know is the beginning of new knowledge. For some people, this knowing is never grasped. (25 Aug 2006)

> The scholar labors to know the unknown.
> The fool strives to know the unknowable.
> But where is the boundary between the unknown and the unknowable?
> Upon this question rests the verdict of whether you are the scholar or the fool. (26 Aug 2006)

> Knowledge is power. Absolutistic knowledge is tyrannical power. (29 Dec 2007)

> If you think you are always right, you are a very dangerous person, especially if indeed you are. (6 June 2008)

Someone says: "If I think I am right, I will continue to think I am right, regardless of what others might say; and if I think I am wrong, it is only because I think I am indeed wrong." Is this borne of conviction, or tyranny of the mind? (8 June 2008)

Knowledge is the sum total of information required to render it impossible for any sentient being to distinguish truth from falsehood, or reality from virtual reality, anytime, anywhere in the cosmos and beyond. In other words, to deceive a being like you or me cocooned in a virtual world into believing that it is reality. Who is the deceiver? A super mathematician called God. (1 Jan 2014)

The Rorschach test is the best-known projective technique. The subject is asked to look at ten inkblot cards, one at a time. He is to say what the inkblot represents or looks like to him, what comes to his mind. My initial reaction to the Rorschach was skepticism. As I went deeper, skepticism turned into amazement, of how much one can learn about the psychology of personality in general and individual persons in particular.

Around the time I was completing my doctoral training in the United States, I went to one of my professors whose specialty was hypnotherapy. The professor interpreted my Rorschach protocol, which was unusual in many respects, while I was under hypnosis. The protocol contained some two hundred responses, an exceptionally large number. The examiner (i.e., myself) recorded a remark I made during testing: "All kinds of idea come to my mind so fast; sometimes I can't tell you fast enough." Even though I was by no means experiencing flight of ideas, my experience with the Rorschach test was similar to the bouts of madness that occurred later in my life.

Along with responses indicative of obsessive compulsivity (e.g., small details) were those of creative imagination, just as obsessive compulsivity and creativity have been the dual aspects of my personality. These aspects are like antagonistic twins engaged in a continual battle within my psyche. Winning this battle would be momentous for not only my mental health but also my spiritual fulfillment. It amounts to freedom from fixation and liberation from self-imprisonment.

One of the percepts I identified in the Rorschach test was a devil, followed by a spontaneous remark, "The best defense is mockery, for the devil fears nothing more than your laughter." Indeed. The significant point is that the usual direction of fear is reversed: I am in control; it is the devil who fears my mockery.

As a matter of fact, I have never been afraid of devils, vampires, or ghosts. Once I went to a cemetery alone in the middle of the night, hoping to obtain a glimpse of these beings. I didn't; instead, I saw for the first time the beauty of the bright moonlight shining on tombstones and angels made of white marble all over the cemetery.

When I was about ten years old, someone told me that beautiful ghosts of banana trees would come out at night. So I went to the backyard of the house where I dwelled, alone at night, because it was full of banana trees. I waited and waited under the trees. I saw nothing but a snake. Could the snake be that beautiful female demon who assumed human form, according to the Chinese legend of the white snake, before her transfiguration?

Another percept was a butterfly, to which I alluded in a poem I wrote many years later (1 Aug 2005).

Who's Dreaming?

Awakened from my slumber, still
Enchanted by the butterfly,
Flying happily in Zhuangzi's dream,
Dreaming about the philosopher.

"A wish forbidden to be fulfilled,
In a dreamer's wet dream," Sigmund declares.

Zhuangzi retorts: "What's forbidden?
The Dao is all embracing!"

"Oh, Sigmund, trying to analyze the Daoist?"
"The royal road to the unconscious leads nowhere.
I'm lost in this Daoist labyrinth.
Hermann, you give it a try."

"Please tell me more about the butterfly."
"As dainty as Dame Margot, as serene as Guanyin,
Emulating varied floral coloration,
Metamorphosing itself into a flying orchid."
"Metaphoric, combining movement, color and its nuances:
A rare percept indeed!" Hermann mumbles to himself.
"Now, which part of the inkblot looks like the butterfly?"

The butterfly flies away, leaving behind
The smoke of Sigmund's cigar.

This is really weird. Who's dreaming
Another dreamer's dream,
Privy to others' inner thoughts?

I calm myself: "Don't worry. *You* are only dreaming."
But then, this means I'm still *in* the dream.
"So, when will I wake up, to know
I'm awake, or dreaming I'm awake?"

Still perplexed.

Note. The personalities that "appear" in the dream are
Zhuangzi (Daoist philosopher), Sigmund Freud, Hermann
Rorschach (Swiss psychiatrist who invented the inkblot
test), Guanyin (Chinese goddess of mercy), and Margot

Fonteyn (one of the greatest classical ballet dancers of all time). The poem is inspired by the famous tale of Zhuangzi's dream of the butterfly.

To this day, I still feel the *presence* of the butterfly. Empathy and emotional reactivity are evident in my test responses as in real life. In Hypomania 2, I wept in front of a class of students when talking about the June Fourth massacre in Beijing. Even when I am normal, tears sometimes flow from my eyes in poignant moments. On occasion, watching starving children in Africa on television can overwhelm me.

Empathic and emotional responsiveness in the extreme may have negative consequences. Being as sensitive as a *living* Rorschach inkblot enables me to be a good psychologist; it can also tax my emotional life. Sympathy, empathic sensitivity, kind-heartedness, and the like are admirable attributes; in the extreme, however, they can be hazardous to mental health. A person who experiences all the pain of battered women, the homeless, the enslaved, and so forth—like Mother Teresa carrying the woes of humankind on her shoulders—would be loaded to the extreme.

I value my capacity to experience pain, as well as delight, as an attribute of psychological health. But I also know that there is a limit to that capacity. Moreover, the natural tendency is to defend myself from emotional overloading. The danger, by which I have been threatened, is that I may become callous: There are times when I succumb to the pressures of life, become indifferent to the pain and suffering of others, and descend into spiritual emptiness.

This leads me to interpret callousness as a defensive reaction against emotional overloading, at least among individuals who have the capacity for empathic sensitivity. Balance holds a key for spiritual fulfillment, as it does for Body-Mind-Spirit (BMS) interconnectedness.

The conclusions of two particular self-reports are informative. One, the case history concluded that I was "quite well adjusted on a psycho-social level, but at the expense of a great deal of psychic energy"; that I had "serious internal conflicts"; and that the symptomatology pointed to "a compulsive personality, even neurosis."

Two, the integrative report on all test results gave a similar clinical picture. It depicted me as a driven person who viewed his life as "an intense struggle"; my personality is "extremely complicated," and "seems to include extremes." Strengths and potentialities were also mentioned: a strong ego; highly motivated, with a fighting spirit in the face of adversity; intelligence and language facility; reality bound, yet imaginative; empathic capacity; emotional responsiveness.

Reviewing now the test protocols and reports I have kept, this time with the critical eye of a professor, I have to agree with these conclusions. They contain nothing inconsistent with my life history or with the sentiments I expressed in diaries and correspondence with friends and relatives written during my student days in North America. The germs of my spiritual quest can be discerned; so can the theme of liberation from compulsivity and the realization of creative potential. But I now must ask: Does a spiritual quest or liberation have to be an intense struggle?

One critical point, in terms of the following self-diagnostic exercise, is that there was no clear indication of a mood disorder. Moreover, the strengths mentioned would predict against the occurrence of severe mental disorders in the future. Thus, in the light of the early self case study, the episodes of madness come as a surprise.

The most significant issues to be addressed concern two of the atypical features of my madness. One is that the episodes occur late in my life. Why? I frankly don't know. Two, all of the episodes are spells of exuberance, none of depression. Thus, my mood disorders are rather odd, unipolar instead of being typically bipolar. Why? The early self case study provides a clue: Having "a fighting spirit in the face of adversity" is a potent antidote to depression.

A Self-Diagnostic Exercise in Psychiatry

The self-diagnostic exercise begins with a psychiatric focus: to find out what mental disorder(s), if any, I suffered during the episodes. I first turn to the DSM-IV (*Diagnostic and Statistical Manual of Mental Disorders*, 4th edition), which provides explicit criteria for the diagnosis of mental disorders.

To make such a self-diagnosis is an odd and difficult task. How would one maintain objectivity? In essence, I am asked to assess how sick I have been. For instance, did Mania 1 and Mania 2 qualify as full-blown mania? To this day, at the time of writing this chapter, I am still debating within myself.

So, why not share the debate with readers? An internal dialogue ensues to make the self-diagnostic task clearer. Readers certainly don't want to miss the delight of seeing the bible of psychiatric diagnosis debunked. And predictably, David and YF are so absorbed in their dialogue that they cannot stop until the end of the chapter.

David   According to DSM-IV, Manic Episode is a distinct period of abnormally and persistently elevated, expansive, or irritable mood. Unlike Hypomanic Episodes, the mood disturbance is sufficiently severe to cause marked impairment in occupational, social, or interpersonal functioning. Psychotic features (e.g., hallucinations and delusions) may be present. Hospitalization may be necessary. (Note that names of episodes are capitalized in the DSM-IV.)

Both Mania 1 and Mania 2 meet the criteria for Manic Episode. You had distinct periods of persistently elevated and expansive mood. You had manic symptoms such as inflated self-esteem, being more talkative than usual or feeling pressure to keep talking, flight of ideas or the subjective experience that thoughts are racing.

YF   In my case, irritability was secondary to elevation and expansiveness. At any rate, hospitalization was not necessary; no psychotic features were present. Grandiosity, if present, never reached delusional proportions.

In Mania 1, I did experience hallucinations, like seeing myself on a cross. But it must be made clear these were *willful* hallucinations, under the control of the hallucinator; at no time was there any confusion between visualization and reality. Hallucinations are not necessarily pathological. To make a stronger claim, they may be a positive, powerful, even transformative, religious experience. To me, they certainly are.

More generally, in what sense is elevated mood abnormal? To whom? According to what standards?

David   Modeled after medical diagnosis, the DSM-IV is based on a rather narrow view of mental disorders. The new DSM-V, released in 2013, shows no radical conceptual breakthrough. To expand our horizons, consider the different ways or criteria by which a mental disorder, or its absence, may be judged.

A person may be diagnosed by a qualified professional as suffering from a mental disorder. He may (or may not) subjectively feel unwell, with complaints such as "I'm going to have a nervous break-down." He may deviate significantly from some statistical norm (e.g., scoring unusually high on a test of psychopathology) or sociocultural standard (e.g., acting in ways that are considered outside the bounds of social or cultural acceptability). He may fail to maintain interpersonal relationships or meet the demands of adaptation (e.g., holding onto a job). He may fall short of some ideal of psychological health (e.g., self-realization). Finally, he may interpret his mental disorder in a larger context, religious or spiritual. This is not unusual, but has not been given sufficient attention by the psychiatric establishment.

These criteria do not necessarily yield the same judgment. A person may be judged to be mentally ill by one criterion (e.g., diagnosis by a professional) but not so by another (e.g., his own subjective feeling).

Diagnosis is no simple matter. To add more complication to the life of a diagnostician, consider the case of a person who wants to lead others to think he is mentally ill (a form of manipulation), does not think he is mentally ill himself, but is judged to be mentally ill by professionals. I have in fact come across such cases, you know.

YF   I am all too aware of the tension between how I view myself and how I am judged by others.

David   You have said many times that one's social self presented to others is not necessarily congruent with one's social image perceived by others. You have admitted that your social image was damaged. What about your social self during the episodic bouts of madness, as you now perceive it?

YF   The presentation of my social self to others left much to be desired. Still, what did I do that was so abnormal or horrible? There was no hatred, no violence. I was not a danger to myself or to others.

David   Your mood disturbance was sufficiently severe to cause marked impairment in daily functioning; in Mania 2 especially, enough to incur heavy occupational and social costs (losing a job, losing friends).

YF   My functioning was indeed disturbed. But marked impairment? In Mania 1, I functioned well enough to go to Thailand for a few days. In place of hospitalization, I took a vacation, by the end of which I had recovered. As to Mania 2, losing a job and losing friends are not an "impairment" of my person. I was quite capable of functioning as a teacher; I had many friends not lost.

David   You may make a self-diagnosis. But it is the diagnosis by others that counts. You yourself have alluded to the importance of managing your social image. Reflecting on Mania 2, you wrote:

> My self-perceptions differ from the perceptions by others about my mania: I find the experiences inspirational; people around me are worried, perhaps even petrified. This remains a contradiction I have to face. Attending to perceptions by other people about my behavior is no less important to effective social functioning than self-perceptions.

Once the tendency to perceive your behavior in psychopathological terms is solidified, you've had it. You get stigmatized. People become suspicious of you. Even your normal behaviors may be perceived through a tainted lens.

YF   You're telling me! I've had plenty of personal experiences of being stigmatized.

David   Etiology and prognosis are two questions we have not yet discussed. Let's talk about etiology, or causation, first. There is nothing in your case history to suggest that psychological factors (e.g., internal vulnerability, external stress) play a significant role in causation. As you have pointed out, some of the bouts of madness occurred around the golden age of your life, when things were going well. Moreover, there seems to be no correlation between onset and life events: You have no inkling of when or why the episodes occur.

On the other hand, clinical features such as mental fatigue and difficulty falling asleep point to neurophysiological factors. You have alluded to a hyperactive sympathetic autonomic nervous system leading to brain fatigue as a possible mechanism underlying your hypomania or mania. But we don't know what triggered or caused the hyperactivity.

It is natural to ask if there will be a recurrence of exuberant spells in the future. This is a question about prognosis.

YF   Of course, no one knows for sure. However, the fact that I have managed to prevent episodes from developing into full-blown mania gives credence to a favorable prognosis. If something does occur, I am now in a better position to control it. Difficulty falling asleep and racing thoughts are two early telltale signs of an impending exuberate spell. It would not be difficult to nip it in the bud by taking medication.

But do I want to throw the baby out with the bathwater? I would prefer not to take medication or to delay taking it for as long as feasible. I will first try to exploit the dynamism of a hyperactive brain to serve my ends, without falling victim to it.

David   Finally, the diagnosis. Let's recapitulate what we have already arrived at. You had episodes of hypomania, although there is still debate on whether you meet fully the criteria for mania. Now, by definition hypomania is an abnormal condition.

YF   I accept the verdict: I've been mad all right.

Being Atypical in Madness as in Normality

David   However, there are atypical features of diagnostic significance. The first feature is the most striking. The presumption of a shift in polarity between mania and depression is inherent in the use of the term *bipolar*. You have had your share of unhappiness, pain, and anguish. Deeply felt, these experiences resulted mostly from disturbed relationships with family members and intimate others.

YF   But I have had nothing resembling a major depression (morbid preoccupation with worthlessness, suicidal ideation, psychotic symptoms, or psychomotor retardation). Ten episodes of exuberance, not a single one of depression! I cannot be said to have suffered from a bipolar mood disorder at all.

If this be so, a new diagnostic category has to be added: unipolar disorders characterized by only hypomanic and/or manic episodes. In fact, terms like *unipolar mania* and *mania without depression* have already appeared in the psychiatric literature.

David   Second, your case history was rather atypical. A recount of your golden age provides a new context for a deeper understanding of your unusual experiences. The golden age was also a period during which four of the episodes (including the more serious Mania 1 and Mania 2) occurred.

This fact runs counter to the usual course of psychopathologies: Abnormal conditions or mental disorders typically occur at times when a person is under great stress, facing serious problems for which there appears to be no solution, undergoing a particularly difficult period of life, or has been severely traumatized.

YF   I had none of these, preceding, during, or after the four episodes in my Golden age. Significantly, the very first episode occurred rather late, when I was already fifty-eight years old, which is atypical.

David   The third atypical feature concerns the symptom of distractibility. DSM-IV describes distractibility as "attention too easily drawn to unimportant or irrelevant external stimuli."

YF   True enough, I had trouble performing simple tasks (e.g., taking 20 minutes to find my underwear). But the distractibility was secondary to fatigue. When my energy level permitted, I could be highly focused, purposeful, and goal-directed in my activities.

David   The fourth atypical feature concerns sleep disturbance. Manics can go for days without sleeping and yet not feel tired. DSM-IV states that one of the symptoms present in a Manic Episode is "decreased need for sleep (e.g., feels rested after only 3 hours of sleep)."

YF   Contrary to the typical clinical picture, I experienced no such decreased need; rather, I suffered from insomnia and fatigue, mental and physical. I tried my best to fall asleep, unsuccessfully, during the hypomanic or manic episodes.

Two important points deserve attention. First, fatigue is clearly distinct from sleepiness. Fatigue, both physical and mental, was intensely felt. But I did not feel sleepy. Second, mania is characterized by unusually high levels of energy and activity. In my case, I fluctuated between high and low levels of activity. I felt that my energy reserves were depleted. I was running on a "low battery," and I had to conserve what little energy I had.

David   There is support for your conjecture of extraordinarily high energy consumption by the brain during manic or hypomanic states. Proton magnetic resonance spectroscopy shows that acute manic patients have elevated glutamate/glutamine levels within the left dorsolateral prefrontal cortex; PET scans show that brain energy consumption rises and falls with manic and depressive episodes.

However, there is a dearth of scientific attention paid to the phenomenon of brain fatigue in manic states. For this reason, *Fatigue as a Window to the Brain*, edited by John DeLuca, stands out; it points to a new avenue for understanding conditions such as those you have experienced. Clearly, there is a need for investigating mental and physical fatigue during manic states.

YF   Living in Southern California, where temperatures reach 80 degrees Fahrenheit or above, I would still feel cold and have frequent shaking chills, except when I practice Taiji or dance to music and generate warmth momentarily throughout my body. The chills could not be due to a lack of nutrition or calories, for I had a good appetite and ate well.

I asked a neurologist for an explanation, the answer was, "I don't know." But I am convinced that the energy consumption of my brain has something to do with it. I touch my head and I can just feel that it is burning inside.

David   Mania is thought of primarily as a mood disorder; yet you had dramatic concomitant physical as well as cognitive disturbances. High brain energy consumption may provide an explanation for these disturbances.

YF   Cruising around the Mediterranean on board the *Queen Victoria* during Hypomania 5 afforded me an opportunity to glimpse into the workings of my own mind. I gained firsthand experiences of cognitive processes at work. The following is a fairly accurate verbal report I gave to the physician I consulted on board the *Queen Victoria*.

> I know my body is giving me a warning. It has run out of reserve. So I would conserve energy when I am alone. When I am with other people, during dinner for example, I switch on again. So they don't know how depleted I really am.

In my stateroom, I have spells of feeling cold. My body would shiver. I have to lie in bed and cover myself with a blanket. The spells last for 10 to 15 minutes.

I have trouble performing even the simplest task. For example, to use a lift, I would push a sign with a number on it, instead of the correct button. I then wondered why there was no reaction. This happened several times. At the same time, however, I was aware of how stupid I had become. Getting oriented inside the *Queen Victoria*, which is not easy in any case, has been more difficult than what I would normally expect. Not so much a lack of visual-motor coordination or spatial orientation as what I would call a disturbance of executive function for task completion.

For several days, I have had cognitive dysfunctions. I have great trouble comprehending what I read. Single words are all right. But I have great difficulty comprehending whole sentences. Oral speech is less of a problem, except for occasional difficulties with articulation or finding the right word. My memory fails me, especially about specifics, such as numbers and people's names. Sometimes, I get confused easily. Never before have I experienced such cognitive deficits. The thought that they might be irreversible, if only in part, really scares me.

My brain is like a battery running low, and not recharging properly. However, my reflective faculty is intact. I am aware of my situation and people around me. For instance, I am aware that, right now, far from being confused, I am coherent and able to give a detailed account of my condition.

Would you please tell me what the shaking chills and cognitive dysfunctions, two symptoms which worry me the most, are about?

The physician's diagnosis was "acute stress/constipation." He didn't satisfy my curiosity about the two symptoms. He prescribed some medicine, which took care of my constipation and insomnia in two days. I began to recover physically, but the mood elation lingered. The cognitive dysfunctions were more severe than the "brain fatigue" I had during previous episodes.

David   Your verbal report was not in the least indicative of a disordered mind. On the contrary, it was detailed, informative, and self-reflective—the kind that clinicians would like to obtain from their patients. In particular, it gave an experiential demonstration of how cognitively demanding linguistic functioning, especially syntax parsing (e.g., dealing with whole sentences), really is.

Now, observing the workings of the mind is tricky business. For, in principle, they cannot be directly observed. We have no idea, for instance, of how we arrive at the answer to a simple arithmetic problem or how we generate our thoughts. All we know is that the products of the mind's workings flow as naturally as water out of a tap.

Once in a while, however, extraordinary circumstances provide opportunities to come close to observing the workings, the mechanisms and processes, themselves. Brain researcher Jill Bolte Taylor had a massive stroke and witnessed her brain functions, motion, speech, and self-awareness shut down one by one. Eventually, she recovered to tell her amazing story. Interested readers may visit the website http://www.ted.com/talks/view/id/229 and watch a video about Taylor's experiences, *My Stroke of Insight*.

YF   Additionally, a special feature concerns a syndrome commonly known in China as *zouhuorumo*, which translates as "catching fire, entering demon." This syndrome is found among qigong practitioners thought to have gone astray (literally, qigong means "breath work," and may be translated as "vital energy work"). It is different from the demon possession syndrome, the causation of which is thought of as exogenous. One essential feature of *zouhuorumo* is a loss of cognitive control and reality testing; transient psychotic-like or bizarre behaviors may manifest. I was self-enchanted all right, resulting in a blurring between the virtual and the real. But at no point were there psychotic-like or bizarre behaviors. Fortunately, metacognition saved me from being captured by the allure of virtual pleasures.

David   I am reminded here of Satan's temptation of Jesus and Mara's temptation of Gautama, the founder of Buddhism; surely, metacognition played a part in their triumph over satanic forces. (Mara involved his three daughters to tempt Gautama—surely a depraved, if not an ultimate, scheme.)

YF   During Mania 2, I said to myself: "I don't want to be a Buddha." In other words, giving up sexual pleasure was too much even for supreme enlightenment. I want to celebrate life, not to be celibate. I wonder if Gautama might have given up his quest for enlightenment had his sexual drive been amplified tenfold.

The rest had better be left to the imagination (but not too much imagination, because there was in fact nothing to whet the appetite of voyeurs). I'm keeping some of my most private experiences private. By now, readers might be envious of my privileged experiences. But I don't want to be guilty of inducing anyone into *zouhuorumo*.

David   There is nothing in the idea of BMS interconnectedness to negate sexuality. On the contrary, sexuality is inherent in all three BMS domains. It is the most intense of physical pleasures; it adds passion to love; it energizes spiritual feelings. This will reassure our fellow travelers in quest of spirituality. However, severe imbalances may disrupt the interconnectedness. And disconnected sexuality may debase, rather than enrich, life.

Being atypical has been an issue all your life, in madness as in normality. So, all these analyses of atypical features miss the point, if they do not result in greater self-acceptance. In any case, what condition were you suffering from?

YF   To this day, I am not sure.

Sequential Learning and Coping: Practical Suggestions

David   Some readers may have had experiences similar to those of yours. How can this book be of service to them? What have you learned in terms of coping, now that you have had ten bouts of madness already? What are some practical suggestions?

YF   Bearing in mind that different cases vary, I don't want to offer definitive, formulaic answers in the form of do's and don'ts, or "An Idiot's Guide to…." Rather, I delight in respectful sharing with an intelligent audience.

First and foremost, refrain from driving if at all possible, especially in the height of mania. Distractibility leads to reckless driving that can kill you.

In Hypomania 8, for a while I dared not drive, on account of mental fatigue and confusion—rather than of recklessness. I value my life too much to endanger it, in madness no less than in normality.

David   In the midst of Hypomania 2, you wrote in your diary (Nov 1998), "Men are not stupid, except when they are bewitched by women." This reflects an awareness of the dangers of "falling in love" during spells of exuberance: An outpouring of emotions is characteristic and may be directed to a specific person.

YF   Being self-bewitched is closer to the truth.

David   Romantic entanglements established during madness may well rest on perilous grounds, because perceptions may be distorted and judgment impaired. If the target person does not reciprocate, one may not read or discount the signals of rejection.

As well, my cautionary remarks apply to depressive episodes, during which the sufferer may be more vulnerable to temptations of emotional support from someone he is attracted to.

YF   Romantic relationships are, I suspect, of foremost interest to many readers. And I do want to come to the defense of romantic love. All my life, drummed into my head is the injunction, "Think before you leap." If I do, too much, what would become of me? Paralyzed, I suspect.

Plunge before you think: That's falling in love. The most important decisions in life are leaps of faith, not of thinking.

David   You are an incurable romantic.

Being overly enthusiastic, optimistic, and self-confident is another problem. You are probably running too far ahead of people around you. In the midst of a spell, your enthusiasm may be unshared by others; reality may be clouded with wishful thinking.

YF   When I read my diaries now, I am dumbfounded by how my self-confidence was inflated and how difficult it would be for my wishes to be realized.

David   That's why it is ill-advised to make major decisions when your mood is abnormally elevated.

YF   With greater familiarity of the symptoms, which are basically similar in my case, detection gets sequentially easier. Early in Mania 2, I called a friend and said, "I feel that I am beginning to get overly excited, but I am clear about my physical condition. I will be all right after several days of good rest." Clearly, I was aware that I was about to enter into another period of unusual excitement. As it turned out, however, I was overly optimistic about recovery.

Similarly, in Hypomania 8, I could tell exactly when I first sensed trouble brewing: One day, while having lunch with relatives, I noticed a more-than-usual pressure toward being talkative. Early detection enabled me to take preventive actions. The lesson learned: Nip it in the bud when you sense that something has gone awry, physically or psychologically.

David   Maintaining contact with friends and relatives is important: Their feedback on your behavior may help to keep you on track. The trouble is, however, you may not want to listen to them when you are high. At the very least, be receptive to your own inner voices of caution. But what if your suffering is inflicted upon you by your friends and relatives?

YF There is no point to self-inflict more suffering. As I wrote in Hypomania 5, "Let not the folly of others torture you. That's the Dao of remaining sane in an insane world."

Sequential learning bore fruit. I took measures (consulting a physician and taking the medicine, including sleeping pills, he prescribed) in Hypomania 5 to take care of physical symptoms. Recovery was relatively fast and easy.

By the onset of Hypomania 6, I had probably learned enough to forestall a full-blown episode. I was determined to keep it under control, but I didn't want to kill it. My goal was to reap the benefits of creativity and heightened sensibilities, without costly social consequences. As in other episodes, the key factor was sleep: I knew that if I could fall asleep, I would be all right. That's exactly what happened. There was no insomnia. I was mostly able to control the madness myself, without taking medicine. It did not result in damage to my social image.

Hypomania 7 was kept under control early on. I took sleeping pills for two nights, enough to get rid of insomnia. But I knew that mental hyperactivity remained an underlying problem. Somehow, I managed to keep the spell dormant. So there were few overt hypomanic manifestations that might disturb others. Eventually, just before my departure for the United States, balance was restored, thus ending the episode.

My main concern in Hypomania 8 was not to scare my friends and relatives. I kept my manic-like manifestations secret successfully. As far as they were concerned, what I went through was an unexplained, mysterious medical condition.

David But I am convinced that a psychological mechanism underlay Hypomania 8. The months following your relocation to the United States were the worst time in your life: You uprooted yourself from Hong Kong, where you had spent most of your life, and were feeling socially isolated; you had to adjust to life after retirement and to aging. Thus, the psychological mechanism may be thought of as counterdepression.

YF   Yes, I was liberated from feelings of depression. And together with that liberation, creative-artistic impulses were unleashed. Rid of inertia, my body was propelled to exercise. Counterdepression was probably operative, to various degrees, during previous episodes also.

Counterdepression is as powerful as it is seductive. Who wants to be stuck in the depth of hellish feelings? And who doesn't want be liberated from compulsivity and, even more, to have creative-artistic impulses unleashed?

David   Acknowledging psychological mechanisms does not mean rejecting medical solutions. To take or not to take medicine for treating mental disorders is an important, and difficult, decision.

YF   I generally prefer to let the body's own wisdom take care of itself. The ideal is to cultivate BMS Health, without medication.

During Mania 2, I was unable to fall asleep for about a month. Coincidentally, the apartment right above mine was undergoing renovation; loud sounds of hammers and electric drills made falling asleep doubly difficult. Staying at home most of the time, I learned to "tune out" these sounds with self-hypnosis; success was limited.

I stubbornly resisted taking medicine. Eventually, I capitulated, for fatigue as a constant companion was too much to bear. For the first time, I took antipsychotic medicine (a low dosage, two Risperdal tablets, 1 mg each). I slept for several nights consecutively and came out of madness.

As to Hypomania 8, taking sleeping pills for a few nights didn't help much, but taking risperidone (generic name for Risperdal; also a small dosage, three tablets, 2 mg each) was definitive in ending the episode.

Still, I was disconcerted by my capitulation because Risperdal is, after all, an antipsychotic medicine usually prescribed for severe psychiatric disorders, such as schizophrenia.

David   You would be more disconcerted to learn that the Johnson & Johnson is now plagued by lawsuits over its marketing tactics involving Risperdal, one of the most commonly prescribed antipsychotic drugs. The healthcare giant is accused of having concealed

Risperdal's many nasty side effects, some of which may be life-threatening.

Here is an excerpt from the information sheet on risperidone provided by a well-known pharmacy.

> Drowsiness, dizziness, lightheadedness, drooling, nausea, weight gain, or tiredness may occur.... Tell your doctor immediately if you have any serious side effects, including: difficulty swallowing, muscle spasms, shaking (tremor), mental/mood changes (such as anxiety, restlessness), signs of infection (such as fever, persistent sore throat).... Tell your doctor immediately if you develop any unusual/ uncontrolled movements.... Get medical help right away if you have any of the following symptoms: fever, muscle stiffness/pain/tenderness/weakness, severe tiredness, severe confusion, sweating, fast/irregular heartbeat, dark urine, change in the amount of urine. Rarely, males may have a painful or prolonged erection lasting more than 4 hours. If this occurs, stop using this drug and get medical help right away, or *permanent* problems could occur.... This is not a complete list of possible side effects.... [Italics added]

Scary, isn't it?

YF   Scary side effects are by no means unusual. Aside from this issue, medication is inherently limited. Taking medicine alone is no solution to problems of living. It does not promote health, lead to new ways of relating or of viewing the world.

However, we have to balance the benefits against the costs. I am now more receptive to medication, on the basis of need. In particular, I accept that taking sleeping pills alone may not be enough; they do not address mood elation, mental hyperactivity, fatigue.

David   We have now learned that being able to sleep is a necessary, but perhaps not sufficient, treatment of fatigue. Putting an end to mental hyperactivity is also necessary.

Consistent with the idea of BMS interconnectedness, restoring balance, physical and mental, is essential to recovery. This is systemic thinking, on which Chinese medicine rests. In the long run, Chinese life-fostering practices such as qigong are preferable to medication; at least, they would reduce overreliance on medication.

Balance holds the key: You will be a happy person if you can reap the benefits of creativity in madness, without costly adverse consequences.

YF   I can testify to a success story. During one of my hypomanic episodes, I was able to lower my blood pressure to healthy levels without medication through intensive practice in martial arts and dance to music. Later, I told my physician what I had accomplished and asked him if I could stop taking or reduce the medicines he had prescribed for lowering my blood pressure. He was skeptical and said no. At that point, I decided not to adhere to his medical regimen.

David   Frankly, what abhors me is the extent to which Americans rely on drugs to treat mental disorders, alleviate anxiety and depression, control hyperactive children, and so forth. Some even rely on psychedelic drugs, marijuana, and the like for "peak" experiences of spirituality, in denial of the perils of brain damage that these drugs may bring.

FY Immersing myself in peak experiences through music and dance entails no such perils. I go for self-intoxication, not intoxication by wine or any other means. A Chinese proverb, rooted in the Buddhist conception of self-enchantment, puts it this way:

Not wine, we intoxicate ourselves;
Nor beauty, we enchant ourselves.

David   The proverb expresses the same basic idea, almost word for word in translation, in what Shakespeare wrote:

> Not wine, men intoxicate themselves;
> Not vice, men entice themselves.

In all, the main lesson we have learned is to speak of solving problems and enriching life, rather than of curing a disease.

Spiritual Fulfillment versus Spiritual Emptiness: A Dynamic Process

YF   Still, intriguing diagnostic questions remain. My writing in the midst of madness was not the product of a disordered mind. Rather, it was a self-reflective mind, supersensitive, audacious, experimental, intent on a transcendental-spiritual quest. Christ-like pathos for humanity—that is, love—triumphs over hate. Aside from diagnosis, the data we have assembled from diverse sources yield a composite picture of my thoughts and actions as I go through my life journey. They give me plenty to reflect on the joys and tribulations of my life.

As I look back, it dawns on me how fortunate I have been, with so many inviting tales to tell. Often, the happenings do not result from a deliberate search on my part; rather, they are serendipitous. I simply seize the opportunity to create meaning and revel in narration when they occur. It also seems clear that I have gone into different directions. In the end, what unifies my activities is spiritual meaning.

David   Unfortunately, the DSM-IV is silent here; in fact, it discounts positive features, especially when they are outside the normal range of human experience. We have to go beyond its scope.

YF   More than that: My case serves to reveal how deficient psychiatric diagnosis, based on the DSM-IV or otherwise, can be. It tends to locate disorders within individuals; it pays insufficient attention to the interpersonal dimension underlying disorders. It lacks a dynamic conception to appreciate the coexistence of positive and negative forces. It is silent on how conditions that merely resemble a mental disorder but are fundamentally positive in nature may be distinguished from those that are truly pathological. I refer to extraordinary religious-spiritual experiences of numerous people (e.g., mystics), historical and contemporary, in diverse cultures.

Abnormality comes in great varieties; witness the vast number of diagnostic categories in the psychiatric literature. Why should normality be more impoverished in diversity?

Religious-spiritual experiences can be highly problematic to a person's life—not being understood, or worse, misunderstood by family, friends, and yes, psychiatrists. I bring this up only to illustrate once again how inadequate psychiatric diagnosis can be.

David   Here is all that the DSM-IV has to say about Religious or Spiritual Problem:

> This category can be used when the focus of clinical attention is a religious or spiritual problem. Examples include distressing experiences that involve loss or questioning of faith, problems associated with conversion to a new faith, or questioning of spiritual values that may not necessarily be related to an organized church or religious institution.

YF   Why is the focus of attention "clinical"? This is disingenuous, inasmuch as Religious or Spiritual Problem, the DSM-IV makes clear, is not a mental disorder. Obviously, we have to move beyond psychiatry toward spirituality.

David   It is rather ironic that these scathing remarks come from the mouth of a person who has taught psychiatric and psychological diagnosis for most of his professional life. You must have seen the light, to come up with such an antiestablishment argument.

I'm sure there are readers who have suffered from mental aberrations. The usual course of development is psychiatric diagnosis followed by treatment (psychotherapy and/or medication). The diagnostic label (e.g., schizophrenia, literally "split mind") can be scary and lead to stigmatization; treatment can be worse than the disorder.

Rarely is there an attempt to help the patient understand his disorder in a larger context, as an existential quest for meaning. That's why your insistence that madness may be a part of one's spiritual journey is refreshing and reassuring. Others can benefit from your experience. What perspective, beyond psychiatric diagnosis, promises to shed light on a fuller understanding of your journey?

YF   A dynamic conception of the struggle between spiritual fulfillment and spiritual emptiness cries out to be heard. The attainment of spirituality is a dynamic process in which struggle, change, and self-transformation are central.

Speaking from personal experience, the process may be described as a movement, back and forth, from disorientation-alienation to reconstruction-reorganization. Spirituality and spiritual emptiness have coexisted, alternating at different moments, in my lifetime. Certainly, my journey in search of spirituality has not been easy, peaceful sailing.

A spiritual journey can be lonely and hazardous. Lonely because it is intensely personal; segments of it, at least, have to be taken without accompaniment; feelings of being different or distant from others may appear. Hazardous because the traveler may go astray, wander into the path of evil cults or be overcome by madness. It is especially hazardous for those who 3have gone far enough to experience ecstasy, the mystical, and the like; for it is not uncommon for these advanced travelers to be viewed as weird, abnormal, or exceeding the bounds of social acceptability.

Spiritual journeys make no promises. There are no shortcuts, like taking drugs; that's fundamental. And if the traveler finally succeeds in reaching enlightenment, he would have a hard time making himself fully understood by fellow humans, not having experienced his experiences, about his state of being. Only a Buddha knows a Buddha, so to speak.

David   Why bother with spiritual journeys, if they are arduous, lonely, full of hazards and predicaments? Some might ask.

YF   Because spiritual fulfillment is like a lighthouse, alluring and drawing the lost, the empty toward it. A journey can be fundamentally rewarding in itself, adding color to all aspects of life. And because failure to embark on one will eventually result in spiritual emptiness: Life becomes stagnant, unfulfilled. I would go as far as to say spirituality is built into human nature: We really have no choice but to seek it out; failure to do so violates our being.

The trouble is that deep self-reflection and immense effort are required. Not surprisingly, inertia often gets the better of us, like a dead weight inside our psyche. At every turn, we may see plenty of people who want to be spoon-fed ready-made answers on questions of faith, religion, or spirituality.

David   How many of us dare to take the journey? I suspect that genuine spirituality may not be easily found. Rather, spiritual emptiness is the norm; its symptoms may be discerned everywhere. We lead our lives with complacency, perhaps even numbness. We lack courage to make commitments, and we avoid taking risks for a fundamental change in direction. We may even be unaware of, and hence do not reflect upon, the empty state of our existence.

Of course, failure to take risks is the greatest risk of all. Sometimes, however, critical incidents or alterations in our life condition occur: bankruptcy, financial or social; cheating death and given a new lease on life; inspired by a trusted mentor. They wake us from our complacency. Even spontaneous awakenings may occur.

YF   As long as there is the will to struggle, there may be torment, anguish, despair—but not spiritual emptiness. Struggle confers meaning on life and thus negates spiritual emptiness; it has in itself positive value, even when success is not assured. But struggle is not enough; one must be committed and take action. Hardly anything is more uninviting than to be caught in perennial struggle. Action leads to change, perhaps eventual self-transformation. A self-transformed person experiences the joys of spiritual fulfillment and realizes his potential.

Herein lies the answer to why some people are willing to take the journey: The goal of spiritual fulfillment is seductive, and the process itself is exciting. Besides, failure to take the journey is decidedly unattractive. When a person gives up struggling, spiritual emptiness sets in: He becomes passive, withdrawn, self-absorbed, fixated, stagnant, and eventually embittered.

If this sounds too grave, let me hasten to add that the dynamic struggle between spiritual fulfillment and spiritual emptiness does not have to be as intense as I have described it. However, the struggle is relevant to a person's life regardless of his mental condition, normal or abnormal. It may be openly recognized or latent in your life. But it can no more be avoided than you can by burying your head in the sand. I have simply articulated a central nature of human life.

And if it sounds too abstract, let me reassure the reader that everything I have said I have experienced in flesh and blood.

David   Spirituality and religiosity are distinct ideas. Religiosity puts the emphasis on personal salvation, deliverance from punishment in the present life or afterlife, and the promise of everlasting life. Often it is driven by insecurity, anxiety, and fear of punishment, hell, God.

In contrast, spiritual pursuits are growth oriented, not driven by fear; they demand intense personal effort, soul searching. What is crucial is to seek some higher goal in life and principles that serve as a guide to leading the good life.

Why not apply the dynamic conception to your own case? A fruitful way to proceed is to spell out the positive as well as negative forces of your madness.

YF   The positives were many. Positive feelings (e.g., love of humanity, "Life is wonderful," "Eros triumphs over Thanatos") predominated. I was aware of my aggressive-hostile impulses, of course, but they did not threaten to be acted out in unchecked, destructive forms. The capacity for depth of feelings, both pleasant and painful, was magnified. I experienced heightened artistic-esthetic sensibilities (e.g., "The world is beautiful"); empathy and compassion; creativity and linguistic fluency. I was freed from obsessive-compulsivity, self-doubt, and shame.

The spells of exuberance afforded me precious opportunities to gain unhindered access to the unconscious, experience the extraordinary, and glimpse into the mystical-transcendental state of enlightenment.

Among the most dramatic, memorable, and inspirational of my experiences were those gained in Mania 1. These included experiencing myself as bodily vanished, empty; self-healing of an injured knee while I was in the state of emptiness; coexistence of yin and yang in an androgynous body; willful visual hallucinations, in which I saw myself vividly on a cross and, likening myself to Jesus, felt great pathos for the sufferings of humankind. With repression gone, access to the unconscious was total.

David   There's another positive that deserves to be mentioned: Madness adds color to your spiritual journey. The child in you comes out during your madness; you return to your "original face." You become more spontaneous, playful, humorous—also naughty, adventurous, audacious. Your creative potential is realized.

The great irony is that, in so many ways, you are a more attractive person when you are mad than when you are normal. Your interactions with friends are full of laughter. People respond to you positively—as long as you keep your behavior within bounds. Is that the reason why you have so many bouts of madness?

Why can't spiritual journeys be playful and joyous? This is an important point, because too many people think of the pursuit of spirituality as a grave and staid undertaking, in which playfulness has no place. Struggle is essential, but spiritual journeys don't have to be based on viewing life, in your student days, as "an intense struggle." The pursuit of spirituality is more sustainable if it is made attractive, as when playfulness intermingles with dedication. Spiritual journeys can be fun, especially when the spice of madness is added.

YF   Actually I have made quite a career of entertaining people. As a schoolboy, I cracked jokes that often made the entire class, already bored to death by boring teachers, burst into laughter.

While I was an undergraduate, I had a summer job as an orderly at a hospital for French Canadians. My job was to prepare patients for surgery. Why not entertain them as well, I thought. And I did. The fact that I spoke little or no French did not diminish my ability to make the patients laugh. I wrote in my diary, "I cannot control myself not to be funny." One of the patients who had undergone abdominal surgery laughed so heartily that I became concerned about his belly bursting open. I had to control myself.

Years later, in my golden age, I succeeded in combining entertainment and education in the classroom, one of the secrets of being an effective teacher.

David   Now, what about the negatives?

YF   At times, I have felt alienated and enslaved by work. I have been too much of a workaholic. Academic and professional pursuits have brought me prestige, not happiness; they might even be detours or, worse, escapes from my quest for spirituality. Achievement is important, but not nearly as important as happiness, which comes only with the participation of others. With this understanding, I will recount my search of communion in the next chapter.

Have I felt spiritually empty? No, I have never felt that life is meaningless or purposeless, although I have experienced a loss of direction sometimes. If anything, I tend to be overcommitted to too many goals, but I take action toward reaching some of them. And I don't run away from struggle.

David   Thinking about important questions concerning life characterized by metacognitive, reflective thought, as in your case, would involve doubt or struggle. It does not fall back automatically on stereotyped or superstitious beliefs, blind faith, religious dogmas, doctrinaire beliefs for ready answers.

YF   Depth of feelings, both positive and negative, marks my madness. I experienced fluctuations between exuberance and anguish in different episodes, but never psychic numbing, the incapacity to feel happiness or sadness. Heightened aesthetic sensibilities were prominent: I had the capacity to experience simple, unabashed delight in ordinary things (e.g., the root of a tree, the droning sound of cicadas). I experienced serenity and inner peace, but also inner turmoil.

In the self-report on my case history submitted as an assignment, I wrote:

> I am all alone, in a new country; and, for the first time in my life, I experience loneness and emptiness…. Well, this is what really makes an existentialist: he has to create his own values, from the beginning of despair.

Decades later, I woke up suddenly one night in the midst of Mania 2, feeling I was the loneliest person in the world, understood by none and fighting lonely battles all my life. As expressed in a famous line by a renowned Chinese writer of bygone age: "All earthlings are intoxicated. I alone am sober."

David   It is never easy to remain sober while all others are intoxicated.

YF   So underneath the mania was a deep sense of anguish, loneliness, and yearning for human contact, expressed in a poem I sent out to friends (5 July 2007).

Black Hole

Into a Black Hole I plunge,
From which nothing can ever escape.
Its center singularity I reach,
Where Loneliness Eternal dwells.

I ask the Physicist,
"Is there really no exit?"

"If there is, you might continue
Your journey from one universe
To another, but never
To return to your home."
My body droops,
My eyes downcast,
On the ground I prostrate,
As Loneliness turns into Despair.

I turn to the Philosopher. He says:
"The Dao is ONE, omnipresent, timeless.
Nothing is, everything becomes.
Everything connects
With everything else, with itself,
With the whole Multiverse."
Enfleshed in my body,
Hope drives Despair away.

The Physicist jumps in:
"Ah, Theory of Everything. Wait!
The topology of the Klein bottle suggests
Black holes can connect
To the universe as a whole."
As a child, I did think:
An atom is a universe unto itself,
Our universe is but an atom
To a larger universe; so each atom contains,
And is contained by,
An infinity of universes up and down.

I turn to the Poet. He says:
"Now the language of science surpasses
The language of idle words, in connecting
Sentients throughout the Multiverse,
WhereverWhenever they may be."

A whispering voice says:
"Haven't you heard of
Karma Invariance?
You are gone,
Truly gone.
You are here,
Here with us:
Just as our karma lives
In your consciousness,
Your karma lives
In ours, and continues
To work out its effects on our lives."
I see myself smiling back to bring
A smile on your face again.

Spirituality: Relational and Ecumenical

David   To be eternally cut off from humanity: What greater horror can there be? But you are an incurable optimist. That's why you wrote at the end of the poem, "I see myself smiling back to bring / A smile on your face again." That's relational spirituality.

You view the self in a larger context; spirituality is reached through transcending egocentrism and moving toward universal love. Transcendence is relational spirituality, reached through transcending egocentrism. Relationships are integral to one's meaning and purpose in life. The antithesis of transcendence is self-encapsulation, in which the self derives meaning and purpose solely or primarily from its own individual existence, without reference to a larger context. Self-encapsulation is a form of egoism or self-contained individualism.

YF   Ironically, at the time I wrote the poem, I had warm relationships with quite a few friends and fellow workers. In my madness, I feel greater warmth toward people. I become more generous, more loving, more prosocial in words and deeds.

By nature, I enjoy having a good time with other people. I shun solitary recreation and I dread social isolation. So being gregarious does not save me from having lonely feelings.

Intermittent tension between closeness and distance underlies my relations with other people. In Hypomania 7, I wrote, "At every turn, I encounter people with fixated mentalities who want to be spoon fed on how to 'grow psychologically.' They don't see what is in front of their eyes, or hear voices that should be loud and clear to them." And "As I grow wiser, so too the distance increases between myself and others."

David   As you grower wiser, other-acceptance becomes commensurate with self-acceptance. You would view people with greater understanding and acceptance, particularly of how they differ from you. Alternating between solitude and companionship is all right. There are times when we wish to retreat into our private selves, undisturbed by others, and there are times when we feel the need for human contact. The ideals are solitude without loneliness and companionship without loss of individuality.

We must talk more about the interpersonal dimension of spiritual journeys. Up to now, we have been talking about the quest for spirituality mostly as if it were an individual undertaking without the involvement of others. This dawns on me as we are engaged in the present dialogue. No, I say to myself, this is not meant to be. The quest should be a much more rewarding search of spirituality-in-partnership.

YF   A great irony is that taking a spiritual journey may indeed increase the distance between the traveler and others. As the traveler become more advanced in his journey, he is likely to become more atypical, more unlike other people. This has been largely my experience. The question arises, How does becoming more atypical affect the traveler's relationships with his significant others?

David   Siddhartha Gautama, we may recall, went to the extreme of abandoning his family, parents, wife, and newborn son. Among my Buddhist friends, some have renounced marital life in their search for enlightenment. In these cases, the spiritual journey is taken individually, devoid of the participation of significant others.

What about journeys taken by intimate partners together? Ah, finding a suitable partner is as difficult as looking for a needle in a haystack, and more challenges await the traveler who succeeds in finding one. A journey taken by a single person is trying enough; a journey taken together with others, especially significant others, will tax all to the limit.

YF   To me, however, the idea of spirituality-in-isolation has little or no appeal; spirituality-in-partnership is attractive enough to take on whatever challenge it presents. The whole is greater than the sum of its parts.

Emergent relational properties, unique to the partners involved, arise from two travelers coming together in an intimate relationship. The partners transform, and are transformed by, their relationship: This is spirituality-in-partnership.

David   An operatic love duet provides a beautiful analogy. The opera depicts the individual character of the lovers in the duet. Yet the opera on the printed page is dead music. It becomes alive only when the musical notes, each and all, are articulated and the lyrics are sung by the performing artists. The performance of each singer acts as a powerful stimulus to the other. The "chemistry" between them gives life to the duet, resulting in a performance that cannot be reduced to a summation of individual artistic qualities.

YF   Synchronicity holds the key to having a happy spiritual journey together, as it does to sustain intimate relationships in general. Consider the case of a dyadic relationship. Change in one partner acts as catalyst for change in the other, and vice versa; this leads to change in the nature of their relationship, such as greater trust, affection, and complementarity. This invigorated relationship, in turn, sets the stage for further changes within each partner. In sum, together the partners grow spiritually.

On the other hand, an asynchronous journey, in terms of pace, direction, determination, and so forth, can be hazardous. It may increase the distance between the partners and tear their relationship apart. Both partners may be wonderful persons, but both may suffer terribly.

David   But there is an absolute limit to companionship or partnership in any spiritual journey. Ultimately pivotal decisions and commitments in life must be made alone. Just as we come into the world alone, so shall we leave the world alone—unaccompanied. In between the coming and the leaving is when we may choose our companions wisely.

YF   However, in a sense relationships do not end when a person dies: His karma continues to live in the consciousness of other people, such as colleagues, friends, and relatives, unrestricted by space or time.

David   Our conceptualization is also ecumenical in orientation, not biased toward or anchored in a particular Christian denomination, or even in a particular religion. By ecumenicity, we mean universality, more than merely transcending denominational or religious boundaries.

Universal love is the lodestone of ecumenicity. It finds expression in the Greek idea of agape, the Confucian idea of *ren* (benevolence), the Buddhist idea of *daai* (great love), the Christian ideas of *caritas* and love feast. At root, it champions the intrinsic value of human life and cherishing care for one's fellow human beings. Buddhism extends the regard for life to all living creatures. Daoism views human life as person-in-cosmos; the regard for mother earth and nature follows.

YF   "Within the four seas, all men are brothers." This Chinese saying expresses an embracing, ecumenical sentiment. In a modernized version, it might read: "In our global village, we are all sisters and brothers." This is an expression of ecumenicity: All members of humankind are welcome to embark on a spiritual pilgrimage; no one is excluded.

David   In keeping with pluralism, ecumenicity allows for, even welcomes, cultural or religious diversity. For instance, the value of suffering is recognized in Buddhism, Christianity, as well as other religions. Ecumenicity affirms the spiritual value of suffering but leaves open what that value may entail.

Closely allied with ecumenicity is equifinality, the idea that the same ultimate goal may be reached from different paths. A fellow traveler is at liberty to define his own chosen path for spiritual fulfillment. In principle, there may be as many paths as there are travelers.

No stranger to suffering, especially in your age of turbulence, you appreciate its value, although you do not profess to be Buddhist or Christian. You reaffirm your belief in "the dignity of each and every person, without exceptions"; "cultural uprooting" is an extreme that marks the path you have chosen.

Your intercultural interests and experiences may enrich our understanding of ecumenical spirituality. Ours is both principled and tolerant. Ecumenicity without tolerance succumbs to absolutism; unprincipled ecumenicity absorbs unwanted elements and risks becoming tainted. The tension between principled discernment and tolerance drives its further development—in a process much like the "creative synthesis" of the East and the West you have described.

YF   Spirituality is being-in-the-world. It includes political activism for peace and justice, anywhere; it is not just an abstract idea. Like religion, the idea of mental health can be an opiate of the mind. In the face of ugly social reality, we make a travesty of enhancing the individual's potentialities. Self-actualization is escapism, unless it entails active participation in social change, helping others.

Yet, I sometimes feel that I can't even help myself, let alone others.

Witnessing My Ineptitude and Decline: Acceptance

David   "Be yourself" includes your positives as well as negatives. By all counts, among the negatives ineptitude in mechanical or practical things are the most salient. They make an in-your-face mockery of your intellectual prowess.

YF   My ineptitudes are manifest in different episodes: I experience great difficulty locating "lost" objects or recalling "lost" ideas, comprehending what I read, making a phone call, performing a simple arithmetic calculation, finding my way around in my neighborhood. The list goes on and on.

But ineptitude is nothing new: All my life, I have found that many things other people find easy to do make me feel incompetent. (Equally, many things difficult for others seem so easy to me that I have great trouble, emotionally if not intellectually, understanding how they can be found difficult.) Once I took a U.S. Army's test of mechanical aptitude, during a mass induction exercise. I scored in the "idiot's range," prompting the sergeant who administered the test to suspect that I was faking.

I suffer from computer phobia, especially when I receive an invitation to be a "friend" on Facebook or the like. I have trouble with surfing the Internet, registration, user names, passwords, and so forth. Isn't living in this technological age overloading our memory capacity? Once, in the midst of Hypomania 7, I wrote the following message to my friends and colleagues, confessing how inept I felt.

> My apology to you for having sent multiples messages. My CSQ (Computer-Savvy Quotient), mechanical, clerical aptitude, etc. is in the imbecile range. Nothing irritates me like a temperamental computer does.
>
> I'm just not cut out for modern gadgets, and hereby swear on the Altar of the Almighty that I shall continue to refrain from using cell phones to avoid being enslaved by them.

I have never owned one, because I don't want people to locate me when I don't want them to. People in Hong Kong think I am old fashioned. They can't comprehend why I refuse to have one, unaware how they themselves have been enslaved by modern consumerism, commercials targeting women on how to lose weight, etc.

Oh no, I'm beginning to sound like Andy Rooney, the octogenarian who has become an institution in 60 Minutes. I concede, however, that he does have a knack for saying things that both entertain and instruct, especially to the ears of a nonnative speaker of English like myself.

Another confession I have to make: Having moved to the United States later on, I agreed to get a cell phone for safety reasons.

David   Ineptitude takes many forms. I imagine your daily life is a gold mine reinforcing the stereotype of an absent-minded professor.

YF   Yes, I make silly mistakes, like dialing the wrong telephone number, forgetting where I had put my things and then looking for them in frustration, and so forth.

One of my techniques in teaching is to transform my weakness into strength, and thus to amuse my students. During lessons, my mind sometimes raced so much faster than my tongue that I would say one thing when I meant another. Thus, I uttered unintentionally a novel nominal construction: XI Zedong, which collapsed XI Tele (the Chinese name for Hitler) and MAO Zedong. (I hasten to add that I didn't mean to imply MAO and Hitler were the same.)

I forewarned my students: "Once in a while, I might say things that are false or misleading, just to see if you would jot them down in your notebook." An example: "There are three kinds of logic, deductive, inductive, and seductive." Most of my students dutifully recorded that utterance.

David   This is not to deny the linguistic-logical-creative prowess you possess. Abstract, logical, systematic thought has never been a problem, except in the sense that it can sometimes make you overly conscious of conundrums, paradoxes, and inconsistencies in utterances or writings by yourself or by others. Such overconsciousness, or perfectionism, can make students uncomfortable and put them on guard.

YF   It can also cause writer's paralysis, especially with regard to academic writing, from which I have long suffered. To avoid the task at hand, I would run around, looking for other things to do. Typically, the torment would last for about two weeks, after which I would settle down to write. Creative writing frees me from compulsivity, though not from perfectionism, and is in this sense truly creative. And during bouts of madness, I enjoy freedom from perfectionism. Better to be imperfect and remain human, as our maker's creation, than to be perfect and equal to our maker.

But now, I am confronted by something far more formidable than ineptitude: No question about it, I am witnessing my own decline. One day, I took my three-year-old grandson, hand in hand, for a walk along a country road. I drew his attention to something lying on the ground, "See this dead animal, poor thing." Whereupon, the three-year-old injected, "It's a lizard." My inner reactions were twofold. One, what grandfather wouldn't find delight in being bested by his grandchildren? Two, actually I was fumbling to find the right word *lizard* in my mind. Unable to do so fast enough, I used *animal* as a poor substitute. Such is the evidence compelling me to accept that my brain is aging.

David   As you age, your working memory is not as efficient as before. You have trouble remembering telephone numbers, names of people newly introduced, and the like; performing simple clerical or computational tasks cannot be completed easily and error free; processing information requires longer time periods. In short, your relative weaknesses, in what psychologists call fluid intelligence, have been exacerbated as a function of aging.

The difficulty seems to be confined to registration and storage of new information. As of this moment, retrieval of old learning presents no problem whatsoever. Your prowess in remote associations, retrieving, and synthesizing knowledge, undiminished in the least, continues to sometimes overwhelm yourself: You can't write down your thoughts as fast as they come.

Perhaps you are getting even stronger in what psychologists call crystallized intelligence. So your decline in cognitive abilities has caused you no more than inconveniences and embarrassments.

YF   I am grateful for what I still possess and not mourn what I have lost.

Eventually, however, cognitive decline may reach a point where spirituality in the fullest sense can no longer be sustained. What then? I'm not going to get away from facing a question that no spiritual traveler can avoid. I pray that I will still be able to express and receive affection by whatever means unto my last breath.

David   Isn't acceptance of the inevitable, and of what cannot be changed, wisdom to be attained in any spiritual journey? To make a stronger point, such acceptance is a basic value essential to spiritual fulfillment. Remember the timeless wisdom of the Serenity Prayer?

> God, grant me the serenity to accept the things I cannot change,
> The courage to change the things I can,
> And wisdom to know the difference.

YF   Or of acceptance Shantideva, a Buddhist scholar of Nalanda University, expressed in the eighth century?

> If there is remedy when trouble strikes,
> What reason is there for dejection?
> And if there is none,
> Of what use is there in being glum?

David   The Jewish philosopher Solomon ibn Gabirol expressed a similar thought in the eleventh century:

And they said: At the head of all understanding is realizing what is and what cannot be, and the consoling of what is not in our power to change.

YF   I would also enlarge the scope of acceptance. Many things can be changed, but there is no moral necessity for changing them. For instance, take my being atypical, different from other people. If I try hard enough, I suppose I might succeed in being more like others and perhaps gain greater social acceptance; I would then lead an easier life.

But what is the point and at what cost? I suspect that the color in my life would be subdued. Gaining self-acceptance is part and parcel of my spiritual journey. I have struggled to arrive at a point where I value the way I am and feel "at home in the cosmos." So rather than trying to be what I am not, I would spend my energy on more worthwhile endeavors, such as helping our fellow travelers.

David   The irony is that you seem to accept yourself more when you are mad than when you are not. Moreover, your firsthand experiences of madness have been instrumental to obtaining a deeper understanding of spirituality, and in particular to the development of Guide to Spiritual Self-Evaluation (see Appendix A).

The Guide derives from your knowledge of comparative religion, Eastern and Western intellectual and religious traditions, clinical experiences in multicultural settings, and personal insights. I urge readers to make good use of it most earnestly. For them, it may be a pivotal step toward tipping the balance from spiritual emptiness toward spiritual fulfillment.

What is intriguing is that you have applied the Guide, an instrument of your creation, to yourself. In doing so, you have presented a convincing case for moving beyond psychiatry to spirituality.

Now tell us more about how your encounters with madness have shaped your professional growth. In particular, using the lessons you have learned from these encounters to help others and enhance their mental health would be a fulfillment of generativity. You should mention two other contributions you have made in recent years: Dialogic Action Therapy (DAT) and Dynamic Relaxation and Meditation (DRM). A recurrent theme, in line with relational spirituality, in your approach to helping may be identified: Helping others is the best way to help oneself.

Dialogic Action Therapy

YF   DAT integrates two cardinal ideas, dialogics and action, into a coherent framework for effective problem solving and effective living. Both ideas are quintessential to defining what it means to be human. Dialogics refers to the study of all forms, aspects, and processes of dialogues. Virtually all therapeutic systems entail dialogues between persons, therapist and client(s).

DAT stresses the importance of internal dialogues within persons as well. The therapist may exploit dialogues, both between and within persons, to achieve therapeutic gain (e.g., sharpening the client's thinking on the nature of his problems). But that is not enough. DAT promotes the unity of action and thought. It stresses that taking action is essential to successful therapy and therefore accords with the time-honored adage "Actions speak louder than words."

In DAT, the term *external dialogue* refers to an actual dialogue between persons. *Internal dialogue* (or *self-directed dialogue*) refers to a person "talking with oneself," that is, inner self-talk involving only one person, acting as both "speaker" and "listener." This self-talk may take the form of a dialogue between one's different (e.g., present and future) selves, or of an *imaginary* dialogue between oneself and another person.

Internal dialogue may be overt (spoken aloud) or covert (silent). In daily life, we shift back and forth between outer speech and inner self-talk (covert, to be discreet) when we converse with others. We fall into internal dialogic states, often without conscious effort, as naturally as we walk.

I make use of internal dialogues in normality as in madness. As an "absent-minded" professor, sometimes I may be seen talking with myself, dead serious in my quest for a solution to some intriguing problem. During my spells of exuberance, my proclivity toward internal dialogue increases. I am aware, however, that being seen to be talking with myself in public invites suspicion of madness. So I exercise caution to keep my internal dialogues covert, or I explain to others present that I am merely "thinking aloud." Even absent-minded professors have to suspend their self-absorption at some point and attend to external reality at hand.

David   Internal dialogue may serve self-guiding, self-consolation, even self-healing functions.

YF   During bouts of madness, in particular, talking with myself preserves and even strengthens my sanity and gives me hope. I say to myself things like "Life is beautiful and precious, even when it descends into dark moments. There is value and meaning in suffering. Endurance gives me strength…. You are too harsh on yourself. Be kind and forgiving to yourself."

Going beyond self-consolation, internal dialogue may serve as a guide and propellant for dialogic action: "You revel in your exuberance, but you must also pay attention to how other people perceive and react to your elation. Learn to harvest the benefits of madness, without incurring unnecessary social costs."

The fantastic experiences (e.g., vanished self, visual hallucinations) I had in Mania 1 were a treasure trove, which I later exploited for a useful purpose—to develop ideas of selfhood and identity in DAT. Assuming the identity of another person may be very powerful for enhancing interpersonal sensitivity and confronting prejudices. A therapist may invite clients, individually or in a group, to assume the identity of a member of the opposite sex, a minority group, a low-status group (e.g., domestic servants) or caste (e.g., untouchables in India), or a mentally or physically disabled group (e.g., people who are deaf or blind).

David   Yes, the self is dialogical in nature. It may be split into different selves, as in talking with oneself in everyday life or talking among our different selves in a dream.

The very idea of self, moreover, sets psychology apart from the natural sciences: Unlike an atom, the self can investigate itself. Indeed, there are few ideas as pregnant with potentialities as the self.

YF   In DAT, the dialogic self engages in both internal and external dialogues, summates from its experiences, formulates and tests plans of action to solve problems. It participates in its self-transformation, even self-creation. Capable of healing itself, my dialogic self has helped me in my journey at every point.

DAT may be regarded as a general approach to effective and meaningful living, or as therapy for helping people in distress. Although articulated as therapy, DAT may be generalized to become a methodology that has universal applicability for problem solving, learning from experiences, and taking corrective actions in daily living.

David   This marks DAT apart from dogged perseverance. To persevere without learning and without corrective actions is a fixation that runs the risk of energy squandered.

YF   DAT is "Therapy for All Seasons." Haven't you already sensed the therapeutic effects on us at this very moment, when we are engaged in dialogue? And in the process of writing this book?

Yes, the potency of DAT is awesome. I know because I have applied it to myself. It has helped to take me out of egoism into greater union with others. Let me illustrate. I still get nervous sometimes when I have to give a presentation in front of a large audience, despite the fact that I have done it innumerable times. The technique I use is to reorient my attitude:

You are here to perform for them, not for yourself. Uplift yourself from your egoistic concern over performance;

instead, redirect your attention on how you may better communicate with the audience. Now be joyful, and delight in the delight that your presentation brings to them.

Next, I scan the audience with composure, paying special attention to those members who smile kindly. Once eye contact is established, my anxiety level drops to near zero instantaneously. I can then proceed with renewed spiritual energy. You see, you can "borrow" energy from people with whom you are in the process of forming a dialogical relationship.

David   The most effective way to reduce anxiety is to make others more comfortable in your presence. The best way to help oneself is to help others. I urge readers to be *committed* in applying the methods of DAT in their lives. What's the point of dwelling on how mistreated or miserable you have been? It is basically egotistic. Start to redirect your attention to making others around you happy.

Now, empty your mind, unload the negatives, and be reborn.

Dynamic Relaxation and Meditation

YF   I owe much to Hypomania 1. It gave me the idea of doing a self case study of madness. It enabled me to experience disinhibition; hence, spontaneity, flashes of insight, and selfless-oblivion. It was the first significant step toward the discovery of my artistic bent. My first love was music and dance, not psychology. My simulation of conducting music sowed the seeds for advancing art-aesthetics-psychology integration as a way of healthy living. Eventually, this integration was articulated in the idea of BMS interconnectedness.

David   Achieving BMS unity is the ultimate goal of holistic health: vigorous in body, tranquil in mind, uplifted in spirit. It is an essential part of my spiritual journey. Spirituality is integral to health, physical and mental; it cannot be reached without the participation of both the body and the mind. This thesis has been amply demonstrated in your episodic experiences.

YF   Mania 2 awakened me to the fact that my passion for the performing arts has remained undiminished. I would love nothing more than to put everything I have learned to advance BMS Health.

I have learned many things in my life, wushu (martial arts), playing the violin, singing, dancing, fencing, meditation, yoga, qigong, none very well. Together, however, the whole is greater than the sum of its parts. Incorporating elements of all these together with hypnotherapy, I have created a unique approach to relaxation, stress management, and health enhancement. I call this approach Dynamic Relaxation and Meditation.

David   People usually think of meditation as being required to sit still, static.

YF   Therapists practice therapies that match their peculiarities, naturally, just as clients react favorably to therapies and therapists that match their needs. Given my disposition toward mental hyper-activity, the sit-still form of meditation doesn't work well for me. However, I enter a dynamic state of meditation with ease while moving or dancing to music.

While practicing DRM, I experience the body, mind, and spirit working as a unity. Adding a measure of madness, I enter into a state of complete selfless-oblivion, an altered state of consciousness, in precious moments. Repression is gone; primitive impulses animate creative self-expression. And DRM becomes poetry in motion, without words.

David   Some people may find it difficult to enter into a dynamic state of meditation, at least initially. Practice is required to progress from mere relaxation to meditation. Advanced meditative states of selfless-oblivion demand far more.

What about DRM for beginners?

YF   DRM is suitable for men and women, adults and children. Practitioners do not have to know anything about hypnosis, meditation, music, or dancing; the only requirements are that they can communicate and move around. In short, DRM integrates self-expression and health. Its aim is to not only manage stress but also promote health in body, mind, and spirit. Above all, DRM is meant to be enjoyed.

DRM is applicable to the training of dancers, singers, actors, and other artists who take their chosen paths seriously.

DRM may be done individually or in groups. In a group situation, verbal and especially nonverbal interaction among participants is emphasized. A therapeutic group is not just a collection of individuals; it is a dynamic field of forces acting on individuals-in-communion. The presence of others magnifies the therapeutic effects on each member of the group. Underlying this conception of the therapeutic group is, again, relational and ecumenical spirituality.

David   Could you point to specific techniques or practices that magnify therapeutic effects?

YF   A simple, but effective practice is Carnival of the Animals, named in honor of the French Romantic composer Camille Saint-Saëns. I ask participants each to imitate an animal of their choice. Naturally, children love it. So do adults when the music and movement bring forth the child hidden within their psyche.

Other techniques are as follows.

Unloading of an Unwanted Baggage: Each participant is asked to think of a specific negative (e.g., a persistent bad thought or habit), which need not be verbalized or made public, and to make a commitment to get rid of it upon passing through a door from one room symbolic of darkness to another symbolic of light. The process may be generalized to life outside: Participants are encouraged to get rid of at least one specific negative on a daily basis.

Posture of Emotions: I ask participants each to express through the language of the body a particular emotion, such as disgust, sadness, fear, anger, surprise, and happiness. They would soon learn the correspondence between emotion and posture. Identification and alteration of negative emotions may follow.

Synergistic Energy Flow: Participants sit or stand in a circle and join hands together in a meditative state induced by the therapist. Participants may be then induced through suggestive messages from the therapist to feel the flow of energy passing from one to another, first in a clockwise direction, followed by a counterclockwise direction. They may be asked each to activate their inner energy for self-healing. They may be encouraged to "borrow" energy from or to "lend" energy to other participants.

Awakening of the Lotus: Arising gradually from a prostrate position on the ground to a fully upright position, with both hands in the form of a lotus reaching for the sky. The process parallels those of growing up from babyhood to adulthood, from dejection to delight, or from ignorance to insight.

David   The symbolic meaning of the lotus has deep roots in Asian cultures and religions (Hinduism and Buddhism). Visualizing the image of Guanyin Sitting on a Lotus blossom is enough for me to forget, momentarily, all my troubles.

YF   Here is the Awakening of Lotus I have written recently (15 Jan 2014).

Awakening of the Sacred Lotus

What miracle of rebirth and longevity,
Save the Sacred Lotus,
Has a flower performed?
You are *the* survivor of all time:
A seed from the Sacred Lotus,
More than a thousand years old, spouts
Into life, undiminished
In her shining karma.

What other flower has inspired
Deeper, loftier spirituality?
See now the Goddess of Mercy
Sitting atop the Lotus blossom
And you too will be inspired.

What capability more advanced
Has another flower evolved to possess?
You generate heat to keep yourself warm
When the temperature around drops—
In triumph over adversity.

What other flower dares to embody
The noble virtues that mark your existence?
You remain immaculate, unstained
By the muck of the pond
From which you arise.
No glory in luxuriant adornment,
But in pure and simple dignity.

David   Looking at photographs of Chinese people taken a century or more ago, I am struck by their characteristic postures: stiff, rigid, lifeless. You would trace this to pervasive inhibition and impulse control rooted in Confucianism. What specific DRM techniques are suitable for loosening Chinese participants up?

YF   My own physical transformation may serve as a guide to treatment. My body was stiff and rigid too, though not lifeless, more so than I would like; this paralleled my mental rigidity, compulsivity, and obsessiveness.

So you can imagine how overjoyed I was when I discovered the DRM route to undo oppressive inhibition and control: BMS Interconnectedness. Suddenly my body becomes supple and expressive, more so than I could have imagined. I cried out loud in celebration, as if I had breathed life into Chinese civilization after centuries of suffocation.

David   And for alleviating the sense of shame that you have described as "a shackle on the Chinese soul"?

YF   Posture of Emotions may be adapted to unshackle the sense of shame among Chinese participants. Invite participates each to express in posture and movements something *they feel* ashamed of (not the same as something to be ashamed of), only to find out that it is not so terrible after all.

This technique is especially effective in the context of a therapeutic group because the presence of an audience, real, imagined, or assumed is interwoven with how shame is experienced. Do people around approve of, or laugh at you? Do you feel accepted, or humiliated by them?

David   I imagine that DRM cannot be understood fully in words. Experiential learning is essential. Are there nonverbal analogues of techniques like those used in DAT?

YF   There are. For instance, physical distance may be used as an indication of psychological distance between individuals. One exercise is to ask two participants to engage in reciprocal movements, with one person advancing and the other retreating, and vice versa. A more advanced exercise is to approach synchronicity in body, mind, and spirit.

David   Witness Rudolf Nureyev and Margot Fontyn, two of the greatest ballet dancers of all time, dancing with one body, one soul. That's ultimate synchronicity.

The possibilities seem legion, limited by only the therapist's creativity.

Therapy, however, is of no use if participants do not translate into action in their daily lives what their have learned in therapy sessions. How do you facilitate such translation?

YF   We spend an incredibly large portion of our lives on eating, though not as much as animals do. But we seldom devote time to reflect on about how we eat. So let me illustrate how DRM may be extended to various realms of living with some (deceptively) simple advices on eating that are easy (but not really) to put into practice. They represent a distillate of my insights derived from health psychology, Buddhist teachings, and the Christian tradition of the love-feast.

A Chinese idiom says, "The people regard eating as their heaven [primal want]." No wonder, the culture of eating and drinking has deep roots in China. You hardly see a person eating alone; but you see plenty families of three generations eating together. So having a meal is as much about eating as about sociality. But it is now threatened by the onslaught of fast-food chains, by the likes of McDonald and Kentucky Fried Chicken. Against this backdrop, I offer the following.

> Get away from the desk where you do your work. (Eating at the same desk where you work is a bad habit. It is unhygienic, unsociable, and unhelpful to free your mind from thinking about work while you eat.)
> Turn off the TV if you are eating at home. (This may be difficult to do in the face of opposition by members of your family. So it is essential to establish a norm. The implication is enormous: not to allow the TV to replace dialogues.)
> Begin to regulate your pace. Sit down slowly, with your back upright.
> Clear your mind. Rid yourself of negative thoughts, especially angry thoughts.
> Close your eyes, breathe slowly, relax, and enter into a state of quiet calmness, if only for a brief moment. Then open your eyes with a sense of renewed life.
> Reach out and hold hands together with your family or friends. (Remember Synergistic Energy Flow?)
> Treasure the food in front of you and appreciate the labor that has gone into its preparation.

Eat slowly, allowing your mind to be fully present in the process of eating.
Don't go back to work immediately. Take a break, even if brief.

These are not meant to be just good habits, but habits of the heart. The whole process of preparing yourself for a meal takes no more than one minute or two. But your perception of time may change, as if the clock has slowed down and you will live long.

I guarantee that you will discover the joys of eating you have not dreamed of before, prevent digestive problems from brewing, and in some cases restore balance to your disturbed gastrointestinal system—if, and only if, you adhere to the habits of the heart with persistence. You will then "eat like a Buddha."

David Now why don't you take a break from writing this book, practice DRM, and experience again the joy of the body, mind, and spirit working in unison?

Whoops, we must not forget to make a transition to the next chapter. Madness has added color to your life. But has it facilitated enlightenment or detracted from it? How are madness and enlightenment to be differentiated? Have you been just mad, or mad and enlightened? A deep sense of loneliness, of being atypical, permeates your life, prompting you to search for spirituality-in-communion. These are the questions to be answered in the following chapter.

Chapter 4:
Glimpses of Enlightenment in the
Midst of Madness

Faith begins where, and only where, reason ends.

A life that has failed to harness the creative forces of madness is an impoverished life.

This chapter goes to the heart of my journey in search of spirituality, punctuated by episodes of madness. It depicts my glimpses into enlightenment during the episodes. It confronts the central issue of how spirituality may interact with madness. In doing so, I will have to clarify the complex meanings of manic-depression, paranoia, creativity, religiosity, spirituality, and enlightenment.

My glimpses of enlightenment are the raw materials that have given me insights on the interaction between madness and enlightenment; and on relations among madness, creativity, and religiosity.

What can I share with fellow travelers? Strategies of coping with depression and life's misfortunes that I have found useful in my own journey? How can one fall in love with madness? How does poetry and spirituality drive each other? To answer these questions, an internal dialogue ensues.

Fleeting Experiences of Enlightenment

David   Your extraordinary experiences during the episodes of madness provide an avenue for exploring the hypothetical nature of enlightenment, through extrapolation from a glimpse to the fully developed state. I say "hypothetical" to underscore our limited understanding of enlightenment.

YF   There are times when I can say to myself, "I have arrived." I act according to my wishes, without inhibition or paralyzing inner conflicts. I feel a sense of supreme self-confidence, even self-mastery. My capacity for keen perception, appreciation, and humor is immense. I delight in things, large and small, complex and simple, and I proclaim, "The world is a wondrous place."

I enter into a mystical state of serenity and magnanimity, free from anxiety or inner turmoil. Guilt, shame, self-rejection, and self-mortification are minimized. I feel connected with people, at home in society, nature, and the cosmos. All the good things are present, in enhanced magnitudes. Gone are the fixations, prejudices, obsessions. Life is sweet, meaningful, and fulfilling.

Above all, the enlargement of love dominates my being and leads me to act in selfless ways for the betterment of humankind. Vivid willful hallucinations and the selfless self may be experienced, more readily than usual. In short, enlightenment is an extremely pleasant state to be in; it touches a person to the core of his being.

So even a fleeting experiencing of enlightenment is to be cherished as a beacon for the rest of my life. So I feel privileged. Like others who have experienced mania, I would prefer, if given the choice, to live my life without being deprived of manic exuberance.

David   Direct experiences of enlightenment or of the transcendent are inherently solitary. You may experience them together with someone else, but that someone else can't experience them *for you directly.*

Moreover, they may be perilously close to madness when we fail to respect the distinction between subjective experiencing and reality. I would tread, therefore, with great caution and perhaps trepidation in the unknown territory of the transcendent.

YF   Not all of my experiences are enlightened or enlightening. They include, for instance, aggressive or hostile elements. However, most of the time, hatred, embitterment, and aggression are gone.

More critically, my experiences include both positive and negative feelings. I experienced pain, pathos, and anguish intensely; I cried. But these negatives were also positive in a sense: From the crying came total catharsis, which has a powerful healing effect.

I don't know if these emotions can still be found in the final state of enlightenment.

David   The capability for deep spiritual experiences is not the same as enlightenment. Some people have this capability but are not necessarily wise and may lead disorganized lives. Mozart comes to mind as an example. His music bears testimony to his inward spirituality, yet his biography is a case study of a disorganized life.

YF   On the other hand, wisdom does not necessarily include spirituality. There are wise persons who are not known for being particularly spiritual. Enlightenment is the summit: It includes both wisdom and the capacity for deep spiritual feelings, such as compassion; madness is excluded, however.

David   I gather you don't think of enlightenment as a place or physical destination to reach. You describe enlightenment as a state of serenity and magnanimity hypothetically. Your conception is based on an extrapolation of fleeting experiences—an admission of incomplete knowledge.

However, the value of firsthand experiences cannot be overstated, to the experiencing person as well as people with whom they are shared. But we must examine further the nature of firsthand experiences and the difficulties they present to sharing.

In this book are disclosures of your private experiences, at different stages of development from childhood to adulthood. These include intercultural encounters, some inspirational and some painful; encounters with madness as well as spirituality. Of these, the most difficult to recount are those of spirituality in the depth of madness.

YF   Spiritual experiences are privately experienced; they are highly personal, not easily revealed to or understood by others. Fortunately, these private experiences do not have to remain entirely private; they can be shared meaningfully with others.

Mystical experiences, transcendent consciousness, enlightenment, and the like present even greater difficulties. Like my fleeting experiences of enlightenment, they hover around the summit of spirituality. They are not only private but also unfamiliar, even inaccessible, to most of us. They cannot be publicly demonstrated.

David   Here we encounter what appears to be an insurmountable barrier to communication or external observation. However, physiological correlates (e.g., alterations in brain waves) of these experiences are publicly demonstrable. The experiences may be reported to a public audience, as you have done in this book. Their effects on the lives of people who experience them are observable; in some cases, the effects are dramatic and transformative.

YF   The idea that "only a Buddha knows a Buddha" suggests a plausible approach to observation: comparing notes among advanced travelers who claim to have experienced enlightenment; or, better still, examination of an advanced traveler by a panel of other travelers, equally or more advanced.

David   This approach may render public what would otherwise be open only to private experiential verification: The authenticity of heightened, unusual spiritual experiences claimed by an individual may be subject to examination by a panel of judges whose qualifications are publicly acknowledged. Thus, the difficulties of communicating, observing, and verifying one's private experiences of enlightenment are not entirely insurmountable.

YF   This is a happy thought: My private experiences of enlightenment and the like can be shared meaningfully with others and are, to some extent, accessible and understandable by others. I don't mind being examined by travelers more advanced than I, if it helps the sharing. Besides, I can learn from them.

David   The mind of a lesser order is incapable of understanding fully that of a higher order, just as humans are inherently limited in their comprehension of divine beings.

God is unknowable. The absence of God, however, can be apprehended: It can be seen everywhere, in all the foolish things that people do, especially when they speak and act in God's name.

So to understand the mind of a Buddha, prophet, or saint is a formidable, if not impossible, task. However, we are not totally helpless. Reading the autobiographies, journals, or confessions of religious luminaries (such as George Fox and St. Augustine) is a good starting point. They can be a gold mine of madness, no less than of spirituality.

YF   Ultimately, however, enlightenment has to be experienced; it cannot be known by other means.

David   Presumably, enlightenment is the destination of a religious or spiritual journey. Is enlightenment like being in Heaven? And madness like being in Hell?

Madness and Hell both conjure imageries of a burning inferno, volcano explosion, and cauldron of untamed impulses like the Freudian id, as you wrote in this poem (circa January 2010):

Thus Speaks Lucifer

Cast into a lake of fire and brimstone,
Tormented day and night for ever
And ever, this is the mother of all tortures!
Hoping against hope that never comes,
Down and down we descend,
Layer upon layers of the Inferno,
Into the vast abyss
That knows not where to end.
No heavenly angels sing;

We hear only the Devil's Trill.
Lure and lust red hot inflame
Burning desire unconsumed.
O what sadist has invented Hell!

It is tempting to associate madness with Hell. However, madness has no necessary connection with evil. Hell has the connection, because it is where the evil are punished in everlasting agony, according to traditional Christian as well as Islamic theology.

YF   Perhaps the most extreme of hellish torments is that desires are not extinct, but there is no possibility for their consummation—too much of a predicament for contemplation. Hell must be a human, not divine, invention, for it is hard to contemplate that divine beings are capable of such extreme sadism. I prefer, therefore, to think of Hell as a state of mind, especially about human relationships. Hell is other people, as the existentialist Sartre says.

David   Like Hell, Heaven is not a literal place, but a state of mind. What is it like to be in Heaven? The New Testament's Book of Revelation (21:4) gives an image of Heaven:

> And God shall wipe away all tears from their eyes; and there shall be no more death, neither sorrow, nor crying, neither shall there be any more pain: for the former things are passed away.

YF   No tears, no death, no sorrow, no crying, no pain—and no need for memory. Eternal peace, eternal boredom! What can one do with angels?

Could Hell be more attractive, with its collection of fallen angels and the likes of Salome, still dancing her Dance of the Seven Veils? My vision of enlightenment differs from the Christian imagery of Heaven. It is anything but boring.

Dialectics between Spirituality and Madness

David Many people yearn for and actively seek extraordinary experiences, good and bad. William James, the American philosopher-psychologist who authored *The Varieties of Religious Experience*, once wrote to his family:

> I have learned a lot, but I'm glad to get into something less blameless, but more admiration-worthy. The flash of a pistol, a dagger, or a devilish eye, anything to break the unlovely level of 10,000 good people—a crime, murder, rape, elopement, anything would do.

YF A devilish eye, elopement, and rape conjure up romantic-sexual fantasies, in an ascending order of salaciousness. Violent fantasies are also abundant; "anything would do" is really scary. In James's case, we may be certain that the boundary between fantasy and action was not breached.

David In your case, you didn't actively seek for extraordinary experiences, through drugs, meditation, or other means. They occurred spontaneously. In point of fact, even now you don't know how to switch them on or off at will.

But we must consider the horror of this possibility: Your extraordinary experiences could be pathological and destructive through and through, without the redeeming value of the positives. Do you have any assurance that your extraordinary experiences are, or will be, positive when they do occur?

YF I have of course pondered this question. And I can give you some assurance, but not an infallible prediction. To enter into a state of selfless self *safely* presupposes a developed, healthy self already in existence.

In terms of development, the achievement of a healthy self is a prerequisite for experiencing its disappearance. The state of selfless self must be distinguished from nonexistence of self.

David   In Western psychology, the healthy self is conceived as stable over time; it is a coherent, integrated, and unitary whole. I have no dispute with this conception. To experience the selfless self or empty mind, as in Dynamic Relaxation and Meditation, is to go beyond, not supplant, the normal and healthy.

In a similar vein, the achievement of impulse control is prerequisite to experiencing the extraordinary, which implies overcoming repression and gaining access to the unconscious. If what comes out are unchecked rampant impulses and raw destructiveness, the result would be horror. Therefore, experiencing the extraordinary in the absence of adequate control is not to be recommended for all.

How do you know if and when it is safe?

YF   There are no shortcuts to the accumulation of experiences under normal and abnormal circumstances. Digging deeply into my own experiences, I see a preponderance of positives (e.g., love of humanity) over the negatives (e.g., aggressiveness), and I foresee no horror when they come out in magnified intensities. In Mania 2, for instance, the free association was replete with aggressive or hostile impulses, which I never acted on.

David   An idea that comes to mind is germane to our discussion at hand: In some cases, religiosity takes on a life of its own, coexisting with madness, and transforms the person's life. We should develop this idea further. Can we not contemplate the possibility that, in transforming the person, religiosity may also be instrumental in severing madness from the person's life eventually?

YF   In this context, I prefer to speak of spirituality, rather than religiosity, because of its closer conceptual linkage with enlightenment. Also, I don't think in terms of severance, but of harnessing or mastering.

David   Even before your encounter with mania, you made this very point (30 July 1996).

Harnessing Madness

Madness unharnessed is dangerous;
Sanity devoid of Madness is boredom.
Madness,
Oh Madness, if only
I can control you,
Switch you on
And off at will,
Then I shall have
Not only sanity,
But also tranquility.

YF   The secret is to develop a master switch that can control madness. This has proven to be extremely difficult to do. Time and time again, I thought I had learned enough to keep my hypomania or mania under control, only to realize later that my optimism was premature.

However, what I want to achieve is clear: to reap the benefits of my extraordinary, mystical experiences, without having to incur the social costs. That means I have to pay more attention to the perceptions of others, including their views of my behavior, and adjust to the distance between myself and others.

For instance, during episodes, my mind runs too fast, and I need to slow down for other people. I tend to forget that other people may not be as enthusiastic, fired up, as I am about my ideals, and I have to learn not to expect too much, or be disappointed afterwards.

In short, I must learn to master myself, to "act according to my wishes," without arousing fear and inviting rejection from others.

David   The idea of harnessing goes beyond coexisting with madness. Coexistence with madness is like living at the foot of an active volcano, and you don't know when it will explode. Harnessing madness is more radical: The creative forces of madness are made subservient to spirituality and drive its further development. The healing forces of spirituality temper the volatility of madness and keep it from causing harm or destruction.

In this way spirituality and madness are not just in peaceful coexistence with each other. Rather, they exist in a dialectical relation. Spirituality without a measure of madness is devoid of energy; madness without spirituality loses its redeeming value. Spirituality derives creative energy from madness to reach new heights; madness receives the healing, calming effects of spirituality to become benign.

YF   I like this conception. It means that madness may continue to be intertwined with spirituality, not something I have to get rid of.

A dialectical relation entails tension and conflict. Many people, including psychologists, tend to regard inner conflicts as negative and self-consistency as positive for mental health. However, the notion of self-consistency may lead to a sterile conception of human functioning in which conflicts have no place. Conflicts are, however, a part of life—a source for change, adaptation, and creativity in the process of their resolution.

David   Your own self case study, conducted when you were a graduate student in clinical psychology, is a convincing demonstration of how conflicts drive human development!

I sense the positive attachment you have toward madness. You say madness becomes benign under the effects of spirituality. This is a critical point. But what does benign madness mean?

YF   Elevated and expansive mood; hyperactive mental activity, flight of ideas, and racing thoughts; inflated self-esteem; and touches of grandiosity are all symptoms of madness I have experienced. So I know they can cause a great deal of trouble. They cannot be expunged from the mind, in the fashion of extirpating a tumor from the body. But they can be kept under control and rendered harmless.

David   It is important to distinguish between thoughts, words, and deeds in terms of impulse control. This is especially important when repression vanishes, as in your case, and access to the unconscious is unhindered.

Impulses are harmless, as long as they remain in the domain of thought. Nothing is unthinkable, for in themselves thoughts are innocent—a person cannot be found guilty for just having "bad" thoughts.

YF   And when nothing is unthinkable, there is no boundary to creativity. However, not all impulses should be expressed in words, and even fewer should be in deeds. We may keep all our thoughts, be creative, and be all right, as long as we exercise adequate control over the expression of our impulses in words or in deeds. In this sense, madness may become benign.

David   Adequate control is not easy to achieve. People are always looking for shortcuts to Heaven. You bet technologies are already being developed, claiming to bring people closer to the dream of being able to erase unpleasant and unwanted memories from their minds selectively.

A lot of people may think: Wouldn't it be wonderful if you can forget what you want to forget, simply by taking a wonder drug, like a "forgetfulness pill"?

Remember the Christian image of Heaven: "No tears, no death, no sorrow, no crying, no pain—and no need for memory"?

YF   No thanks. Such a pill, if available, may turn a dream into a nightmare. Every memory loss alters my identity, my being. What kind of a being would I be if I have only pleasant memories?

David   Unpleasant and unwanted memories are not to be extirpated, in the fashion of deleting junk files from a computer. Rather, they coexist with pleasant memories to define and enrich human nature. But we mustn't allow unpleasant memories to continue to do their destructive work. Healing is an essential part of any spiritual journey in which the past does not determine the present or future.

YF   As spiritual forces prevail, unpleasant memories lose their destructiveness and madness becomes more benign. Eventfully, spirituality triumphs over madness, not so much by vanquishing it as by dissolving it into the total being of the person.

When the ultimate goal of enlightenment is reached, destructive thoughts are extinct, and the mind is completely healed. Then, finally, madness is dissolved into the total being of the person, and can be found as a distinct part of it no longer. Such a goal draws us toward it like a magnet, even if it is beyond the reach of most of us.

In this regard, I have had only limited success: experiencing moments of serenity, most ironically, during episodic madness. The success is less limited when spiritual forces augmented during madness carry into normal times.

David   We have clarified the key issue of how spirituality may interact with madness, which goes to the core of what this book is about. Still, the book's very title demands an answer to the question: Are you enlightened or mad?

Everything we have discussed points to one conclusion: You are spiritual but not enlightened, at least not yet; you still have touches of madness, albeit now quiescent. So, the answer cannot be given in the form of an either/or statement.

YF   I have to modify your conclusion. I have been mad, quite a few times: That's beyond debate. Enlightened? That's better for the reader to decide. We have more to say about this question in the Epilogue.

Madness, Creativity, and Religiosity

David   Two broad themes, about the roles that madness plays in creativity and in religiosity, appear to encompass your extraordinary experiences. The first concerns the relation between creativity and madness, particularly manic-depression. Inspirational creativity is the hallmark of genius.

Since ancient times, a common perception is that genius and madness are closely associated. Socrates declares, "If man comes to the door of poetry untouched by the madness of the Muses, believing that technique alone will make him a good poet, he and his sane compositions never reach perfection, but are utterly eclipsed by the performances of the inspired madman." Aristotle asks, "Why is it that all men who are outstanding in philosophy, poetry or the arts are melancholic?" The novelist George Sand says, "Between genius and madness there is often not the thickness of a hair."

YF   Most people are not mad; most people are not geniuses. But the few who embody both madness and genius capture public attention. Vincent Van Gogh is an example par excellence. At times, his paintings reflect inner tranquility; at other times, they exude explosive emotions and horror.

A very educational exercise is to arrange his paintings, alongside his psychiatric history, in chronological order. It would reveal a close synchronicity between the paintings' features and the mental status of the painter.

There is good reason for genius to be associated especially with manic-depression, among the rich variety of mental disorders. Hyperactive mental activity and grandiosity are conducive to creative productivity. Feelings of anguish, self-rejection, and hopelessness in the depths of depression provide the raw materials for creative productions.

David   The Danish existentialist Søren Kierkegaard says, "A poet is an unhappy being whose heart is torn by secret sufferings, but whose lips are so strangely formed that when the sighs and cries escape them, they sound like beautiful music." The question arises: Is manic-depression merely a catalyst, or is it an essential condition for genius?

A powerful ferment, but I wouldn't want to say that manic-depression is essential to genius. The conditions for genius are inspiration to drive creative production, linguistic or artistic mastery to execute production, and singularity of purpose to ensure the completion of production. All three conditions must be met and are hence essential.

YF   Being no genius, I prefer to talk about inspirational and inspired creativity. Inspiration derives from experience; the more extraordinary the experience, the greater the inspiration. And without experience, no creative production is possible.

During madness, I was inspired; creative ideas rained down faster than I could cope. I had supreme confidence in my creative ability. I yearned to share my creative insights with others. These were favorable conditions for productions of inspirational creativity.

Alas, having come out, many of the "creative ideas" appear less creative; confidence in my ability takes a beating; doubts about sharing have appeared. Still, the inspired creativity I experienced continues to make its presence felt. Otherwise, I wouldn't be writing this book now. The question, which I can't answer, is: Will the inspired transform into the inspirational?

David   Next, we deal with the relation between religiosity and madness, particularly paranoia. The most extraordinary of your experiences (willful visual hallucinations, the vanished self) appear to be religious or spiritual in nature. We may use the term *religious-spiritual experiences* to refer to extraordinary experiences such as yours that pertain to existential-transcendental questions concerning the meaning of life and the individual's place in society, nature, and the cosmos.

YF   I would say I have had more of spiritual than of religious experience. I liken the spiritual to the flow of water through a creek and the religious to an earthquake. The spiritual works to transform my being gradually through time; the religious shakes me up to reach new heights.

Religiosity and spirituality are not the same, but they do overlap. It is possible to be religious without being spiritual or spiritual without being religious, be both, or be neither. Religiosity refers to beliefs, sentiments, and practices that are anchored in a particular religion; its expression is often institutional and denominational, as well as personal. Attending church and going to a temple are examples of religiosity.

Spirituality has no necessary connection with institutional or denominational affiliation. Though not necessarily anchored in a particular religion, spirituality embodies overarching values, meanings, and principles according to which I conduct my life. It concerns enduring transcendent-existential questions that have been raised in diverse cultures since humanity began reflecting on its own existence and nonexistence.

David Religiosity is inclined toward personal salvation, deliverance from punishment in the present life or afterlife, and the promise of everlasting life. Insecurity, anxiety, and fear of punishment, hell, and God are often the driving forces of religiosity. Answers to questions of life and death are available from religious authorities.

YF We see ironic instances of compartmentalization, by no means uncommon, where religiosity occupies a central position in a person's life and yet leaves his life unexamined, unchanged. In contrast, spiritual pursuits demand great personal effort, soul searching; for some, they are a do-it-yourself endeavor. Spirituality is growth oriented, not driven by fear.

David Another difference concerns the propensity toward violence. Religiosity may carry with it potential perils of dogmatism, cultism, extremism or, worse, fanaticism. Because religious experiences pertain to the ultimate questions of life, the danger of their occurrence in violent forms rings a grave alarm. The likes of evil cults ending in mass suicide and religious militants who kill in the name of God are magnified consequences of violent tendencies wedded to religious fervor.

In contrast, spirituality has inherent immunity to guard itself against these perils, because of its propensity toward humility, contemplativeness, and self-reflection. Exemplars of spirituality (e.g., prophets, mystics, arhats) may be tormented by self-doubt or guilt; they may be given to self-denial—but not to suicide bombing or other forms of wanton outbound aggression.

The absence of violence and even the propensity toward violence is a defining characteristic of your case.

YF   Like religiosity and spirituality, religiosity and madness are overlapping concepts. Logically, this implies that neither is a necessary or sufficient condition for the other. It is possible to be religious without being mad or be mad without being religious, be neither, or be both.

The last category, being both religious and mad, may comprise only a minority, but an important minority. Religion may enter into madness in the form of hallucinations or delusions with religious content. In some cases, these psychiatric symptoms are merely by-products of madness; they disappear with its termination. In other cases, symptoms with religious content form the core of madness—that is to say, religion is now wedded to madness, a highly incendiary condition.

In still other cases, and these are the most interesting of all, religiosity takes on a life of its own, coexisting with madness, and transforms the person's life in two possible directions, one toward the good and the other toward evil!

David   When that happens we may witness the arrival of a new prophet or another monster. That's why a study of the psychopathology of religious luminaries throughout the ages may be so illuminating.

What about your own religious-spiritual experiences in this regard?

YF   My experiences pale in significance compared with those of religious luminaries. Willful hallucinations, such as those of mine, are under the control of the hallucinator and should not be construed as pathological. The psychopathology of my madness is circumscribed and relatively tame; in particular, paranoid ideation is absent. I have no ambition to be a religious leader. I just yearn to lead a good life.

David   Not so with the great religious leaders of the world: Together, they manifest a museum of psychiatric symptoms (e.g., hallucinations, delusions of grandeur). Whereas genius tends to be associated with manic-depression, religiosity-spirituality tends to be associated with paranoia. Medical authors have long adduced biblical evidence to allege that no less a leader than Jesus suffered from paranoia. Albert Schweitzer, the renowned medical missionary to Africa, wrote his doctoral thesis, entitled *The Psychiatric Study of Jesus*, to refute this allegation.

No one to my knowledge, however, has come out for a psychiatric defense of George Fox, who founded Quakerism (later called the Religious Society of Friends) in seventeenth-century England. Fox was a troubled and searching youth drawn to religious concerns. He was shocked by what he saw as the failure of the "professors," that is, the professing Christians, to live their beliefs.

At age nineteen, Fox left home on a spiritual quest, during which he challenged religious leaders everywhere to answer his questions. Nowhere did he find satisfaction. In 1647, having "forsaken all the priests" and in despair, he heard a voice, saying "There is one, even Christ Jesus, that can speak to thy condition." To Fox, this was a direct, immediate, and transforming experience of God. It was to become the heart of his message and ministry, marking the beginning of the Quaker movement.

Predictably, Fox was persecuted. He was imprisoned eight times. He suffered cruel beatings and deprivation. But he was an indomitable figure. Nothing would drive him to detract from his dogged persistence to spread his message. His journal and other writings continue to be the basic works of Quakerism.

YF   Anyone who succeeds in leading a religious movement into maturity, surviving untold hardship and persecution, has to be a religious genius. The probability of success, though statistically significantly different from zero, is still near zero. But Fox was also a mad genius. A reading of his journal makes clear that Fox was a deeply disturbed man. Paranoid ideation leaps out from the pages.

As a clinical psychologist, I detect one extremely disturbing aspect in Fox's case: his obedience to, and acting out, hallucinatory commands attributed to some external authority. An example (emphasis added):

The word of the Lord came to me, that I must to thither [to the city of Lichfield].... Then was I commanded by the Lord to pull off my shoes. I stood still, for it was winter: but the word of the Lord was like a fire in me. So I put off my shoes.... Then I walked on about a mile, and as soon as I got within the city, the word of the Lord came to me again, saying: Cry, 'Wo to the bloody city of Lichfield!' So I went up and down the streets, crying with a loud voice, Wo to the bloody city of Lichfield! ... As I went thus crying through the streets, there *seemed* to me to be a channel of blood running down the streets, and the market-place *appeared* like a pool of blood.... After this a deep consideration came upon me, for what reason I should be sent to cry against that city, and call it the bloody city! ... *afterwards* I came to understand, that in the Emperor Diocletian's time, a thousand Christians were martyr'd in Lichfield. So I was to go, without my shoes, through the channel of their blood, and into the pool of their blood in the market-place, that I might raise up the memorial of the blood of those martyrs.

What if the commands had been of a more violent-destructive sort? The use of the words *seemed* and *appeared* suggests an awareness of the distinction between appearance and the real thing. The "deep consideration" is a clear indication of a self-reflective mind (or metacognition) at work. The word *afterwards* is significant, for it informs us that the crucial historical information about Lichfield comes after the actions. The martyrs' blood then gives Fox's actions perfect rationalization and elevation to the status of religiosity.

The journal also reveals total commitment to his religious quest; indifference to his physical and, more significantly, social costs that the quest entails. To Fox, how others perceive and react to his actions are irrelevant. Surely, here is a mark of madness.

But is there anything evil in his actions? The answer is no. That is the critical question that may differentiate religiosity from evil. To conclude, Fox is a religious genius, paranoid but not evil.

David   Judgments of good and evil are made, not on psychiatric or scientific, but on ethical grounds. So the severity of psychiatric disturbance, if any, is irrelevant.

YF   Though fully capable of acting in naughty, mischievous, even out-of-bound ways, I confess that I lack the capacity to do evil. This I count as a blessing. Less inclined to inflict pain on others than to hold myself responsible for wrongdoings, I find it easier to forgive others than to forgive myself. This I now count as a liability.

David   "Every tree is known by its fruit": This provides a hint on how we may proceed.

YF   Suppose we look at two trees, Fox and Hitler, and see how they are known by their fruits, Quakerism and Nazism. Ah, suddenly, the contrasts at every turn can't be sharper. Thus I conclude that religiosity is not always benign; when it is based on absolutism or wedded to freneticism, it can be outright dangerous.

That's one reason why my journey is not a religious but a spiritual one.

David   But is religion irrelevant to your journey? No. I sense that, deep down, you find yourself attracted to religion like the earth is to the sun. This strange attraction, which survives countless intellectual questioning, informs you that you must look deeper into the role that religion plays in your journey. This we will follow through in the next chapter.

Forbearance, Forgiveness, Hope, and Meaning Reconstruction

David   A pressing question is how you cope with negative emotions that stubbornly refuse to go away and continue to wreak havoc within the psyche. Depression is by far more common than exuberance in the human experience. So we should talk more on "madness in the opposite direction of exuberance."

YF   People react in different ways to disaster, trauma, personal failure, serious illness, or loss of a significant other. Spiritual orientation makes a big difference: A negative orientation makes people more vulnerable; a positive orientation makes them more resilient.

Thus, some people remain bitter for life, feeling that the world owes them a better deal; others commit themselves to make the world a better place; still others, who have been treated with gross injustice by others, let go of their anger and forgive. Some plunge into depression out of despair; others prevail with hope. Some lack the energy to fight on and remain stagnant; others not only rebound but also grow psychologically and emerge from their ordeals better adjusted, stronger, healthier.

David   What are the strategies for facilitating fellow travelers to augment spiritual forces in their lives, especially in the face of adversity or in the depth of a depression? I must push you again, this time to share more of how you have coped with frustrations, despair, or spiritual emptiness.

YF   I offer four coping strategies to those who have soon to face or are already facing life's misfortunes: forbearance, forgiveness, hope, and meaning reconstruction. These strategies have pulled me out of black holes and restored me to spirituality. I would love nothing more than to see that they do the same for fellow travelers. (See Appendix B on how to apply these strategies in detail.)

First, forbearance: the capacity to endure pain, suffering, or ill fortune without complaint. The antithesis of forbearance is intolerance. In the present context, it refers to unwillingness or inability to endure frustration, pain, suffering, or ill fortune, coupled with a tendency to complain. A person with low frustration tolerance tends to be impatient, irritable, and prone to emotional outbursts; such a person is likely to make a habit of whining.

There is no point dwelling on how mistreated or miserable I have been. It's basically egoistic. Applying Dialogic Action Therapy (DAT), I try to redirect attention to heal others, and thus heal myself through them. Besides, being Chinese, I have the capacity to endure pain, suffering, or ill fortune without complaint. Throughout Chinese history, forbearance is dictated by necessity: People fall victim to harsh socioeconomic or political realities beyond their control; they are hobbled by poverty, fearful of punishment or retaliation by the rich and powerful.

Forbearance may or may not entail fortitude—the moral courage to stand up for one's conviction in the face of threat or danger to oneself. Chinese people commonly regard self-cultivation a great virtue. However, appeasement, placation, or conciliation motivated by fear is often mistaken to be self-cultivation.

Restraining oneself from getting angry in the face of provocation is the mark of a cultivated person. Of course, not showing anger externally is not to be confused with not getting angry internally.

A Chinese idiom puts it this way, "Forbear insults and swallow sounds of protest": Exactly what I have observed many people do in response to humiliation, revealing a mixture of fear and repressed rage, all bottled up. So forbearance is not always a good thing.

David   Neither is uncontrolled rage that leads to fist fights, domestic violence, or in the extreme abominable mass shootings in America.

American history is as short as Chinese history is long; its baggage from history is as light as the Chinese is heavy. Americans tend to be optimistic. They want to expunge unhappiness from their collective consciousness. But true happiness includes the wisdom to embrace unhappiness as a part of life. Happiness comes more easily when we are no longer obsessed with pursuing it. It ensues naturally from taking actions aimed to make others around us happier and the world a better place.

The value of suffering is recognized in many religions. Take the Buddhist belief that suffering ceases through selflessness; the moral implication is that, likening others to oneself, one should reduce suffering in others. Its counterpart in Christianity, though not identical, may be discerned. Suffering presents opportunities for acts of courage, forbearance, or kindness, as well as for strengthening one's faith. The exemplar is the suffering of Jesus for the salvation of all humankind. Thus, adding religiosity or spirituality to forbearance amplifies its potency.

YF   Forbearance in the face of natural calamities is difficult enough. It reaches a higher level when the deliberate acts of others inflict suffering on us. To forbear provocation, insults, oppression, and the like is probably the most demanding of all. This brings us to forgiveness, which has deep roots in religion and ethical traditions in diverse cultures.

Forgiveness takes two directions: To forgive someone, and to ask for forgiveness from someone. To forgive is to excuse someone from an offense, in thought and action. It does not entail negating the offender's responsibility for the offense: Forgive, but do not forget!

Full forgiveness is unconditional: It entails refusal to blame or to condescend, and letting go of resentment. Giving people a second chance is conditional and therefore does not qualify as full forgiveness. Granting a pardon is of a lesser degree; it may involve merely permitting the offender to go unpunished. Forgiveness reaches a pinnacle when it inspires the offender to be a better person.

Beyond the pinnacle is a magnanimous state of mind where the thought of forgiveness would not even arise: That's Buddhahood. I had a glimpse into this magnanimous state during moments of madness.

David   The antithesis of forgiveness takes two forms. Vengefulness: to harbor resentment or hatred, resort to personal vindictiveness, get even or seek revenge against the offender. Irresponsibility: to admit no responsibility for harm done to another, feel no remorse, and take no action that may undo at least in part the harm done.

Repentance is important because it means assuming responsibility for one's wrongdoings. It may be particularly effective for dealing with guilt, but not with shame, in which personal responsibility is not necessarily involved. Repentance may or may not be a prelude to ask for forgiveness: A person may feel remorse, contrition, or self-reproach, and yet take no *action* to ask for forgiveness or, better still, to make reparation or restitution as an attempt to undo, at least in part, the damage done.

We must also pay due attention to forgiving oneself, which stands in a dialogic relation with both forgiving someone and asking for forgiveness. Forgiving others and forgiving oneself are mutually reinforcing. But asking for forgiveness from others without forgiving oneself is incomplete forgiveness. And to forgive oneself without forgiving others is a mark of egocentrism; it negates the right to ask for forgiveness.

YF   The trouble is that I don't find it difficult to forgive others or to ask for forgiveness from others, but I do find it very difficult to forgive myself. My superego weighs heavily on my psyche with feelings of guilt and shame, as psychoanalysts would say. After years of self-therapy, I find much relief from this burden. Applying DAT gives me further relief. It is the madness of exuberance, however, that gives me total relief.

Now I have tamed my superego; I am getting nearer my goal of being "shameless." I have learned to be kinder to myself. Shame is not in the lexicon of the enlightened, I would imagine. Indeed, the consequence of refusing to self-forgive is to lead a life loaded with guilt and self-blame.

David   One point has to be emphasized. There is nothing worse than an insincere or half-hearted apology. So don't apologize unless it comes from the heart. Asking for forgiveness, which goes beyond apologizing, is especially difficult for the proud and mighty. The moral-therapeutic route beginning from denial to acknowledgment of responsibility is difficult enough; taking corrective action, including asking for forgiveness, may be even more so.

I must also question the basic premise that forgiveness is always possible. Some crimes against humanity are so heinous that they make it very hard for us to contemplate forgiving their perpetrators. What readily comes to mind are the Holocaust, the self-genocide of Cambodia, systematic rape as an instrument of ethnic cleansing, and so forth. Are the perpetrators of such crimes forgivable?

Even for lesser crimes, not all victims are willing or ready to forgive. Thus imposing forgiveness on victims may add conflict, pressure, even guilt to the trauma they have already suffered. Forgiveness cannot be done by religious decree.

YF   "I forgive not, at least not yet. But life goes on, and I will not allow bitterness and vindictiveness to lessen the value of my life": Forgiveness is not mandatory and is not a necessary condition for moving forward.

For many, this may be a more realistic solution that may circumvent the moral dilemma entailed in asking people to forgive. The solution puts the emphasis on letting go of fixations (e.g., on past traumas, revenge), an idea rooted in Buddhism and Daoism.

David   In line with what you have stated, forgiveness does not preclude anger. Prophets get angry, even Jesus. Those who cannot experience anger (not the same as hatred) cannot love. I wish more people would experience righteous indignation over social injustice that might lead to corrective actions and ignite hope.

However, defiant actions against injustice may lead to retaliation and more oppression, as the histories of China and other countries have shown. That's why hope can be a dangerous idea. Once ignited, hope propels people to defend themselves even when their chances of success—of survival—are grim. Beware: The path of hope may lead to the grave.

YF   Be that as it may, I sent out a festive message on hope to friends and relatives in December 2005, a few months after Mania 1 ended.

> **Hope** is the mother of life: It gives us reason to live, to endure the unendurable.
>
> Hope is the archenemy of despair: That there is a way out and that all is not lost.
>
> Hope orients toward the future: What is bad will pass and what is good will be restored.
>
> Hope impacts the present: It activates action for change and holds despair at bay.
>
> Hope is not rationalization, denial, or self-deception: Authentic hope perceives reality accurately and accepts the present as it truly is.
>
> Hope is no mere optimism: The future will be better than what it is now, even in the face of calamity.
>
> Hope is a dangerous idea: It impels us to take action that may imperil our lives.
>
> Hope is also a hopeful idea: For the great peril is to take no action at all.
>
> Let hope triumph over despair, especially for all those who have endured enough.

David   Hope should be differentiated from rationalization, denial, and other forms of self-deception. Authentic hope is devoid of self-deception and distortions of reality; it is predicated on perceiving objective conditions accurately, and accepting the present as it truly is.

Despair is the archenemy of hope, as you said. It is extreme pessimism, believing that all is lost and that there is no way out of a present predicament or misfortune. It derives from exaggerations of fatalism, feelings of total abandonment, or prolonged learned helplessness.

YF   Hope goes beyond forbearance: With forbearance, I shall endure; given hope, I say, "I shall prevail." I have maintained hope even in my darkest moments. In Mania 2, I plunged into a "Black Hole" out of deep feelings of loneliness, not despair. I have had only fleeting moments of despair—as of enlightenment. So I do have strong immunity against despair. I strengthen my psychological immune system further when I view my life as a spiritual journey of discoveries.

David   What exactly have you discovered? We do not presume to know in advance where or, more significantly, what a spiritual pilgrimage will lead us to.

In your case, you weren't even cognizant that you had embarked on a pilgrimage in the beginning. You certainly do not conceive of a pilgrim's destination in terms of a geographical location of religious significance. In fact, you reject the idea of a final destination. For you, a pilgrimage is a lifelong process of discovery, in which the direction toward destination and even the nature of the destination itself have to be discovered.

YF   This question brings us to the fourth strategy, meaning reconstruction. Meaning reconstruction drives the spiritual self to find its place in society, nature, and the cosmos. My spiritual journey is not about discovering something "out there," like a treasure island. It is about the search for meaning; the treasures to be found are in the meaning that emerges from reconstruction.

The recognition of profound ignorance is the first step toward discovery. There are times when I find myself in a state of ignorance or, worse, directionlessness. Indeed, my spiritual advancement is a history of discovering greater depths of ignorance than what I had previously acknowledged.

David   In the extreme, your situation may be likened to a person searching for something, the nature of which he is ignorant, in the dark, or to a detective dealing with a case in which there are no clues to permit even formulating an initial hypothesis as a starting point.

YF   I cannot claim to know what exactly I am searching for or what the final goals to be reached are. Without trodden paths or procedures to follow, there is only a global, undifferentiated notion of the goal to be reached, which is subject to change as I proceed.

I do not even presume to know what questions should be asked, let alone the answers. That is, I admit not only that I do not know, but also that I do not know what I need to know. In short, much of the time I have been groping in the dark. What else can I do but to embrace humility imposed upon me by the recognition of such ignorance? Together with hope, humility uplifts me from the terror that might come when I grope in the dark.

The dynamic process of constructing meanings is what our dialogue is about. We are now engaged in DAT at this very moment. The will to meaning is uniquely human.

But some may still ask, "Why should we bother to engage in meaning reconstruction?"

YF   Because unwillingness or inability to find new meanings or purpose leaves old constructions untouched. Entrenchment of mental conservatism, fixation, or rigidity sets in and further inhibits meaning reconstruction. A life so entrenched is impoverished; it has no creativity.

Speaking for myself: A life that fails to harness the fecundity of madness is a life that throws away its opportunities for enrichment. It is not in love with all of itself.

David   Sadly too many people fall into the trap of entrenchment, the negation of meaning reconstruction, as their option for life. One reason is that reconstruction can be painful and demanding. Remember how painful your own reconstruction of self-identity was; you had to perform a kind of "psychological surgery" to cleanse your soul of the pernicious influences of your own mother.

Meaning reconstruction can also be hazardous, as when the reconstructed meanings are acerbic and deleterious. Many a person may react to betrayal by a trusted friend in this way: "The more I think about it, the bitterer I become. I used to be suspicious; now I am convinced I can trust no one, ever." Affirmation of spiritual values comes to the rescue, as in other instances of impasse along our journey.

And reconstruction can hardly be achieved without prior deconstruction, which requires examining and altering previous constructions. However, it would be irresponsible to leave people already suffering from loss of meaning to suffer further from unended or, worse, unending deconstruction. An implication for therapy is that closure has to be achieved.

YF   In some cases, closure may be achieved rather quickly and without pain. Let me give a specific example. Recall that my mother assigned a servant to accompany me to primary school every day? Ironically, this did not protect me from being sexually abused by a male physical education teacher who was very fond of me.

On one or two occasions he took me into his office, where his coworker was present, and kissed me. I was then about nine years old, and unsurprisingly I did not know what child sexual abuse was. I noticed his breath smelled bad because of his heavy smoking. I did not tell my mother because I was afraid she would get upset and cause a row in the school. Then I would be really embarrassed and be worse off, and the teacher might be punished.

The meaning I construed was: "That's his way of showing his affection for me, but I feel uncomfortable about the way he does it." That was the end of it. There was no deconstruction or reconstruction and no need for them. To this day, I do not consider that I have suffered psychological damage in the least.

Actually, I have been reluctant to disclose this private experience. The thought that it may be useful to others who have had similar experiences overcomes my reluctance. My example demonstrates that the way in which meaning is constructed has a decisive effect on outcomes. Psychological traumas, child sexual abuse included, do not necessarily lead to psychopathology and do not have to block the path of a pilgrimage.

David   Historically, the coping strategies you have described have been anchored more in religion and ethics than in therapy. But their place in therapy has to be recognized. Used within the framework of DAT and augmented with spiritual purposes, the coping strategies realize their potential to the fullest.

When the dialogic self constructs meaning and purpose, it entertains possibilities of what it may become—what it has never experienced before—in the future; it renders new forms of thought and action possible. It engages in internal dialogues and participates in its own re-creation. That is, the dialogic self has self-transformational capabilities. The result is the best outcome of coping: self-transformation, rare and precious.

Self-transformation is more than growth; it amounts to a quantum leap. It entails not only quantitative but also qualitative change and not only alterations of previously observed patterns but also new or emergent patterns that were previously dormant or unobserved. A self-transformed person thinks and acts like a new person, visibly to others.

Like being in love with life, even if mad. What greater force can there be?

In Love with Madness

YF   I may be self-transforming, but I can't say I have self-transformed. I have indeed done something I didn't have the courage to do before, such as giving the "impolite speech" at a graduation ceremony in Hypomania 4, and when I am normal I shall go on doing more things I have never done before. It is better to think of self-transformation as an ongoing process, not a terminal outcome—as part of a spiritual pilgrimage.

My entire journey is a dynamic process of constructing, deconstructing, and reconstructing meanings. In response to adverse life events, I make sense of what appears to be unfair or, worse, senseless.

Even after ten episodes, which are considerable, madness still appears alien to me. It should not be a part of my life. But it is, and I am compelled to face it. What can be more challenging than to make sense out of madness?

David   Well, what are the meanings you have come up with?

YF   The constructed meaning: Madness is a welcome stranger, refreshing and joyous. She has brought me many gifts, extraordinary experiences never before experienced. Deconstructed, madness is a harbinger of many troubles. She gives me sleepless nights; she makes me plunge into a Black Hole, unsettle people around me and invite stigmatization. Reconstructed, madness is a companion in my journey, coexisting with spirituality. She can be rendered benign; furthermore, her creative energy can be harnessed to serve spiritual ends.

David   I note a subtlety in your use of the pronoun *she*: Madness is female; she can be troublesome. She is also your spiritual companion and a source of creative energy. It's no wonder why you're so much in love with madness!?

Is there anything more lovable, yet troublesome, than the female in all of God's creation? She personifies both beauty and allure.

The word *lunacy* reflects Western folklore that the Moon induces insanity. Most people think of the Moon, an object of fascination since time immemorial, as being female. And thus the feminine mystique is part of madness. I now understand better your state of mind when you wrote a poem on Chang E, the Chinese goddess of the Moon, on 29 April 2003.

Chang E

The Mistress of the Moon appears
To beguile mankind, in the guise
Of Chang E in the distant East.

She relays messages of amour
Across the heavenly expanse—to sow
The seeds of lunacy on earth.

She smiles the crescent Moon.
Facing the Inferno, death by eclipse;
A moment passes, rebirth by light.

Behind the cloud she hides,
Invisible, almost—but for whom?
Enigma is her true name.

YF   I'm not sure if my mind was conscious of such seductive, twisted logic. The words just effused from my mouth.

David   Daoists use female imageries extensively for cosmic and human fecundity. The Daoist philosopher Laozi is the first to enshrine the feminine mystique in words. In the *Daode Jing* (Classic of the Way and of Potency) we find these lines (translated into English):

The Valley Spirit never dies.
It is named the Enigmatic Female.
The gateway of this Enigmatic Female
Is the root from which Heaven and Earth spring.

YF   Daoist and Buddhist ideas have inspired me to write a recent poem (15 Jan 2014).

Ode to Floral Beauties East and West

What greater pride than the rose
Has a flower ever possessed?
What higher glory than your luxuriance
Has a flower brought to its creator?
What stronger passion than your sensuality
Has a flower aroused
In the man endowed to love?

Enchanted, I swoon, I pluck, I bleed.
The rose is a thorny lady indeed!
Better to admire afar than to suffer
The pain of possession.

The lotus is as elegant
As the rose is sultry.
So shall I compare you not
To a summer rose,
But to the lotus of all seasons?

The elements sustain your life:
Rooted in mother Earth,
You slumber in the season of Water,
Only to blossom in the season of Fire,
Then proudly stand your stalks upright in the Air.
Your buds reach for the Sun,
Your leaves shoot toward the sky.
Each bud unfurls into a chalice
And lets in glimpses
Of your exquisite beauty.

What other flower speaks
The language of enduring love?

Break your rhizome into halves we may,
Only to see lingering threads of silk
Connecting still the disconnected lovers.

In all the kingdoms of living things,
What other sorority surpasses
The Water Nymph of the West
And the Sacred Lotus of the East,
Each vying for attention, yet thriving
Together in the same amicable pond?

Discombobulated, the swains
Can't tell the beauties apart!
What greater folly can there be
Than a beauty contest, to judge
Who is the fairest of them all?
East is West, and West is East—
Beauty is peace, peace beauty.

David I can't but note that you used the name "Water Nymph," instead of "Water Lily." More poetic perhaps, especially when the flower names are capitalized to suggest impersonation.

In abnormal psychology, the term *nymphomania* derives from the coinage of nymph and mania....

YF Interesting, the Chinese equivalent is flower mania. The irony is that men enchanted by women may suffer from this condition more than women do!

David Further evidence of your being in love with madness, discombobulated?

YF Why not focus more on "Beauty is peace, peace beauty"?

Remember the question I asked, "Where have all the flower babies [in mainland China] gone?" The fecundity of the Sacred Lotus brings it up again.

The lotus flower produces a fruit in the shape of a shower head containing lotus seeds, which may be prepared for eating in many ways. The sweetened lotus seeds prepared for the Chinese Lunar New Year, called *tanglianzi* (literally, sugar-lotus-seed), have an important symbolic meaning: *lian* (lotus) sounds close to *nian* (year) and *zi* may mean seed or son. So a lot of sweetened lotus seeds are consumed. Traditionally, one of the most common greetings exchanged is, "*Nian sheng guizi*": In translation, "[May you be blessed with] a precious son each year."

How about two boys in exchange for one girl in future if the outlandish disparity in the sex ratio among newborns continues?

Poetry and Spirituality Drive Each Other

David   Bilingual proficiency is essential to bicultural competence, which is an asset of special importance to a world citizen. It would be instructive for you to say something about your bilingual experiences, including your flair for linguistic playfulness.

Although you are a native speaker of Chinese (Cantonese), you have been using mostly English to express your thoughts in academic discourse. English has become your dominant language. What effect does that have on your cognition?

YF   In a way, I have been permanently altered by the English language-tool I use. It has left its indelible mark on my cognition-being. Such is the awesome power of language-tools to transform their users. A frightful thought? Fear not. I now feel I have more than one tool at my disposal. Goethe goes further, "Those who know nothing of foreign languages know nothing of their own."

David   Can thinking transcend language?

YF   I think yes. Ultimately, any thought can be articulated in any language, in poetry or prose, in speech or writing, in logical-mathematical or ordinary language. I would include nonverbal language as well.

The question is who is master, the language-tool or its user? No trifling question, because I have seen language users enslaved by language-tools, especially among academics.

I would like to allude to a "linguistic experiment," which refers to experimenting with telegraphic styles of writing with relaxed grammatical constraints. It has nothing to do with shorthand text messaging with acronyms. I have been experimenting with constructing English sentences using Chinese grammar. Take, for instance, *I have not seen you for a long time* translates into *long time haven't seen.*

Typically, Chinese grammatical constructions take fewer words than English constructions. They satisfy a key principle of good writing, namely, economy of expression: The fewer the number of words, the better. Not a single word is superfluous, especially for poetry or poetic prose.

David   Poetry is ultimate mastery of the language-tool. You like to write poetry, mostly in a language not your own. Tell us something about your travail and delight.

YF   My initial exposure to English poetry, in my first year in college, was utter bewilderment. Most of the time, I had little idea what the professor was talking about. But the sound of Chaucer's *Canterbury Tales* I heard for the first time got imprinted into my brain: It was pleasant to the ears, even when the connection between sound and meaning eluded my grasp. See, poetry is music in words.

Many years later, as a novice I visited websites for poets, aspiring and established. I even dared to submit a few of my poems for critique, one of which is *Virtual Realities.*

Virtual Realities

About my bedside the bright moonbeam spreads.
Surmise it is the frost upon the floor.
Lifting my head, I gaze at the bright moon;
Drooping my head, I long for my hometown.

Before my desktop images keep dancing.
They parody reality, and mock
Their maker, self-estranged. I ape these creatures,
So ill designed, and yearn for the real things.

The first verse is my translation of a famous poem by the Tang poet Li Bai (701–762 C.E.). The second echoes the first; it was my very first attempt to write a poem in pentameter. That took several months to complete, after what seemed to be endless experimentation. In the process, my head was filled with the sound, tempo, rhythm of words. I could be seen talking to myself while walking around. Never before had I consumed that much brain energy on a single task. The path to poetry led to lexicophilia, an incurable condition.

Critique was brutal. A seasoned poet, witness to how different versions of the poem evolved, had this to say about my "final" product: "I think the new version is metrical. Whether it's a decent poem or not is, however, a very different question."

One authority in English poetry who knew I was nonnative wrote, "Your inability to *hear* the modulating, shifting stress levels is just bringing you to grief." I should add that he also pours scorn on educators who believe in teaching self-esteem rather than grammar. He has a point.

Devastated for a while, I continue to write poems and turn grief into joy.

David   Here you can see dialogic self-healing at work. Action *precedes* emotional change. The action is purposive, to meet a challenge head on. It has saved you from being devastated for good.

I discern spiritual sentiments in many of your poems. Empathy advances when you rewrite the Golden Rule as "Do unto others as *others* would have *you* do unto them." The spirit of ecumenism and world citizenship inheres in "East is West, and West is East: The world will be a better place." All these are ingredients of a spiritual journey.

YF   I'm not sure if I have been conscious, especially in the beginning, of how much writing poetry has to do with our spiritual journey. I was simply too absorbed with learning and experimenting on how to do it.

As time goes on, it becomes clear that the process is more important than the end product. I don't have to be an accomplished poet. I am well aware of my limitations. All I need is to delight in the delight of writing poetry that has enriched my spirituality.

David   Poetry and spirituality drive each other: Poetry is a marvelous way to give spirituality concrete expression; spirituality opens the soul to poetic creation.

To recapitulate, you have stated the conditions under which extraordinary experiences may be experienced safely: adequate impulse control and a healthy self. You find relief from your punitive superego through self-therapy, DAT in particular, and total relief from guilt and shame during madness. You have learned to forgive and be kinder to yourself. Given hope, you feel you shall prevail; you strengthen your psychological immunity when you view your life as a spiritual journey.

Above all, you have learned to harness, even if partially, the creative potential of madness in your spiritual development. The repression of artistic and literary impulses is no longer a hazard to your health. However, your journey has been one of spirituality-in-isolation, in which loneliness is a constant companion. This remains *the* problem you have to face.

Chapter 5:
In Search of Spirituality-in-Communion: Transcultural and Playful

Do unto others as others would have you do unto them—
The Golden Rule restated.

Agency without communion is solitary individualism; communion without agency is but a plain life anchored in conformity.

In this chapter, my journey continues in search of spirituality-in-communion, while I share my karma with fellow spiritual travelers. Once more, David and YF engage in a dialogue to articulate how the journey may be at once transcultural and playful.

Life as a Playful Journey: Intercultural Encounters

David   A spiritual quest does not have to be a journey of solemn, staid drudgery, but of dedication intermingled with playfulness.

You were born in the Year of the Rabbit, according to the Chinese zodiac. What do rabbits do? They leap about and frolic in merriment. So naturally life to you is a gambol.

Recall in this context that Hypomania 5 took place in a luxurious setting, on board the *Queen Victoria* and land excursions around the Mediterranean. The experiences you gained could fill a travelogue. They illustrate your worldviews as a world citizen. They serve to redirect attention from abnormality to the rich diversity of normality, in which madness may be embedded. More important, they demonstrate that spiritual journeys can indeed be playful.

YF   Life on board the *Queen Victoria* was anything but boring. One day, the captain broadcasted an announcement about security measures against terrorism, while crew members went around checking for hidden bombs. The announcement went something like this:

> We take terrorist threats seriously.... So take note and report to the authorities if you see someone who looks suspicious, or if you see someone who does not look suspicious but has been seen in the company of people, among some of whom might have been seen together with someone who does look suspicious.

Upon hearing this, I blurted out, "Ridiculous!" Whereupon, an Englishman nearby was sufficiently amused to initiate conversation with me. I introduced myself as "Double-Oh-Seven"; he introduced himself as "Double-Oh-Six." Thus, both of us were working for Her Majesty's government, in search of potential terrorists on board. Later, he introduced me to his wife.

I ran into his wife over breakfast one morning but failed to recognize her. She was visibly peeved. I thought to myself, "Now you know what it's like not to be recognized by people who ought to have recognized you. I have had plenty of experiences of not being recognized, intentionally or unintentionally, by Westerners."

David   Ah, don't all Orientals look alike?

YF   Mentally settled a moment later, I took corrective action and went over to the table where she and her husband were sitting.

I said to her husband, "007 reporting to 006." I then asked his wife not to take to heart behaviors natural to secret agents that probably look unnatural to normal people. This seemed to have placated her.

The English couple were curious about my occupation. I said, "You mean besides being a secret agent. You may ask me any question, to which I am bound to give a truthful answer. You have five guesses." I did give truthful answers, but with nuances calculated to mislead. I talked about various occupations with authority, coupled with counter questions to suggest that I knew a lot more than I actually did.

David   This comes naturally to you after years of teaching practice: The art of teaching is not to conceal the teacher's ignorance, or to show his knowledge, but to demonstrate how knowledge may be generated through dialogue.

YF   The Englishman came close but missed the target. Finally, I told the couple that I was a professor of psychology. His wife professed disbelief. She asked in a sarcastic tone, "You have a certificate to prove it?" She then took another good look at me and noticed the Gucci shoes I was wearing. "Ah, I believe you. Those expensive shoes befit a professor."

At that moment, I didn't know whether I was amused or vexed. I have seldom bought expensive items for myself. I bought the Gucci shoes so I could dance, not to impress people.

David   Apparently, the Chinese saying "Respect the person's attire, before respecting the person" is not confined to Chinese people. Such great regard for worldly concerns is symptomatic of spiritual emptiness. Sadly, to many, materialistic pursuits offer more attraction than spiritual quests.

YF   Nonetheless, I was very pleased to have met the English couple. Both thought that English was my mother tongue! For the first time in my life, I passed the test of being a native speaker. Nothing made me happier.

Another linguistic encounter was a surprise. After talking with a hairstylist for a while, I asked her what her native tongue was. She replied, "English." This answer instantly embarrassed me, for having possibly embarrassed her. Fortunately, she wasn't. She explained that, being Scottish, she was used to not being understood by the English. It took me a while to get used to her accent. I still remember the way she pronounced *but*, which sounded very strange to my ears.

Accent was certainly no barrier to communication. I sensed that there was something troubling her. After discovering that I was a psychologist, she wanted to talk with me about that something. We had a heart-to-heart talk for about thirty minutes and got to the bottom of it. It turned out that she was concerned about her relationship with her boyfriend's mother, who she felt was rather possessive of her son.

David   So the classic antipathy between mothers-in-law and daughters-in-law is not unique to the Chinese.

YF   I felt gratified that we had both transcended our back-grounds. Indeed, kindred souls countenance no linguistic or cultural barriers to communication.

Displayed inside the ship's gallery were photographs of passengers dressed in utmost elegance. A Chinese couple were looking at some of the photographs, and the lady aimed her camera at one. A staff member dashed in front of the couple and bawled out a pointed threat with an Australian accent: "These photos are copyrighted. If I see you doing this again, I'm going to confiscate your camera."

David   Typical Western active-aggressiveness!

YF   She had a build that dwarfed the Chinese lady. Standing nearby, I could imagine how the Chinese woman reacted, and I approached her to see if I could help. She explained that she didn't really intend to take a photograph of the photograph on display. I said that I would talk with the staff member concerned. In a typical Chinese fashion, she said, "Never mind."

I saw an opportunity to be an agent of intercultural understanding in action. In a typically atypical Chinese fashion, I approached the staff member and relayed to her what the Chinese lady said. The staff member explained: "You know, some people actually steal

photographs from the gallery. We have to protect our copyrights."
I replied, "I understand. However, the couple feels offended. You
could have explained to them in a nicer way." She then went over
to the couple and apologized for her ill manners.

Later, I talked to some Chinese passengers about the incident.
One reacted: "I'll intentionally take photographs of photographs in
the gallery, just to vex them." I thought to myself: Typical Chinese
passive-aggressiveness!

I was witness and intervener to numerous similar incidents of
intercultural strain during the entire cruise. Neither Eastern nor
Western I had found myself, but a supracultural agent of understanding.

David   So you treated the *Queen Victoria* as a perfect place for
conducting field research on intercultural communication, organi-
zational behavior, customer relations, and so forth.

YF   Too busy enjoying myself, I did nothing by design. Still, a
generalization forced its way into my scientific consciousness: There
was an inverse relation between status and friendliness or pleasant-
ness among the staff. The high-status staff were typically European
and fluent speakers of English. Some displayed condescending
attitudes toward passengers who didn't speak English.

The low-status staff came from the Philippines, India, or other
third-world countries. Some had substandard proficiency in English.
One waiter asked, for instance, "Are you all right?"

David   When what he meant was, "Is the food all right?"

YF   I discovered to my amazement, however, that those who
came from Mauritius were articulate in multiple languages, although
they had completed only secondary education. This would put Hong
Kong to shame.

I found out that the low-status staff were not as well paid as one
would imagine. This meant that I had paid less for the cruise on their
account. Almost without exception, they were helpful and friendly.
To repay them in a small measure, I would hoard chocolates given

only to passengers and redistribute them among the staff. They showed grateful delight, far beyond the chocolates' value.

David   Without loving actions in the concrete, talks of universal love in the abstract sound hollow.

YF   Part of the cruise involved land excursions in Egypt and Italy. I visited the world renowned Library of Alexandria, where I saw groups of Egyptian schoolchildren on tour with their teachers. Like schoolchildren elsewhere, they were fun-loving, noisy, and not as attentive as demanded. Their teachers, mostly men, watched over them like hawks over chickens. They had no hesitation in delivering a hefty blow to the head of a child whom they considered to be out of line.

I followed the children around for a while. Occasionally, I caught their attention by making funny faces to reflect how scary the teachers were. They were greatly amused.

David   You had to be cautious, for nothing would infuriate teachers, in Egypt or elsewhere, more than someone who succeeded in distracting students from the crutch of their authority.

YF   In Italy, I saw an entirely different pattern of teacher-student relationships. Groups of schoolchildren were led by their teachers around to tour galleries and museums. The children were jovial and showed no fear of their teachers. I saw students and teachers joking around together, enjoying each other's company.

David   All your life, you have had a special interest in the social-ization of children in different cultures. Here was socialization observed in person. You have often said: The destiny of a nation is conditioned by the manner in which its children are socialized. Remember, even as a child, you thought that traditional Chinese upbringing "produces enslaved nations."

YF   I saw busloads of tourists on their way to the Egyptian Museum in Cairo. Most of them seemed to show more interest in Egypt's antiquity than in its modern history, more fascination with dead mummies than with the living. Few showed understanding of, let alone empathy toward, life outside the museum.

I noticed, however, that the squalid conditions under which teeming masses of people lived did not seem to have taken the spirit out of them. Everywhere I went, people responded cheerfully to gestures of goodwill. I asked someone to write down on a piece of paper the equivalent of "Greetings, and thank you for your help" in Egyptian Arabic. All I had to do was to show it to people around when I got lost (sometimes in pretense) and they would come to my aid.

David   That piece of paper is a passport to pleasant and meaningful intercultural interactions. Serendipitous encounters tend to be the most interesting when you travel in another country.

YF   Inside the museum, I took a special interest in the death mask of King Tutankhamun, particularly the hieroglyphics inscribed on it. A young Egyptian woman appeared unexpectedly and asked, "Would you like some help?" It turned out she was a university student majoring in history. She could read the hieroglyphics, which she translated into English for my benefit!

She then took my hand and gave me a personal guided tour around the museum. Pointing to a statue of a cat, she explained that it was crying with tears because it wanted another "man." Perplexed, I endeavored to discover the mystery behind such feline desire. It then dawned on me that she meant "meal."

Her name was Amany. Her stature was as diminutive as her charm was immense. Her head was covered with a hijab, which did nothing to conceal her facial expressiveness. Her large, enchanting eyes, like a pair of black pearls, would move even the most unmovable Bodhisattva. She taught me to write my name in hieroglyphics, and I showed her how to write hers in Chinese.

When it was time to depart, I took out a banknote of twenty euros and gave it to her. She asked me to write my Chinese name on it, which I did. "I will treasure this for the rest of my life," she said. At that moment, I felt what began as a casual contact had turned into a communion between two ancient civilizations, of which we were ambassadors.

David   A woman in a Muslim country taking initiative to approach a man in public? And taking his hand to go around? This defies the stereotype of heterosexual relations in Muslim societies.

YF   I remember my visit years ago to Mindanao State University in the Autonomous Region in Muslim Mindanao of the Philippines. On the way there, my travel companion, a Christian, warned me repeatedly: "Don't ever touch any woman, not even accidentally. Otherwise, dire consequences will follow!"

However, Amany showed no unease and must have felt that her behavior was perfectly acceptable. As a matter of fact, nobody around paid much attention to our interaction. She provided a living demonstration of how misleading stereotypes can be.

David   The Muslim world is not monolithic. It is far more heterogeneous than is acknowledged by most outsiders.

YF   More fundamentally, my past encounters in diverse cultures give me little or no reason to be surprised: Everywhere women governed by strict codes of conduct will, nonetheless, find ways to express their humanity.

David   Manuals in the form of do's and don'ts written for tourists often perform a disservice: They reinforce common ethnic or cultural stereotypes and put tourists too much on guard. Now you have published many scholarly papers on transcultural psychology. Are you guided by your extensive knowledge of how people from different cultures interact when you travel to foreign lands?

YF   Having traveled around the world three times, I can say that attitude matters much more than academic knowledge. People all over the world appreciate gestures of good will. Ultimately, I have only one basic principle: Be yourself, whether you are living in your own country or traveling abroad.

David   You are saying, in effect, that there is no distinction to be made between traveling as a tourist for pleasure and traveling as a pilgrim for spiritual fulfillment? If so, you have taken a radical stance, in conformity with your identity as a world citizen.

But "be yourself" also means being occasionally mad. Did you scare anyone around the Mediterranean?

YF   Being myself, I was playful. Not surprisingly, my playfulness was amplified by a measure of madness. Significantly, none of the people I interacted with thought I was mad. So, it is possible to control or conceal my madness during episodes.

Insights from the East: Psychological Decentering

David   In chapter 1, we speak of your life in two worlds, the East and the West, and of being a world citizen. A creative synthesis embodies the best elements from both worlds. I now ask: In what ways can this creative synthesis enlighten a traveler taking a spiritual journey?

To speak of creative synthesis of the East and the West demands a better understanding of what each has to offer. Yet another glaring lacuna in our dialogue is demanding to be filled, I have just come to realize. The ideas on spirituality you have mentioned thus far derive largely from the West. I have to push you to say more about how intellectual traditions from the East have informed your pilgrimage.

YF   As I now look back on the journey of spiritual discoveries I have taken, philosophical Daoism has colored my development in many ways, particularly my relations with coworkers, my role as an educator, and my artistic fulfillment. Daoism fosters individuality and individual freedom. It is the Chinese counterculture. Not surprisingly, I am attracted to it, intellectually and temperamentally.

Regrettably, Daoism has not received due attention from therapists or healers of the mind. Spontaneity and selflessness are two of its key concepts.

David Daoists disdain the Confucian affinity for social convention, hierarchical organization, and governmental rule by the scholar class. For Daoists, the good life is the simple life, spontaneous, in harmony with nature, unencumbered by societal regulation, and free from the desire to achieve social ascendancy—in short, a life lived in accordance with the Dao. Thus Daoism champions spontaneity, freedom, and empathic understanding. These Daoist ideas play a significant role in developing our conception of relational and ecumenical spirituality.

The sage acts without action and the ruler rules without governing. The intelligent person is like a little child.

YF To "return to my original face," as I wrote in my diary in the midst of Mania 2, expresses a similar thought. All things are relative yet identical because the Dao is unitary. Being and nonbeing produce each other; each derives its meaning from the coexistence of the other. That's dialectical thought.

David Daoism disavows a hierarchical view of the self, society, or cosmos. Unlike Confucianism, Daoism does not regard the self as an extension of, and defined by, social relationships. Rather, the self is but one of the countless manifestations of the Dao. It is an extension of the cosmos. Laozi's *Daode Jing* (Classic of the Way and of Potency) speaks of knowing others as being wise and of knowing one's self as being enlightened.

That seems to imply a differentiation between self and others. Yet the sage has no fixed ideas and regards the people's ideas as his own.

YF All my life I have struggled with the problem of getting rid of "fixed ideas." This problem is especially acute and difficult for professors. In madness, however, I find it easier to do.

David Regarded as a mystic of unmatched brilliance in China, Zhuangzi explicitly negates the centrality of selfhood: "The perfect man has no self; the spiritual man has no achievement; the sage has no name." The ideal is thus selflessness.

Yet the selfless person is not without attributes: He becomes a sage in tranquility and a king in activity. The selfless person leads a balanced life, in harmony with both nature and society. In sum, Zhuangzi's conception of enlightenment entails conscious self-transformation leading to the embodiment of "sageliness within and kingliness without."

When selflessness is attained, the distinction between "I" and "other" disappears. One may then act with complete selfless spontaneity. The mind becomes like a mirror, free from obstinacies and prejudices. Thus one's thinking is to be liberated from not only external social constrictions but also internal psychological impediments. This idea of thought liberation, transcending one's egoism, occupies a central place in Zhuangzi's writings:

> To be impartial and nonpartisan; to be compliant and selfless; to be free from insistence and prejudice; to take things as they come; to be without worry or care; to accept all and mingle with all—these were some of the aspects of the system of the Dao among the ancients.... Their fundamental idea was the equality of all things. They said: ".... The great Dao is all embracing, without making distinctions."

Here is a paradox indeed. Zhuangzi's assault on analysis ("making distinctions") reflects the power of his own analytic faculty.

YF His idea of thought liberation is central to my pilgrimage. Again, in some important ways I am closer to his conception of enlightenment in madness than in normality: more spontaneous, more empathic, and more like a child.

Indigenous to China, Daoism has permeated the Chinese mind, despite the fact that most Chinese have never read the Daoist classics. Laozi's ideas such as *wuwei* (nonaction, not inaction) permeate the language of everyday life. *Wuwei* means avoiding actions that go against the Dao of nature. The Dao of swimming comes to mind as an illustrative example of *wuwei*: Swim *with* the water, not against it; regard it as your partner, not something to be afraid of. I acquire a physical understanding of *wuwei* when I practice taiji push-hands.

David   Daoism fosters psychological decentering and egalitarianism. Psychological decentering is implied in the notion of selflessness, the distinction between I and other being absent; it follows naturally from the perspective that the individual is humbled in the cosmic scale of things. Egalitarianism is embodied in the idea of "the equality of all things."

YF   To me, of particular significance is that the relation between women and men is not hierarchical but complementary, like the yin and the yang. Female imagery is used extensively for cosmic and personal creativity. This is especially remarkable in the patriarchal context of Confucian societies.

David   An East-West comparison of conceptions of selfhood and identity would help us grasp the idea of psychological decentering. Let me characterize briefly conceptions in the West. Of course, Western conceptions, as are the Eastern, are rich in diversity. Still, it is possible to distillate the core common to prevailing Western conceptions.

What emerges is an individualistic self that is intensely aware of itself, its uniqueness, sense of direction, purpose, and volition. It is a center of awareness, at the core of the individual's psychological universe. The self is at center stage, and the world is perceived by and through it.

Self and nonself are sharply demarcated: The self is an entity distinct from other selves and all other entities. The self "belongs" to the individual and to no other person. The individual feels that he has complete and sole ownership of his self, which has an identity unique to the individual.

The self is sovereign, or at least should have a sense of mastery, in its own household. Having a sense of personal control is essential to selfhood. In a healthy state, the self is stable over time; it is a coherent, integrated, and unitary whole. It is individual, not dividual. Rooted firmly in individualism, the Western self is in short the measure of all things.

YF   In contrast, the Eastern self is not the measure of all things and is not at center stage. It is rooted in the relational character of human existence. Identity is defined relationally, in terms of the position that a person occupies in his social network. The self is not sovereign, but selfless and humble.

Take a look at Chinese paintings, especially the Daoist-inspired, and you see the insignificance of the individual against the cosmic scale—in contrast to the dominant, triumphant individual in Western paintings, such as those by the Italian Renaissance artist Raphael.

David   These Eastern and Western conceptions form the dialectical tension for expanding our understanding of selfhood. I believe the formation of a healthy self is a precondition for the emergence of selflessness. To put it differently, the healthy self is the womb within which selflessness is nurtured. At the same time, selflessness makes the healthy self healthier. This is one way to arrive at a synthesis of East-West conceptions.

YF   Eastern perspectives on communicating and relating cannot be characterized by anything short of psychological decentering. They suggest different approaches to decentering, a key to confront the problem of egoistic predicament and thus to rid oneself of prejudices.

In Confucianism, the principle is to extend the consideration for oneself to the consideration for others, in the self-to-other direction; likewise, others are expected to extend their consideration to oneself, in the other-to-self direction. This I call the bidirectional principle of self-to-other and other-to-self reciprocity, or reciprocity for short. The Confucian Golden Rule states:

> The humane man, wishing to establish himself, seeks to establish others; wishing to be prominent himself, he helps others to be prominent. To be able to judge others

by what is near to ourselves may be called the method of realizing humanity.

The negative form states: "Do not do to others what you would not want done to yourself."

David   Much like the Golden Rule in Judaism, as expressed by Hillel: "What is hateful to you, do not do to your neighbor."

Reciprocity should be distinguished from empathy. In reciprocity, the consideration for others is based on the consideration for oneself. In empathy, it is based on a perception of others' consideration for themselves; the consideration for oneself is suspended. Reciprocity is an extension of one's own self-understanding to understand others. Empathy is the understanding others through perceiving the self-understanding of others.

YF   I'm afraid all these may sound awfully complicated. So let me try to relate our discussion to something we are all familiar with. The common English phrasing of the Golden Rule is: "Do unto others as you would have them do undo you." Let us simply rewrite it: "Do unto others as *others* would have *you* do unto them." This I did in the first poem I ever wrote, "Rewriting the Golden Rule" (chap. 1). Thus rewritten, empathic understanding stands out.

David   An illustration from the art of giving and receiving, derived from your own experience, will make the momentous implications of this rewriting clearer.

YF   As a child, I used to collect postage stamps. My mother bought a collection as a gift for me. I pleaded with her not to do so, saying that I wanted to make my own collection and didn't want her to spend money on something I could collect for free. Moreover, at the time my family was poor, barely able to make ends meet, so I thought the money should have been better spent. The next thing I knew was that she bought me another collection. At that point, I was overcome with unhappiness.

What was going on? Did my mother follow the Golden Rule: "Do unto my son as I would have my son do unto me"? Not necessarily, because she might or might not be pleased if I spent money to buy her a gift. Her reaction would depend on many factors, the most important of which was most likely my heart behind the giving. She definitely did not follow "do unto my son as he would have me do undo him," because her son's pleading was ignored. In other words, she was not empathic in her act of giving.

As I now ponder further, I have to ask myself: If my mother was lacking in the art of giving, did I do any better in the art of receiving? Empathy on the part of both parties, then, is the hallmark of a truly dialogic relationship.

David   This discussion on the art of giving and receiving has practical utility. Next time, on Valentine's Day, readers may want to rethink what makes a "perfect" gift. Roses, chocolates, or other common items that spin doctors of consumerism peddle? Or something, which may or may not be a material thing, that your partner deeply desires?

A spiritual journey is like opening a box of delicious chocolates in various shapes and tastes from which the traveler can pick and choose. So give her a box, and she, if seasoned in the art of receiving, will lure you to consume the chocolates together with her.

YF   Break the rules, but not until you have mastered the grammar of life.

The Golden Rule, in either the original or the restated version, cannot be followed unthinkingly. A fundamental problem in the original version is that what you want others to do to you may be unwanted by others.

As regards the restated version, would you "do unto others as others would have you do unto them," if what others want you to do to them is destructive or self-destructive? The grammar of life cannot be reduced to simplistic rules.

David   George Bernard Shaw quips, "The golden rule is that there are no golden rules." Of course, he negates his golden rule by his own remark.

YF   If the Confucian prescription for combating egoism is not radical enough the same cannot be said of other Eastern prescriptions. The concept of selflessness, common to Daoism and Buddhism, holds the key.

To be selfless is to be decentered; to be decentered is an effective antidote to egoism, rigidity, cognitive conservatism, and the like. The decentered self attends to not only what others are thinking, but also what others are thinking about what the self itself is thinking. It is thus better prepared to form dialogical relationships, which are reciprocal and bidirectional.

To Zhuangzi, the sage "uses the eye to look at the eye," "has ears and eyes as images he perceives," and "takes his stand "at the ultimate eye." The mind of the perfect person is like a mirror. The selfless, by seeing through all dichotomies, including self and other, is able to "mirror things as they are." Through his metaphors, "losing myself" and "forgetting everything," we may glimpse at the empty mind. Zhuangzi says, "Exercise fully what you have received from nature without any subjective viewpoint. In one word, be absolutely vacuous."

I know the more I become empathic, selfless, and empty of mind the better a listener-therapist I would become. To think of others as "I" comes as close to transcending egoism as it is humanly possible; it is the ultimate of empathy. To have "no self" is the ultimate of selflessness. To be "absolutely vacuous" is the ultimate of emptiness. These ultimate states of mind are beyond the normal range of human experience.

During my episodes of madness, however, empathy, selflessness, and emptiness came readily and enabled me to conduct some of the best classes and therapeutic sessions in my career. I have now an experiential grasp of the exotic states of being that Zhuangzi described. He would be pleased to know that his karma continues to have such a positive effect on human activity more than two thousand years after his death.

David   Daoism serves as a counterpoint to Confucian preoccupation with impulse control, social propriety, and status hierarchy, at the expense of personal sentiments and aspirations. It offers a path to spontaneity and personal liberation. To be decentered is to embark on a royal route toward liberating oneself from egoism, culturocentrism, and prejudices—toward empathic understanding and relating.

The concept of selflessness lies at the core of Daoism. In this regard, Daoism parallels Buddhism. The Buddhist renunciation of selfhood aims to destroy the mother of all illusions. Because the illusion of selfhood is the root of egoism, overcoming it brings forth insight into the true nature of things. Like Zhuangzi, Buddhists use the mirror as a symbol of the mind purified of prejudices.

In Buddhist thought, the state of enlightenment is nirvana (literally, "blowing out," as of a lamp), achieved through moral-intellectual perfection only after strenuous personal effort. It is a state of absolute, eternal quiescence—a transcendent state of supreme equanimity. It is decidedly a state of being, not a literal place. Nirvana is beyond the comprehension of ordinary persons unawakened from the illusion of phenomenal life. "Only a Buddha knows a Buddha": This would preclude me from knowing what Buddhahood or nirvana is like.

Buddhism provides a prescription for enlightenment: Self-renunciation holds the key to salvation. Because life is viewed as intrinsically futile, the goal is deliverance from the self, not from worldly sufferings that have arisen from social conditions. The ideal to be attained, nirvana, is a state of transcendence devoid of self-reference.

Buddhism has worked out an elaborate system of practice to enable one to attain transcendence. Meditation is an instrumentality central to this system. In a state of transcendent consciousness, the subject-object distinction disappears. Cognition is suspended; the self is absent. As claimed by both Buddhists and Hindus, the transcendent state, being transcognitive and hence free from prejudices, enables one to attain higher, even "perfect" knowledge.

The Buddhist path to salvation prescribes ridding oneself of passions and desires, including in particular one's attachment to life. It is based on a total nonattachment from not only worldly objects but also the ego itself. In the language of psychoanalysis, such decathexis is the antithesis of hypercathexis, the profuse and excessive investment of libidinal energy in objects.

YF   I experienced hypercathexis during madness: I erotized myself, other people, and the world. From a psychological perspective, nirvana is the antithesis of madness.

David   Nirvana differs from the Christian or Islamic concept of heaven in one crucial respect: Heaven opens its door to the faithful; nirvana is beyond the reach of most of us. Buddhas are rare in number, as are prophets and saints. They are the few who are willing and able to renunciate worldly pleasures and make the supreme effort toward moral-intellectual perfection—the goal of enlightenment.

YF   Humbly, I feel that nirvana is just beyond my reach. However, I find the idea of karma most relevant and useful to my spiritual journey because of three implications. First, karma places responsibility squarely on me for my actions and their consequences. Second, my karma affects the lives of others and is affected by the karma of others; in a sense then, my spiritual journey is linked to those of others, and other people's journeys are linked to mine. My journey is not an individualistic undertaking! This understanding prepares me for developing the idea of spirituality-in-communion. Third, karmic effects have temporal extensions into the future, beyond my individual life.

David   The Buddhist view may be explained with an analogy. When nirvana is reached, primal ignorance is extinct, as is the causation for the cycle of births and rebirths. An individual candle, when consumed, ceases to be. Yet the light it produced may be transferred to other candles; its "life" continues.

A person dies and is truly gone; there remains only the cumulated result of all his words and actions—the karma that will continue to work out its effects on the lives of other sentient beings. Thus, transmigration is really a transfer of karma, not of any individual soul. Reincarnation is really metamorphosis, not metempsychosis: Birth is new birth, not rebirth.

YF In all, the implications of psychological decentering for spiritual development are enormous. The treasures embodied in the intellectual traditions of the East have pivotal significance for a contemporary understanding of one's place in the world and one's journey through life. They have given me insights on how to develop the Guide to Spiritual Self-Evaluation (see Appendix A)

Spirituality-in-Communion or Spirituality-in-Isolation?

The East and the West appear to resonate in current conceptions of understanding and relating with others. In the East, conceptions grounded in a worldview that stresses the relational character of human existence have always been dominant.

In the West, there is growing awareness of the tension between two conceptions of selfhood in terms of self-other relationships: The first, rooted in individualism, is primacy of the autonomous self, through which the world is perceived and understanding is achieved; the second is the dialogic self, to which engagement in self-other dialogues is fundamental. Long eclipsed by the individualistic, the relational conception is now demanding to be heard.

The individualistic and the relational conceptions parallel two fundamental modalities of being, agency and communion. Agency is an autonomous modality, wherein the will to mastery is supreme; it is manifest in actions such as self-protection, self-assertion, self-expansion, self-control, and self-direction: "I am in charge of my own life."

Communion is a relational modality, wherein the sense of being at one with others defines meaning; it is manifest in communal actions like participation, cooperation, attachment, and engagement in dialogues. Agency is accompanied by separation, isolation, aloneness, and alienation; communion by togetherness and union.

Balance between agency and communion is the hallmark of a healthy life. Freedom is achieved through agency; security is obtained through communion. In unison, agency and communion promise a life both free and secure. However, agency without communion is solitary individualism; the life it offers is that of the polar bear, free to roam alone in the desolate cold. Communion without agency has no character; it offers a plain life of security anchored in boring conformity, the extreme of which is like a swarm of bees in a hive.

Agency and communion do not merely coexist; rather, each relies on the other to thrive. Agency may be achieved through communion, as when the agent chooses to surrender aspects of personal freedom for the collective good, and to become more selfless in maintaining solidarity with others. Communion may be realized via agency, in an open and tolerant society that encourages plurality.

Ah, my life has been imbalanced, hence unhealthy, according to what I have just written down: too much agency, not enough communion. My journey of spiritual discoveries has been primarily "personal." It makes a mockery of my claim of being a world citizen: Devoid of fellowship or communion, being a world citizen would be hollow isolation wherever you go, across national, ethnic, or cultural boundaries.

This realization prompts me to take communal actions. But it is difficult. Groups that offer communion are mostly religious and institutional, and I have always kept distance from religious institutions on intellectual grounds. I have religious sentiments, but I find it difficult to accept the fundamental beliefs of theistic religions.

But is religion irrelevant to my spiritual journey? This is a pointed question raised in the previous chapter. There is simply no way to escape it.

I have a secret envy of religious folks who have communion. The life of a lonely soul in search of spirituality is heavy. Like fighting a lonely battle, it requires great stamina. There are times when I simply feel tired, emotionally if not intellectually, lacking the strength to go on. Could I not derive more strength in the company of religious folks? That is a comforting thought. But I cannot pretend to be what I am not.

Virtually all of my religious experiences pertain to Christianity. So, to Christianity I now turn to examine the role that religion plays in my journey of spiritual discoveries.

Christianity: Ambivalence

Brought up as a Christian, I have, however, strong ambivalence toward Christianity. On theological grounds, I doubt the doctrines of original sin, Trinity, Immaculate Conception, Resurrection, Ascension; I have antipathies toward the conception of Hell as everlasting punishment, the negation of the flesh, the Catholic dogma of Papal Infallibility, and so forth. On social grounds, I object to a good many of Christian teachings, such as the opposition to birth control by the Catholic Church, which has dire consequences for the quality of life in many countries, especially the poor. None of these, however, can extinguish my strange attraction toward Christianity. It has become an inextricable part of my being.

An excursion into my religious history is both necessary and informative. Like other Christian children, I went to Sunday school. The status-conscious behavior of adults in the church put me off; I felt they were hypocrites. To a child, the triangular Methodist church building was huge. Decades later, the building still stands in the same location in Hong Kong; however, to the same child now grown into an adult, it has shrunken in size. Symbolically, as an institution, the church has diminished too.

In the Jesuit school I attended in Hong Kong, religious education consisted mostly of reciting catechisms. That set the stage for my anti-Catholic stance for years. One of my favorite intellectual pastimes was to fire an array of salvos to attack Catholic tenets and push their defenders up against the wall. I would catalogue historical embarrassments of the church: the Inquisition, the persecution of Galileo, the compilation of the *Index Librorum Prohibitorum* (Index of Forbidden Books, which includes works of almost every Western philosopher).

Once, at the age of eighteen, I engaged a priest in conversation while traveling by bus from Ottawa to Montreal in Canada. Before arrival, the priest said something to this effect: "I've held Catholic beliefs all my life. They are basic to my priesthood. My world would collapse if these beliefs are not founded." Sensing the gravity of the situation, I then kept quiet.

When I was a graduate student, I met a priest studying for his Ph.D. in theoretical physics at the University of Chicago. He was obviously an intellect to be reckoned with. One day we engaged in a dialogue on sexuality and sin.

> **David** According to the Catholic Church, masturbation is a cardinal sin. Why?
>
> **Priest** Because in general deriving sexual pleasure outside the context of procreation is sinful.
>
> **David** This would include deriving pleasurable sensations from the body, if the act is unconnected with procreation.
>
> **Priest** Yes.
>
> **David** I have an itch. I scratch it. It relieves me of the itch, and thereby gives me a pleasurable sensation. Is the scratching a sinful act?

Priest   That's a difficult question to answer.
David   Why is that so?
Priest   Because it is.

Why the focus on masturbation? Because drummed into my mind while attending a Jesuit school was that it is a cardinal (as distinct from a venial) sin, the punishment for which is everlasting hellfire, and because, as recounted in chapter 1, as a teenager I suffered greatly from conflicts over masturbation.

In actuality, the priest respected the question. I waited in vain for an answer. He was thoroughly imbued with the antisex theology of St. Paul, St. Jerome, and St. Augustine. The body is as low, filthy, inferior as the soul is high, pure, superior. The lusts of the flesh, prompted by the temptations of the Devil, are locked in eternal battle with the ways of the spirit, supported by the grace of God, within the divided self.

The idea that the body is a hindrance to spirituality is antithetical to holism. In my conception, interconnectedness of the body-mind-spirit as a holistic unit is the ideal, not the triumph of the spirit over the body. In Hypomania 6, it was a physical breakthrough (achieving upright posture after years of hunch back) that led to developments in the psychological and spiritual realms (artistic self-expression and heightened esthetic sensibilities).

Nonetheless, Catholicism has a strong appeal deep inside my psyche, I confess. Such is the allure of religious certainty. My visits to the basilica of Saint Peter in the Vatican invariably arouse religious sentiments. Upon seeing the *Pieta* by Michelangelo or hearing Bach's *Largo* from his *Violin Concerto in E Minor*, strong emotions of pathos would ensue. Great art and music intertwined with religion. But are those religious sentiments purely religious?

Having received my Ph.D., I went for my very first interview for a full-time job in a Baptist college in the United States. The interview with the dean of the college went something like this.

Dean   Dr. Ho, you want to teach psychology. Our college has certain fundamental Christian beliefs, which may conflict with those of psychology. For example, Skinner says that man is not much more than a dog. Would you have trouble with this?

Dr. Ho   Man is much more than a dog. He has the capacity to alter the environment and, in doing so, shapes his own behavior. This capacity is human. Dogs don't have it.

Dean   Dr. Ho, you are well qualified. However, there are morals, more important than qualifications.

Dr. Ho   Of course. Would you please enlighten me on what morals you are referring to?

Dean   We had a faculty member, very well qualified academically. But you know what he did? He ran away with the wife of one of our faculty members. Now, Dr. Ho, would you have any difficulty in this realm?

Dr. Ho   Honestly, I can't answer your question. I haven't seen the wives yet.

The interview terminated at that point. Needless to say, I didn't get a chance to lay eyes on any of the wives. Did I really have the guts to say that? Sorry, the reader will have to make his own judgment.

Fast forward to the year 2009, shortly after my relocation to Southern California from Hong Kong. Eager to search for communion, I attended various religious services or group meetings, Christian and Buddhist. One of these took place in a Christian church. After the service, I was cordially received as a newcomer. A designated host was assigned to introduce to me the basic teachings of the church. Here is the gist of the introduction.

Host   [Going straight to the point] Mr. Ho, are you a Christian?

Mr. Ho   I was baptized when I was a child.

Host   That doesn't mean you will go to Heaven, unless you make a commitment to accept Jesus Christ as your personal savior. [At this point, my host took out a copy of the Bible and proceeded to give me a lecture on who will go to Heaven and who will go to Hell.]

Mr. Ho   I get it. That means countless Christians will go to Hell, and so will I.

Host   That's right. Many Christians don't know it.

Mr. Ho   What about the masses of humanity who are not Christian? Hell will really get crowded.

Host   That's why we must bring the Bible to them. Now, Mr. Ho, are you ready to make a commitment?

Mr. Ho   [politely but firmly] I will think about it.

Host   Are you ready to accept Jesus Christ as your personal Savior?

Mr. Ho   [more politely but firmly, looking directly into the host's eyes.] I will think about it.

It was the most direct, face-to-face encounter I have had with fundamentalist evangelicalism. I visualized a match burning my finger, and felt the pain—then everlasting hellfire engulfing my whole body. What warped mind, human or divine, could conceive of such sadism? I was not angry because there was nothing personal about the encounter, though marked as it was by utter insensitivity. But I was dejected, because there are so many fundamentalist Christians who think and act with such certainty, with such a sense of mission. Like my host, they act as reincarnates of the Crusaders.

Viewed in this light, the encounter reaffirms my observation that in many ways extreme fundamentalist Christians and Muslim militants are mirror images of each other. That's why the acrimony is bidirectional. I feel an inner chill. I fear for the future of peace. I tremble at the thought that the voices of reason, which pale in insignificance against the loud trumpets of extremism, can be drowned out of existence.

As a therapist, I cannot accept the Calvinist doctrine of pre-destination, which classifies people into the "good-elect" and the "wicked-damned." My conception of salvation is ecumenical, hence inclusionary. Salvation extends to all humanity; no one is excluded. Furthermore, personal salvation is linked to the salvation of others. This conception clashes with fundamentalism head on.

I can't help thinking that fundamentalism, chafing under the term fundamentalists applied to themselves in the 1920s in North America, put both believers and nonbelievers in an impossible moral position. Fundamentalism assigns the nonbeliever to eternal condemnation, if he refuses to be "born again"; or makes him a liar if, out of fearing Hell *alone*, he surrenders to his "personal savior." It should not give comfort to believers in the knowledge that a majority portion of humanity will not share with them the joys of their salvation; it would cause them great pain, if that portion includes their significant others.

This is not just an abstract theological issue. Coming from a Christian family, I have many relatives who are Christian. Some are fundamentalistic. What pains me greatly is to witness the progressive closing of the mind stemming from their religious beliefs. How should they feel if they *really* believe they would find me not in Heaven, but in Hell?

In Mania 1, I experienced the near-despair of trying to fathom the infinite with a finite mind; the more I knew, the more I became aware of my profound ignorance. I was simply repeating what countless pioneers of spirituality, much wiser than I, have gone through. Reason alone leads to a dead end in a spiritual journey. However, relying on faith *before* reason has exhausted itself is blind faith, which can be outright perilous. It is the lazy man's cop-out.

Ultimately, questions about faith and reason have no answer. Love, beyond faith and reason, is all I know. Why is this beyond the comprehension of so many who profess Christian love?

It was also in Mania 1 that I had hallucinatory visions of seeing myself being nailed on a cross and having intense feelings of pathos for the sufferings of humankind. I felt what Jesus must have felt. Christianity runs deep in my psyche. Am I perhaps more Christian than I dare to admit? I feel real ambivalence.

This just about sums up what my religiosity is: I am a Catholic when I enter Saint Peter's basilica, an agnostic when I reason, and a Buddhist when I don't think about anything at all.

Quakers and Unitarian Universalists

After that "going to Hell" encounter, in desperation I searched the Internet for the Religious Society of Friends, the Quakers. (Both names appeal to me. The word *Friends* resonates with the second character *Yau*, which means friend, of my Chinese name, HO Yau Fai; *Quakers* conjures up imageries of self-expression with abandon, like dancing in a state of Dynamic Relaxation and Meditation. So, there is a predestined affinity.) I attended their meetings and felt, at last, quite at home.

Why Quakers? To me, Quakers hold a mysterious attraction: They are deliciously odd. My first encounter with Quakerism took place in Hyde Park in Chicago, back in my student days. I participated in protests against the war in Vietnam, resulting in my being arrested and thrown in jail on one occasion (as recounted in chap. 1). Quakers are pacifists. So, a natural alliance is formed out of our common antiwar stance.

I attended a Quaker meeting and was initiated into an unusual experience of religious communion. People sat around in a room, quiet, meditative, contemplative. Then a few stood up and spoke, one by one. The words they uttered came from deep within, enlightened and enlightening. No sermon, sacrament, or scripture reading. The meeting engraved an indelible impression into my mind. (As I learned later, this form of worship is "unprogrammed." Another form is programmed or semiprogrammed, which resembles the worship practices of other Protestants.)

So, my attendance at Quaker meetings in Southern California is a broken continuation of the one I attended in Chicago decades ago. Evidence of predestined affinity?

The central beliefs of Quakerism are at once simple and deceptively simple. Simple, because they are stated in simple words, accessible to most people. Deceptively simple, because their deeper meanings, rooted in Quaker traditions and the "testimonies" of exemplary Quakers, cannot be understood in words alone. They have to be lived, witnessed in the deeds of daily life.

Without getting too deeply into Quaker theology, I find this core belief to be the most illuminating: There is an indwelling Seed, Christ, or Light (which may be interpreted as metaphors) within all persons that, if heeded, will guide them and shape their lives. From this deceptively simple idea springs a wealth of spiritual implications.

The core belief is a statement of ecumenicity: The Light is within *all* persons, that is, everywhere. It erases, therefore, the artificial divide between the secular and the religious, so that all of life may be lived in the Light. Each person I meet is potentially inspired and inspirational. When I shun or reject one, I deprive myself of an inspirational channel to spirituality; when I embrace one, I enrich myself spiritually. What a creative and powerful idea!

God is directly accessible to all persons without the need of intermediary priest or ritual. Quakerism rejects, therefore, ecclesiastical authority and "empty forms" of worship (e.g., set prayers, words, rituals).

All persons are to be equally valued. No wonder Quaker organization is ultimate democracy. Going to a Quaker meeting is an inspirational experience in organization behavior, in which I have great interest as a psychologist. Immediately noticeable is a total absence of hierarchal authority. For instance, there are no chairpersons, but "clerks." The gathering appears to be a leaderless group. Nobody issues edicts. Everybody has a place and a voice, to be heard and respected.

The Quaker way of conducting a business meeting is "notorious" for the length of time that may be required for decisions to be reached. Decisions are not made by majority rule. The presiding clerk, guided by the Light, helps the meeting to search for truth and unity. Strongly opposing views are often reconciled through suggestion of a Third Way (dialectics?); quietly resolved in a period of silent worship; or deferred to a later meeting. No vote is taken. When unity is reached, the clerk states "the sense of the meeting"; approval is voiced or apparent, and the minute is recorded.

My past experience with leaderless groups is that they often degenerate into perennial chaos. Not so with the Quaker communion. Things seem to get done! Individual members share a common purpose, manifest in their personal conduct and performance of tasks. They are not externally driven but internally guided. The common purpose they share is not common at all, but a higher purpose imbued with spirituality. This is communion indeed.

If Quakerism is so attractive, why don't I become one? I have two reservations. The first is that I have difficulty accepting some of the fundamentals of Christianity (e.g., the divinity of Jesus), even though I embrace the Christian idea of love.

The second concerns Quaker pacifism. I have long been antiwar. During the Cuban crisis in 1962, I wrote to a friend, "I am both nervous and depressed about the present [crisis].... when the threat of total extinction by self-destruction is so imminent. Therefore, I have decided, after years of consideration, to dedicate my life to peace." But I am not a pacifist totally, because I hold that there are conditions under which armed struggle (e.g., against tyrannical oppression, ethnic cleansing, genocide) is justified.

Can I still be a Quaker, despite the two reservations? This was the question I put to one of the Quaker "elders." His answer was a definite yes. It put my mind at ease. So I am still treading the Quaker path, learning humbly as I go along.

At a Quaker meeting, I was asked to participate in a talent show. I obliged and gave a report on the following dialogue.

When a Buddhist Meets a Quaker

The lack of talent is no sin,
And sin is not a word that Quakers use.
So, here I am. This afternoon, I heard a "privileged" conversation between a Buddhist and a Quaker, which I would like to share with you.

Buddhist   You meditate. You love to make peace. You want to conserve the gifts of mother earth. You stress the unity of words and deeds. You respect the views and beliefs of others. You are maximally inclusive, not exclusive. You affirm the intrinsic worth of each person. Above all, you believe that Buddha nature lies within each and, therefore, interpersonal encounters are an avenue to enlightenment.
Now, a creature that waddles like a duck, thinks like a duck, and talks like a duck is a duck—according to Leibniz's Law of Identity of Indiscernibles.
So, I say to you, "You are a Buddhist reincarnate in the guise of a Quaker."
Quaker   Quack, quack, quack. But I don't sit cross-legged.
Buddhist   I don't quake. That doesn't make me a lesser Quaker than you are.

Buddhism and Quakerism share much in common. Of the world's major religions, Buddhism stands out in its appeals: nonviolence, compassion, and respect for life in all its forms. Through supreme effort, a person has the potential to reach enlightenment. This idea is truly radical, for it 3implies the possibility of altering the cosmic flow of events, namely, breaking the cycle of births and rebirths, through conscious self-direction. My reservation is that I have a passion for life and I don't want to relinquish my earthly desires.

Unitarian Universalists neither quake nor sit cross-legged. Yet they shine no less brightly. One visit to Tapestry, a Unitarian Universalist congregation, was enough to convince me that I had found a communion of kindred souls. I can't think of a better name than Tapestry.

Here are the seven principles that members of Unitarian Universalist Association of Congregations affirm and promote.

1. The inherent worth and dignity of every person.
2. Justice, equity, and compassion in human relations.
3. Acceptance of one another and encouragement to spiritual growth in our congregations.
4. A free and responsible search for truth and meaning.
5. The right of conscience and the use of democratic process within our congregations and in society at large
6. The goal of world community with peace, liberty, and justice for all.
7. Respect for the interdependent web of all existence of which we are a part.

When I read these for the first time, I was hit by a sense of amazement. I agree with all the principles completely! They are ecumenical, humanistic, and action-oriented. They encompass timeless, transcultural values, and no dogma. Spirituality-in-communion leaps out from the principles. Words like *religion, bible,* and *God* do not even appear. Yet going to the congregation is like attending a Christian church, complete with a sermon, singing of hymns, blessing, and "exchange of gifts" (donation).

Again, the theme of being different emerges in my consciousness. Like Quakers, Unitarian Universalists are small in numbers. Small is beautiful; so is atypicality. Why am I not only atypical but also attracted to the atypical? This is a question I ask myself countless times. Jean-Paul Sartre says that man is condemned to be free. In my case, I am condemned to being different in addition. So be it. As I learned to turn my marginal status into strength a long time ago, so will I learn to truly accept my being different.

Besides, being in the company of the different removes the discomfort of being different. Already, I feel less lonely. I feel I have found, for the first time, a spiritual home. I am no longer a religious refugee. Such is the strength of communion. Like a field of forces, it magnifies the qi (energy) within and between persons, resulting in a greater qi in the whole of the communion than in the sum of its parts.

A Religious Experience

The Meaning of Easter

Good Friday commemorates the crucifixion of Jesus; Easter commemorates his resurrection. That much we all know. But, in a broader sense, Easter is time to celebrate the creative power of women. The egg is symbolic of new life. The Easter egg, in particular, is a symbol of the resurrection of Jesus. It has pagan roots in celebrations of spring, in which the egg represents rebirth of the land. Isn't the creative power of women, then, the secret meaning behind the Easter egg?

Easter evokes the eternal pathos of motherhood. Mary gave birth to Jesus, suckled him, rocked him to sleep, and cradled him in her arms; she witnessed her son's scourging, humiliation, and excruciating pain of dying slowly on the cross—while his male disciples have fled in fear. She was a universal Mater Dolorosa.

Resurrection and Ascension are beyond the range of
human experience. They are of abstract theological significance: Only when captured in art and music is their triumphant spirit given concrete expression. But Crucifixion is
no stranger to human experience. Even thinking about it
evokes physical reactions in us. It represents man's inhu-
manity to man. Easter is time, therefore, to commiserate
with the suffering of humankind caused by the actions of
humankind. Good Friday is good for a cause.
Before his last breath, Jesus said, "Father, forgive them;
for they know not what they do." Friedrich Nietzsche
proclaimed that the last Christian died on the cross. He
contradicted himself, for he was Christian when he said,
"In forgiving and forgetting, things that have happened
can be undone." In truth, however, what has been done
cannot be undone. Forgetting is neither necessary nor
even desirable for magnanimous acts of forgiving. It
makes us oblivious to the lessons of history. And, as
George Santayana said, "Those who ignore history are
condemned to repeat it."

Toward the end of chapter 2, I mentioned a transformative religious
experience I had in the midst of Hypomania 8. In March 2010, I sent
"The Meaning of Easter" to the minister at Tapestry, hoping that it
would be shared with members of the congregation. He asked me
to read the piece during the service on Easter Sunday.

Not even in my wildest dreams had I thought I would be so
honored in a religious-spiritual assembly. I complied. But I was still
not well enough to drive, so someone from the congregation drove
me there. I did the reading, loud and bold. Unexpectedly, I was
overwhelmed with emotion. Halfway through, tears began to flow
uncontrollably (probably invisible to most of the people present).
I might not have been able to complete the reading had there been
another paragraph.

The reading was well received. What was remarkable was that, perhaps for the first time in my life, I felt total liberation from egoism. I was concerned not with how well I performed, but with how effectively my message was delivered; attention was focused on the audience, not on me. I felt an inner peace. I experienced authenticity: Emotion and intellect were synergized; I meant every word I uttered. I had the courage to be myself, sensitive, thoughtful, good-natured—displayed in public, unabashedly.

I have rediscovered myself, my original nature that had been buried deep in mundane life. If so, is there a further point to the search for spirituality? Or for enlightenment? Perhaps whatever I have been searching for is not something out there, faraway. Rather, at least a part of it is already here, within my being. I have now a deeper understanding of what it means to "return to my original face."

Later, I described my experience to the minister. He immediately remarked that it was like a religious experience. Courage is central to spirituality, and this is no time to hide my true self, he said. How I wish I could hear such words of affirmation and encouragement more often. The question now is if and how my courage-to-be will be sustained, infused into my life as a world citizen, and expressed through ethical-prosocial actions in the years ahead.

In a sense, all of my adult life has been a preparation for the occasion. At home with being both Chinese and American, creative synthesis, hopefulness, generativity, and a host of other ideas exude from my mind. These are ideas that have given me encouragement and guidance in my spiritual journey. Now I am a witness to their concrete expressions.

At this point, I thought I had finished writing this book. But fortune smiles at me once more and gives me more opportunities to stride forward to approach enlightenment, which has proven to be far more elusive than I had imagined. This I will recount in the Epilogue.

Epilogue:

I'm Getting There

The Dao is simplicity itself: to delight in the ordinary things of everyday life, interacting with people, just being alive.

At this point, the reader may wonder, "More opportunities to stride forward to approach enlightenment? That means you are going to have more episodes." Right on. In what follows, I describe the continuation of my spiritual journey, again in the form of a dialogue between YF and David.

YF In chapter 2, you raised the question, "Since 2005, at least one episode has occurred each year. How long will this last?" I have now more information to answer your question: My madness has extended into 2014. I have had five more hypomanic episodes. So by now, I have had altogether fifteen episodes—all of exuberance, none of depression. And if the past is a guide, my madness may last indefinitely.

David So, your episodic madness has become not just predictable, but predictably predictable. But I sense that, for two reasons, you have a strange calmness in the face of this predicament. First, you have long accepted madness as a part of your life. Second, you see madness as an opportunity for approaching enlightenment, not as something to be feared. What were your later episodes like?

Madness in China

YF   Let me first relate to an episode in China. In May 2011, I was invited to serve as a Visiting Professor at one of the most prestigious tertiary institutions in mainland China. This was an opportunity I had long dreamed of. My social life was as rich as my material condition of living was poor. In a message to my daughters (6 June 2011), I wrote:

> I am doing very well in Beijing. The students are just wonderful. They are the cream of the cream. I have never seen so many super-intelligent people who are thoughtful and eager to learn in my life…. I am happier than I have been for a long time. I have found greater meaning in doing something good as an educator. Furthermore, my health has improved dramatically, largely through practicing martial arts/dancing. I feel much younger!

Soon after my arrival in China, I sensed a general elevation in my mood and energy level. Gone were the feelings of social isolation and depression I had following my relocation to the United States. My posture was upright. I felt healthy. I experienced an upsurge in mental, physical, and sexual energy. Putting physical inertia behind, I practiced wushu (martial arts) and Dynamic Relaxation and Meditation (DRM). People were surprised when they learned of my advanced age.

The hypomanic episode in China was marked by multiple peaks of mood elevation during a period of about four months. I underwent a self-transformation and became more creative, more colorful, more adventurous, more generous, more appreciative of all the good things in life. Most reassuring was the fact that, although I appeared strange to people around me, I didn't transgress the bounds of cultural acceptability. I thought to myself, "Finally, I have succeeded in reaping the fruits of madness, without being mad."

David   But all was not well, I suspect.

YF   After a month or so in China, disturbing prodromal symptoms appeared. One day, on my way to meet an appointment, I got distracted by a book display for about an hour. I was immersed in books, oblivious to everything else, and nearly missed my appointment. The amazing thing was that my distractibility was matched by my hyperfocused concentration on the books. However, such concentration was like tunnel vision. My distractibility could not be rationalized as behavior characteristic of absent-minded professors.

Also, I suffered from acute cognitive dysfunctions, such as being unable to recall my mobile phone number. For days, I was too mentally fatigued to do any work that required sustained concentration. Again, these were like attacks of mental depletion rather than confusion. I became very worried about my condition.

I put this question to a psychiatrist friend of mine, "Is it unusual for manic or hypomanic patients to suffer from mental fatigue?" The answer was no, which confirmed what I had been suspecting. It was reassuring, in the sense that I felt less atypical: "There are others who suffer the way I do. I'm not alone."

Again, the key was sleep. Most of the time, I was able to sleep remarkably well. This enabled me to maintain my energy level and function adequately on a daily basis.

David   Were there aspects that you had not experienced before, at least not as dramatically as in past episodes? Did you engage in new, previously unimagined activities?

YF   Definitely. I was able to enter into states of selfless-forgetfulness as naturally as breathing. For instance, I practiced "sitting down and forgetting everything."

David   This is an idea originating from Zhuangzi, "I smash up my limbs and body, drive out perception and intellect, cast off form, do away with understanding, and make myself identical with the Great Thoroughfare. This is what I mean by sitting down and forgetting everything."

YF   Actually, I didn't smash up my body and so forth. Rather, I practiced literally sitting down on a chair from a standing position and instantaneously entering into an altered state of consciousness. Through demonstrations, I taught some friends and students to experience what it was like.

Some nights I was too mentally active to sleep, though physically tired. Rather than trying to force myself to sleep, I got out of bed, moved around, and simply followed my natural inclinations.

I found myself practicing a DRM technique that I had been trying to perfect, namely, moving both arms independently of each other. There is endless variation in this independence of left-right arm movements. For instance, one may draw a small circle rapidly with the right hand while drawing a large square slowly with the left.

Soon, drawing figures turned into virtual calligraphy—writing Chinese characters in the air. I attempted to write with both hands simultaneously. I practiced systematically, in steps of increasing difficulty. First, I wrote Chinese characters with only my right hand and then with only my left. Curiously, after practicing with my left for a while, I found it difficult to write with my right.

David   This appears to be a phenomenon of neuro-hemispheric interference.

YF   Second, I wrote the same characters with both hands in synchrony, following the same sequence of strokes. Third, I altered the synchrony and sequence, so they became different for the two hands. I learned to follow these three steps with amazing speed.

Finally, I tried to write different characters with two hands, with or without variation in synchrony or sequence. This proved to be too difficult to be learned in one or two nights. As I practiced virtual calligraphy, I went deeply into an altered state of consciousness; and the deeper I went, the more I was able to perform feats beyond my wildest dream.

David   Writing characters in the air is a technique that some Chinese calligraphers use to perfect their art. This technique helps to solidify the mental representation of Chinese characters in their minds. Because each character has a prescribed sequence of strokes, the technique also strengthens the kinesthetic memory involved in writing. But this is to speak in the language of cognitive psychology.

You speak in the language of Buddhist-Daoist psychology. Being right handed, you would find it difficult to write with your left. In a state of selfless-forgetfulness, however, many things become easier. Your body, mind, and spirit become interconnected. When you stay still, you are totally still; when you move, your whole body—no, your whole being—moves with total commitment.

Did anyone see you doing this?

YF   On one occasion, some students and I were having dinner in a restaurant. It was already quite late, and most of the customers had left, when I gave a public display of writing Chinese characters in the air with both hands. One of the students made a video recording of this "bizarre" event. Interestingly, the restaurant staff were quite accommodating; apparently, none thought that I was crazy.

A Laowantong (Aged-Naughty-Childlike) Professor

David   How did you find the students?

YF   Impressive! I've met the cream of the cream, the brightest of the bright, from China's population of more than a billion people. Quite a few shine through as geniuses. Some appear to have encyclopedic knowledge. Most are well read and articulate. Like other Chinese students, they show deferential regard toward teachers they respect.

Faced with such lovely students, my affection toward them grows naturally. Unlike other Chinese teachers, I make no attempt to conceal my affection. A friend of mine once remarked, "Your likes and dislikes are written on your face." I am simply deficient in my ability or willingness to conceal my emotions.

The students are touched. One class sent me a card wishing me a Happy New Year (1 January 2012). On it were written these words (translated from Chinese):

> The happiest thing is to have spent such an interesting semester together with teacher Ho. We like your distinctive teaching style; we like your frankness and spontaneity—like that of a laowantong ["aged naughty child"]. You encourage us to doubt, to ask, to rebel, to practice. You are most unlike other teachers, also one we love the most.... We will always remember teacher Ho, the most loveable laowantong.

Messages like this lift me from despair that occasionally creeps into my life. The name laowantong is loaded with emotions; it captures not just my personal style but my being. I simply don't behave like a "normal" professor in China: Whatever I may gain from behaving like one wouldn't compensate for the loss of character I will suffer. I am aged, yet naughty and childlike. This ruffles people, especially those steeped in academia. But I want to keep it that way—to preserve my original face. Besides, I can't morph into what I'm not, even if I wanted to.

One of the students, whom I call Little Kitten, was most special. I met her briefly the year before, when I went to the university for a short visit. She wrote a message to me after I returned to the United States, expressing her desire to learn from me. I replied, as I normally would to messages from students or young colleagues asking for guidance. I didn't think I would meet her again. But I did meet up with her again when I reported for duty at the university. She and her boyfriend were about to receive their doctoral degrees.

David   Yuan (a Buddhist idea meaning predestined affinity) brought you together. A Chinese saying puts it this way:

> With yuan, we come to meet from a thousand miles apart.
> Without yuan, we pass each other by face to face.

YF   Little Kitten is one of the brightest, if not the brightest, persons I have ever met. Her empathy is more impressive, surpassing even her intelligence. She has an uncanny ability to comprehend what goes on in my mind. She predicts my utterances before they are uttered. In particular, she helps me to adjust to life in mainland China, many aspects of which I find alien. She guides me through the intricate maze in which people think and act. She gives me sound advice on how to act in awkward situations or to deal with difficult people.

My fondness for Little Kitten grew into deep affection. After about a month of intensive interaction, I told her that I would like to have her as my goddaughter. She readily accepted me as her godfather. As was customary in China, we went through a formal ceremony, during which she offered me a cup of tea in the presence of friends.

David   Without having to kneel, as in the past.

YF   Another one I am especially fond of is a graduate student in theoretical physics. He is the reincarnate of my youth, childlike and naive to a fault. He brings back memories of my days as a physics major in Canada. Curious about everything, his mind roams as quickly and widely as anyone I have encountered. Talented in musical composition, he set to music a poem I have written. His intellectual prowess is awesome, easily surpassing mine.

What's more, he openly acknowledges his talents with neither immodesty nor arrogance. His unusual qualities, delightful to some but disconcerting to others, are apparent even to casual observers. In short, he surpasses me in being odd and atypical.

Once we walked around in Beijing for hours in the middle of the night. We were drawn to a littered flower bed, and as if our minds were interconnected, both of us spontaneously began picking up the litter. How could we bear to see natural beauty spoilt? He would sing in the streets, without being self-conscious or embarrassed. He ran around, back and forth, following his unbridled impulses. Except for his adult size, he was just like a child. It was nearly dawn by the time I arrived home, nearly exhausted but still savoring the time we had spent together.

David   He is not just your reincarnate. He represents what you wish to be, but cannot be. Through him, you fulfill your frustrated aspirations of being a music composer and a promising physicist. Psychologists call this vicarious satisfaction.

Bright students tend to have psychological problems with atypical features. You can understand them better than others, given that you have had a fair measure of atypical problems yourself. How have you helped them?

YF   With Dialogic Action Therapy (DAT), both verbal and nonverbal, not in an office setting, but in everyday life. I don't practice DAT with professional intent; rather, therapy is interwoven with social interaction. This way, I have been able to help quite a few in a short time.

One outstanding case comes to mind. For about two months, I had intensive interactions with a student and his girlfriend. His problems were deep seated and many, among which was avoiding eye contact. His girlfriend wanted him to seek help from me. He refused, thus causing quarrels between them. You can't treat people who refuse treatment. So the trick I used was to avoid using words like therapy or counseling. Yet, therapy was in progress.

One day, I felt that the moment for decisive action was at hand. With his girlfriend by his side, I grabbed hold of his head with my hands and said to him, "Look at me, look into my eyes. Stop avoiding. I like you, so don't turn away. Look how I am smiling. I like you to smile back, smile with me…." I refused to let go of his head until he responded.

We struggled together for a few minutes. Finally, he looked into my eyes and smiled a sweet smile. The eye contact avoidance was at least half gone. His condition improved as our interaction continued. This was my best gift to him and his girlfriend.

David   You were acting more like a mentor than a therapist. Casting aside all theories, you followed your feelings. There was no analysis, only intuition and raw emotions. Your exuberance had an infectious effect on others around you. In a state of madness, you were able to personify therapy.

The Dark Side of Life:
Alienation on an Unprecedented Scale

YF   I must also talk about the dark side of life at the university. Walking around the campus, I noticed many students, especially those in large lecture rooms, dozing off, reading newspapers, playing computers games, or doing their own work, without paying the slightest attention what the lecturers were saying! The lecturers simply kept on talking, oblivious to the students' inattention.

I have not seen such student behavior anywhere else, except in mainland China. Neither have I seen the lecturers' blasé attitude toward such disrespectful behavior elsewhere. Do the lecturers have self-respect?

David   Apparently, the lecturers have not yet learned from the sayings of Chairman MAO:

> There are teachers who ramble on and on when they lecture; they should let their students doze off.... Rather than keeping your eyes open and listening to boring lectures, it is better to get some refreshing sleep. You don't have to listen to nonsense.

So, in actuality dozing off in class may have been prevalent for a long time. In large measure, students learn in spite of, not because of, their professors.

YF   I have been visiting academic institutions in mainland China since 1971—just before the "ping-pong diplomacy" that led to a thaw in Sino-American relations. So I am a witness to dramatic changes that have taken place in China's academic institutions in response to the political climate within which they operate.

The controlled atmosphere is not confined to the classroom. Typically, during an academic or professional forum, the chairperson, who is more likely male, would begin by setting the tone and defining the perimeter of the ensuing discussion. The vice-chairperson, if present, would be the next to speak. After that, others would take turns to speak, according to an implicit order of authority or status. Participants who occupy a low status speak little or keep silent. Toward the end, the chairperson would summarize the main points and conclusions, if any, of the discussion.

Clearly, the right to voice an opinion correlates closely with authority ranking.

David   In 1971, psychology was denounced as a bourgeois subject that has no place in a socialist society. Rooted in the ideology of collectivism, the negation of individuality and personal aspirations was total. The individual was obligated to place collective interests and needs above one's own and to follow the "centralized allocation" of job assignments by state bureaucracies after graduation. Considerations for personal career plans were attacked as "careerism."

YF   During my visit in 1971, I found that cadres in educational institutions negated even the idea of individual differences in aptitude.

By 1981, while teaching in a major university in Shanghai, I discerned a quiet ascendancy of individualism among students, as one put it to me in private: "To think of the state's needs is rather 'abstract.' We have to consider our own future."

On the first day of teaching, the whole class stood up in unison to salute my entrance. Totally unprepared for such an occasion, I was petrified instantaneously. The students seemed as determined as any I have encountered not to participate actively in the learning process. Some informed me quietly that it was considered impolite to ask questions in class. I found out that students have serious misgivings about boring classes. In many ways, the university reminded me of a *sishu* (private school) in past centuries.

Now, what in the world has the docile, obedient, and deferential Chinese student become?

David   How do the professors relate with one another?

YF   Competitiveness, mistrust, and backstabbing define the world they live in. The lack of collegiality among professors seems endemic. Holed up in their offices, many professors live in oblivion of the social world outside. Some don't talk with each other. Some show a singular lack of basic courtesy to colleagues. In all, their behavior defies stereotypes (or romanticized Confucian ideals?) of the traditional scholar-teacher.

David   Academic governance is typically paternalistic and autocratic, as the reader would have guessed, given the concentration of authority in the "leader" (e.g., heads of departments) at different echelons. The leaders don't lead; they issue edicts. There is little to constrain them from practicing "management by terror."

YF   I once mentioned to a department head that students were afraid of him. His reply was, "That's good. I want students to be fearful of me, so they will be more obedient." I was taken aback because the head in question professed to be an expert in management.

Factionalism is rampant. If the leader doesn't like you, you may find yourself being ostracized. It is not personal. The colleagues who shun your company simply want to avoid displeasing the leader.

David   This is called "drawing the line." In mainland China, during political campaigns even family members have to "draw the line" out of self-protection.

YF   I feel a chill down my spine.

Another open secret: BMWs line up to pick up female students in the performing arts in the evenings. Befuddled, I asked some of my students what was going on. The answer confirmed my suspicion: Access to high-class escorts is a special privilege of the rich and powerful in China.

Language use reflects social realities. The term *xiaojie* (literally, little sister) used to refer to a young, unmarried lady from a well-off family. Nowadays, it is a euphemism for fallen women. So be careful when you use it to address a woman lest she may be offended. From this, one can deduce how prevalent prostitution has become.

David   The dark side of life in the university you have described is a microcosm of the ills of Chinese society. The university is not an ivory tower. It cannot insulate itself against outside influences.

Decades of communist indoctrination appear to have done little to cure the ills of China. Has it fallen on deaf ears, like "water passing over the back of a duck"? This is worthy of deep reflection.

YF   Mainland China is communist in name, but Confucian deep down.

Education is not indoctrination. It is integral to the fate of nations and of humankind.

I decry the education I received when I was a schoolboy. Now, as an educator I deplore what I have seen in a ranking university, and others, in China. I long for a creative synthesis of Eastern and Western learning. What I see is an indiscriminate, tasteless mixture in which the worst elements of both worlds are incorporated.

Collective madness? I lament!

David   Your spiritual journey has brought you to China. How do you find life there generally?

YF   A spiritual wasteland. I don't know how to put it more mildly.

The campus is like a sanctuary, encroached from without. Outside, the first thing I notice is that laughter is rarely seen in public places. Workers go on with their business in a perfunctory way, joyless and burnt out. Interpersonal relationships are marked by guardedness and lack of trust.

In the name of development, concrete jungles have transformed much of the landscape beyond recognition. Chinese cities are no longer Chinese. Urbanites have largely lost touch with nature. Urban children see animals mostly in pictures rather than in real life. Air, water, and noise pollution threatens to lower the quality of life beyond human endurance.

In sum, the symptoms of alienation and environmental disregard are manifest everywhere. The more materialistic values predominate, the less spirituality can be found. Anguish!

David   You mince no words. You make your points strongly, at the risk of exaggeration or overgeneralization, in proportion to the depth of anguish you feel. Anguish, because you empathize with the human condition in mainland China. That's living psychohistory.

It may take decades before the wounds of spiritual emptiness can be healed. In the meantime, take comfort in the thought that you have sowed the seeds of spiritual awakening, no matter how humbly, among your students.

Never before in human history has the word spirituality mattered so much to so many people.

Now what about your madness after leaving mainland China?

A Living Buddha in a Schizophrenic City

YF   Another episode that stands out in my mind took place partly in Macau. It lasted about two months, during which I conducted training workshops for counselors. Macau may be characterized as a schizophrenic city split between the casinos district and the rest; the money that changes hands daily dwarfs that of Las Vegas. I was moved by the irony of my situation: What can I really do for the counselors attending my workshops to improve the quality of life in Macau? As I have felt throughout my professional life, mental health professionals are waging a hopeless battle against larger societal forces.

Once I decided to venture into a "casino nightclub," equipped with a large pool where men were there to pick a beauty out of some twenty lined up around. Some of the staff came from the poorest countries in Southeast Asia. They were behaving like enslaved workers, constantly apprehensive of being watched by surveillance cameras everywhere and afraid of interaction with customers. With a state of mind filled with compassion, I told a few Buddhist workers that I was a Living Buddha, there to make an appearance for their consolation. They seemed to have no trouble believing what I told them. Finally, I was appalled enough to cause an incident by lighting cigarettes repeatedly in urns in front of Buddhist statues, and was driven out by intimidating security guards. Looking back at my adventure now, I can still feel the same compassion I felt then.

On a sleepless night, I took a ferry from Macau to Hong Kong. At the port, several boisterous young men plus an unmistakable prostitute they had picked up were lining up at the immigration check point. I asked them politely, "Please don't be so noisy." Soon I found myself in trouble in the embarkation perch, crowded with passengers: One of the men stated to push me around, so hard that I almost hit a wall some ten feet away. Actually, I was hopping away as a reflexive technique to minimize the force of the push. Avoiding a fight but fearless, I walked around the perch demonstrating my fighting skills in full sight of all. The passengers were appalled by the muscular man treating an elderly person in this manner, and the pusher had been restrained by his buddies from making a fool of himself. In a state of sanity now, I would not have the courage to do what I did.

After arriving in Hong Kong, I continued to practice Taiji Quan (an inner school of martial arts), of all places inside a subway train, by maintaining balance without holding onto anything. Of course, nobody took notice, except a woman smiling. She happened to be an advanced Taiji practitioner. We exchanged a few words before I got off the train. It was an improbable encounter, brief but memorable.

This May Not Be the Last Episode

David   You said that your madness extended to 2014. Is this the year when your last episode took place?

YF   Yes.

Incredibly, the latest episode occurred while I was in the process of writing this book. By this time, the benefit of cumulated learning from past experiences amounted to premonition. Prodromal signs appearing about two to three weeks before onset could be read: prolonged hiccups, unexplainable mental fatigue and confusion, fluctuations in energy level, heightened esthetic-literary sensitivities and emotional responsiveness to music.

Presently living in Southern California, where temperatures reach 80 degrees Fahrenheit or above, I would still feel cold and have frequent shaking chills. I once asked a neurologist for an explanation, her answer was, "I don't know." But she did agree with my suspicion of a hyperactive sympathetic autonomic nervous system. I was convinced that high energy consumption due to brain activity had much to do with the shaking chills. I touched my head and I could just "feel" that it was burning inside.

Mental fatigue prevented me from serious writing for several weeks. At the same time, various enchantments added to my distraction. I found myself enjoying the simple activities of daily life, including those that I normally resisted doing (e.g., brushing my teeth, washing dishes). Not least among the enchantments was the music of Mozart, which put me readily into a mood of dancing to it. I thought to myself, "I don't have to be a genius like Mozart. All

I need is to have enough sense to exploit the works of a genius to enrich my own life."

Another enchantment was playing the game of Weiqi (Go in Japanese, Baduk in Korean), without question the most complex board game ever invented. Despite dedicated practice, I was never strong enough to attain the status of an advanced player. Though mentally tired, I was able to play Weiqi because the game requires focus on only one thing, namely, how to plan one's moves to win. One night, in a state of near mental exhaustion, I found myself able to recall what I had studied and seen the strategies of grand masters decades earlier. Then my skill improved by leaps and bounds, enabling me to compete with advanced players. This to me was a convincing demonstration that superefficient retrieval of past learning and memory may occur during episodes.

David   This superefficiency may come at a cost, however: You may be endlessly haunted by embarrassments over faux pas, failures to meet personal standards, disappointments over betrays of trust, and other unpleasantries. You may still harbor resentment toward people who caused you great pain.

YF   Right. To cleanse my mind, I practiced self-healing harder. Finally, one day I found the resentment had subsided, gone perhaps. With humor, I found it easier to interact with difficult people. In social situations, I conducted myself with a renewed sense of self. Surprisingly, I was able to exercise better impulse control during this episode. For instance, I could control the amount of potato chips consumed, something that I often fail to do during normality—while enjoying the taste more. Significantly, even close friends or relatives had little idea of what I was going through and did not notice any "abnormality," as I had gradually learned to better manage my social image.

The episode ended after lasting for about a month. However, the demarcation between hypomanic and normal states is blurred— While I am writing about this episode now, I am not sure if I am entirely out of it. This makes me very happy because, after sequential learning from one episode to the next, I may finally have found a way of harnessing the creative forces of madness without being damaged by it.

David   In all, your episodes are a goldmine of imbalances: ecstasy intermingling with anguish; maintaining a sense of psychophysical well-being while suffering from inability to fall asleep, physical exhaustion, and depletion of reserves; hyperactivity coexisting with mental fatigue and confusion; alterations between bursts of creativity and cognitive disturbances (e.g., extreme forgetfulness).

YF   The chronology reveals that shaking chills have become progressively more severe. Yet, the benefits derived cannot be overemphasized: lowering of blood pressure, to the point where medication is no longer necessary; maintaining good posture, infused with qi (energy), and so forth. Even in a state of severe mental fatigue and confusion, the wisdom of the body could be discerned: I moved around and performed tasks without conscious deliberation, as if my movements were to a large extent automatized. Intensive exercise sharpened my proprioceptive perception, enabling me to be sensitive to tightness or weakness, even mild injuries I had sustained years ago, throughout my whole body. My kinesthetic sense was enhanced in dancing, practicing martial arts, and so forth when I entered into a state of selfless-forgetfulness. The end result was a healed body, more relaxed than I had ever known—visible to those who had witnessed my dance performances.

David   Mania or hypomania is supposed to be a mood disorder. Yet, your description has been focused primarily on the psycho-physical and cognitive, rather than affective, aspects of functioning.

YF   This is dictated by the reality of my firsthand experiences.

David   Once in a while, extraordinary circumstances provide opportunities to observe workings of the mind. Your superefficiency illustrates the mind's awesome capability to retrieve information it has stored and to make remote semantic or conceptual associations.

More generally, in the language of psychoanalysis, you had unhindered access to the unconscious and were able to record the workings of the id. Defenses had broken down so much so that you found yourself in a psychotic state. Yet, the raw impulses of the id were never in danger of being acted out. Rather, they have served you well in your artistic and literary pursuits later through sublimation.

Back to the Original Question

Finally, I am reminded that the main title of this book is in the form of a question, Enlightened or Mad? By now, the reader should have his answer. And I have my own, not a simple one: Madness can be enlightening, not enlightenment.

I don't have the audacity to claim, and I haven't claimed, to have reached enlightenment. Stopping for a moment to survey my present condition, I am humbled by how much I fall short of spiritual fulfillment. Enlightenment, I feel, may be beyond my reach, at least when I am normal.

Have I failed? This question is problematic, and is not a productive way to frame what a spiritual journey is about. A spiritual journey is an ongoing process of development and growth; it has value in itself, regardless of outcomes. Viewed in this light, the idea of a final destination is in itself misleading. After all, the Dao is simplicity itself: to delight in the ordinary things of everyday life, interacting with people, just being alive. Positive forces simply overwhelm negative emotions by their sheer attractiveness.

The word is delight. I now know the direction to go. Without the benefit of firsthand experiences, I wouldn't have been able to say all these things about the interaction between spiritual forces and madness. I have good reasons, therefore, to see my encounters with madness as a blessing.

A different question is, if given a choice, would I rather be free of madness for a life of greater comfort? Again, the reader should know the answer.

I sense heavy responsibility as I write. I aspire to inform, entertain, and inspire the reader. I assume authorial responsibility to be accurate on factual and historical matters. I adhere to the first principle of health-care professionals, "Do no harm." Why? Because spirituality is potentially a dangerous idea that can be abused and mislead people into wayward paths or to evil cults. I thus caution myself not to mislead, and to treat spirituality with the dignity it demands. I shudder when I hear people say with a nonchalant air, "Sex is a spiritual experience." Spirituality is indeed an overused and much abused word.

Cognizant of the many disparaging remarks I have made about psychiatry, I must also expunge from the mind of the reader any possible misunderstanding that it is of no use whatsoever. Being inadequate or incomplete is not the same as being useless. So seeking psychiatric help may be warranted, even necessary, if and when you have a mental disorder.

To bridge different domains of learning, East-West and psychology-spirituality, is demanding; to relate personal and universal experiences is doubly so; to bridge and relate in a way that makes the whole story relevant and meaningful to the reader is even more so. No wonder I find writing this book a challenging journey within a journey, humbling yet fulfilling.

One particular issue in serving as a bridge in East-West learning stands out. The Western tendency is to conceive of spirituality in terms of personal development and growth. The individual self is affirmed, leading to greater autonomy, self-esteem, and self-mastery. These ideas I accept.

Yet, informed by Eastern ideas of the selfless self, more and more I see my spiritual journey as a movement away from the individual self to a self-in-relations (with others, nature, and the cosmos). In particularly, I see liberation from egoism as central to this journey.

Is there a contradiction between the Eastern and the Western approaches to spirituality? No. Again, creative synthesis works best. We can embrace both the Western affirmation of the self and the Eastern ideas of the selfless self.

I would go as far as to say that achieving the selfless self requires a healthy, integrated individual self to begin with; and that selflessness enhances the health of the individual self. Therefore, embark not on a journey of spirituality-in-isolation, but of spirituality-in-communion.

Sharing My Karma with Fellow Travelers

The thought that this book is ultimate self-disclosure is unsettling, especially to an author who is not inclined to self-disclose. For a while, I struggled with whether writing this book was a good idea. In the end, the decision to proceed won the day, motivated by the purpose to share my karma with fellow spiritual travelers. Nothing is more gratifying to an author than to find his work useful to readers.

Karma is an abstract idea that comes to life in the concrete. Most recently, I found one such concrete expression of karma in a chance encounter with a young woman who came from Hong Kong to Southern California, where I am now living, to attend a wedding. After a brief mutual introduction, I discovered that she is now working in the center at the University of Hong Kong, where I worked during my Golden Age. Whereupon, she blurted out, "Are you that legendary professor?"

Central to this purpose is to normalize abnormality as an integral part of human experience, something not to be ashamed of. Abnormality or madness may be kept under control, rendered harmless, and even harnessed to add color to life.

- Madness is not that horrible and not all bad: You may learn to master it, even to harness its creative energy to advance your spiritual development.
- The self-creative self: You have the potential to transform, even create your own self.
- Spirituality-in-communion: Your journey in search of spirituality does not have to be lonely; look for kindred souls as fellow travelers.
- Enlightenment is the acme of attraction (unavoidably, an understatement): Like a magnet, it draws you toward it, even if it is beyond the reach of most of us. Don't feel you have failed if your journey has not brought you there. The search for spiritual fulfillment is rewarding in itself. It can be a playful, joyous process in which you find delight in daily living.
- Beware of the perils of spiritual emptiness resulting from inaction, from being lukewarm or noncommittal: estrangement, meaninglessness, burnout.

If an author says, "I don't want to brag about my own work, because bragging goes against the spirit of humility in which I try to lead my life," is he nonetheless bragging? I will, therefore, neither brag nor self-efface.

What I can say is that, speaking from personal experience, I have derived much comfort from many of the ideas I have written about. Among these are powerful ideas of love and hope that can draw people out of despondency and energize them to proceed with their journey.

The Art of Loving for All Seasons

For all seasons? In all cultures? Grandiose, isn't it? Nevertheless, my message about love reaffirms the universality of humankind, and counters the excesses of "multiculturalism" now in vogue in the Western world.

Some truths about the art of loving are eternal and culture-transcendent. But who has the audacity to proclaim what they are? At the risk of going beyond myself, I offer a distillate of some insights.

- Only when the self forgets itself can total communion with another be achieved.
- Do you have someone around whom you feel free to hit or scold (lovingly, that is), and who feels no less free to return in kind? You are blessed if you do.
- Love presupposes the need to forbear devastating disappointments as part of life. It comes naturally when you are no longer obsessed with pursuing it.
- Blessed is the person who finds the greatest joy in making others happy.
- Blessed is the couple for both of whom the inner and the outer selves are one.

Love is indeed quintessential to any spiritual journey. Now, if only you and I put into practice the art of loving that has just been articulated.... Here, an additional word of encouragement is fitting.

Blessed are fellow travelers in our spiritual journey. You may not feel loved, but you will love others, so they may love more. You may be defeated for now, but you hold your heads high with dignity. You may be near exhaustion, but you will not give up. You may be in turmoil, but you will continue to search for direction. You don't yet see your destination, but you are about to see the light of dawn.

My personal journey is incomplete. I can't help feeling a deep sense of humility, in the face of my many failures and the difficulties ahead. I have a long way to go. In fact, the longer the better, for the end of the journey is also the end of life as we know it.

Gone, but not gone.
I will be here,
Here with you.
My karma will continue
To work out its effects,
Through this book,
On sentient beings,
Of which you are one.

Appendix A:
Guide to Spiritual Self-Evaluation

This Guide is like a map for spiritual travelers. It will help you to reflect on your spiritual condition in diverse domains of life, all of which are of cardinal importance and none of which are trivial. The Guide makes use of concept pairs; in each pair, one concept pertains to a component of spiritual fulfillment and the other to a corresponding component of spiritual emptiness. This facilitates dynamic analyses of both positive and negative functioning, relying on diverse sources or types of information (e.g., life history, diaries). The Guide is a flexible, omnibus tool. It may be used in whole or in part. You may use it regardless of your cultural, religious, or ideological background.

The Guide comprises 32 concept (or item) pairs, each of which may be used to assess contrasting components of spiritual fulfillment versus spiritual emptiness. These concept pairs are grouped into 7 dimensions.

1. Reflectiveness-Decentering versus Dogmatism-Egocentricity (2 items; cognitive)
2. Heightened Sensibilities versus Psychic Numbing/Turmoil (7 items; affective)
3. Acceptance versus Denial (3 items)
4. Humility versus Arrogance (4 items)
5. Existential Quest versus Hedonistic-Materialistic Pursuits (6 items)
6. Transcendence versus Self-Encapsulation (5 items)
7. Self-Actualization versus Alienation (5 items)

Self-exploration is an essential step to be taken in any spiritual journey. I invite or, to put it more strongly, challenge my fellow traveler to a spiritual self-examination: "Take a good look at yourself in the mirror. In what respects and to what extent do you experience spiritual fulfillment, and spiritual emptiness?"

1. Reflectiveness-Decentering versus Dogmatism-Egocentricity

This cognitive dimension of the Guide comprises two component pairs: (a) Reflective Metacognition versus Dogmatism, and (b) Psychological Decentering versus Egocentricity. The focus is placed on how, rather than what, you think about spirituality.

Consider this statement, which illustrates both metacognition and psychological decentering: "I attend to not only what others are thinking, but also what others are thinking about what I'm thinking. I also expect others to do the same thing." And this one, "For now we see through a glass, darkly; but then face to face: now I know in part; but then shall I know even as also I am known" (1 Corinthians 13.12). To know myself is demanding enough; to know myself "even as also I am known [by God]" entails knowing something about the mind of God!

Love is central to religious conceptions of the human-divine relationship. It is important to recognize that there are two distinct directions in this relationship: human-to-divine and divine-to-human. Tension arises from a lack of reciprocities: "I love God, but God doesn't love me"; or "God loves me, but I can't love him because of awful things he has allowed to happen in my life." The benefits of reducing such tension may be generalized to other relationships (e.g., between yourself and your friends).

Directional love	Illustrations of invitation
Love between spiritual traveler and God (direction not specified)	Tell me something about your thinking on love between you and God.
Perception in the human-to-divine direction	What about your thoughts on your love toward God?
Metaperception in the human-to-divine direction	Do you think God perceives that you love him?
Perception in the divine-to-human direction	What about your thoughts on God's love toward you?
Metaperception in the divine-to-human direction	Do you perceive that God is determined in his mind that he loves you?

Note. Metaperception means perception of another perception (e.g., one's own perception, God's perception). Wordings may be altered to suit the traveler's religious background. For instance, for Muslims Allah may be substituted for God.

Reflective Metacognition versus Dogmatism

Metacognition means thinking about the process of thinking itself. Thinking about important questions concerning life is characterized by metacognitive, reflective thought that involves doubt or struggle. It does not fall back automatically on stereotyped or superstitious beliefs, blind faith, religious dogmas, doctrinaire beliefs for ready answers to important questions concerning life. Spirituality tends to be characterized by higher levels of reflectiveness.

Observe the increasing level of metacognitive reflectiveness among these three statements, from one to the next.

> I live from day to day; I don't think about tomorrow.
> That means a lack of purpose in life.
> When I realize I lack purpose in life, I become unhappy and I want to change.

Psychological Decentering versus Egocentricity

Being psychologically decentered is a hallmark of the selfless—an effective antidote to biases and prejudices. You are decentered from the core of your psychological universe. You are now capable of perceiving from other perspectives, freed from the constraints of your own perspective or frame of mind. Correspondingly, there is greater freedom of action. Your decentered self respects the interests of other people, and acts without selfish concerns.

In contrast, egocentricity refers to perceiving the world from the perspective of the self alone, characterized by a lack of capacity to perceive the world from multiple perspectives. It is the antithesis of psychological decentering and of selflessness.

Concept pair	Reflectiveness-Decentering	Dogmatism-Egocentricity
General idea	Cognitive dimension of spirituality	Cognitive dimension of spiritual emptiness
Item 1	*Reflective Metacognition* Thinking about important questions concerning life is characterized by reflective, metacognitive thought; involves doubt or struggle.	*Dogmatism* Falls back automatically on stereotyped or superstitious beliefs, blind faith, religious dogmas, doctrinaire beliefs for ready answers to important questions concerning life.
Examples	"The end of reason is where faith begins. But do not uphold any faith until reason has exhausted itself." "I have sometimes wondered if God exists."	"All the answers are already there, written down. Why bother to think about these questions?" "Generally I simply follow the teachings of my faith."

Item 2	Psychological Decentering	Egocentricity
	Perceives the world from different perspectives.	Perceives the world solely or primarily from one's own perspective.
Examples	"I know what my friends think about me, in the same way that my friends know what I think about them." [Strong capacity for alternating between perspectives] "Americans and Chinese share a common challenge: Each side has something from which the other urgently needs to learn, and sometime else the other advisedly needs to avoid."	"I have no idea of what my friends are thinking at all. There is simply no way to find out what's in the minds of other people." "What do you mean by looking at the world from other peoples' perspectives? We live in this country. All we know is that people from other countries don't behave like we do."

Invitation to Self-Exploration

The following invites you to explore your thinking about spirituality. This will lead you to reexamine your own thinking. You may turn to the tables above as a guide to further exploration.

People have different ways of thinking about questions such as faith, their relationship with God (or the divine), their place in the world, and so forth. What are your own thoughts?

I would like you to talk about not only what your thoughts are, but also the way you think about the questions I mentioned. For instance, how have you arrived at your present beliefs? What do other people think about them? What are your thoughts on other people's beliefs?

What does spiritual emptiness mean to you? Again, I would like you to put the emphasis on the way you think about this question; in other words, please talk about not just the answer, but how you arrive at the answer.

What is your thinking on the human-divine relationship? To you personally, is love reciprocal or one-sided in the relationship? How does your thinking on the human-divine relationship impact your interpersonal relationships, and vice versa?

Is there anything you like to add or clarify?

Please feel free to elaborate further.

You might have left something out; now is the time to add to what you have already said.

2. Heightened Sensibilities versus Psychic Numbing/ Turmoil

This aesthetic-affective dimension of spirituality refers to the capacity for experiencing depth of feelings, both positive and negative. A spiritual person is not happy all or even most of the time, and may even experience anguish at times.

Positive feelings and affect predominate in Heightened Sensibilities. Extreme forms of Heightened Sensibilities are mystical experiences, dramatic conversion experiences, and the like, within or without a religious context. They are intense, profound, and transcendent, yet difficult to describe. We may view them as extraordinary experiences (e.g., ecstasy, flash of insight, self-cosmos connectedness) that accompany the most dramatic forms of self-transformation, rather than as something unexplainable.

The inability to feel predominates in Psychic Numbing; negative affect and feelings predominate in Psychic Turmoil. You may fluctuate between numbing and turmoil.

The dimension of Heightened Sensibilities versus Psychic Numbing/Turmoil includes the following seven components.

Aesthetic Sensibilities versus Sensory Overstimulation

Aesthetic sensibilities are heightened in the visual, kinesthetic, or musical, as well as the linguistic, modalities. Michelangelo's Pieta and Bach-Gounod's Ave Maria evoke spirituality, sometimes, even in people who lead their lives in spiritual emptiness. The majesty of nature, the vastness of the cosmos, artistic expressions, beauty in all its variegated forms are aesthetically felt; deep emotions are evoked. Heightened aesthetic sensibilities touch the core of your being.

In contrast, seeking excitement through sensory overstimulation is symptomatic of spiritual emptiness. It should be distinguished from aesthetic insensibility, which is simply the absence or lack of capacity to note, experience, and be moved by things of beauty represented in different forms, media, or modalities. (Aversion to particular representations, such as modern art, does not mean absence or lack of aesthetic sensibility; rather, it may simply reflect individual differences in taste.)

Contentment versus Discontent

Spiritual persons tend to be content with what they already have, freed from greed; they show gratitude to nature's bounty, God. As expressed in a Chinese saying, "Constant happiness comes from being content." People filled with discontent direct their attention to what they don't have. They register loss, not gain. They see only a bottle half empty.

Delight versus Embitterment

People delighted in living delight others in their company, and delight in their delight. They have the capacity for experiencing simple, unabashed delight or joy at ordinary moments, or in just being alive.

Embitterment is characterized by (a) accumulation of anger, resulting from prolonged frustration, feelings of being repeatedly and unfairly treated or harmed; (b) external attribution (e.g., blaming others for one's own failures), at least in part; (c) a strong sense of injustice of unfairness; and (d) feelings of undeserved defeat, or of unreached goals. It differs from depression in that guilt, dysphoria, and self-rejection are not essential features. Embitterment extinguishes joy like covering a blanket over fire. It may be written on your face.

Depth of Feelings versus Psychic Numbing

Spiritual persons have the capacity for experiencing depth of feelings, both positive and negative. They are not happy all or even most of the time, and may even experience anguish at times.

The antithesis of depth of feelings is not just shallow feelings, but psychic numbing, inability to feel happiness or unhappiness. Indeed, we may regard the inability to feel unhappiness or psychic pain (an instance of emotional numbing) as a symptom of spiritual emptiness. As a Chinese adage states, "There is not greater sadness than the death of feelings from the heart." In place of delight, joy, and exuberance, despondency appears. Habitually sullen, dejected, or despondent people make poor company.

Serenity versus Turmoil

Serenity is tranquil composure that suggests imperviousness to agitation or turmoil. It is akin to the Buddhist idea of maintaining a temperate (or usual) state of mind in the face of challenging circumstances. A tranquil person feels in harmony with others, at home in the cosmos. Turmoil is the antithesis of serenity: It is a state of confusion or agitation. It means more than lack of serenity or disturbed composure.

Spontaneity versus Inhibition

Spontaneity is freedom from restraint, inhibition, or stagnation. Unencumbered by overregulation, spontaneous persons are playful and humorous. This does not mean that they show indiscriminate disregard for social convention, norms, or moral standards.

Inhibited persons lack spontaneity, and tend to be overly self-conscious or ill at ease. They are overregulated, externally by social convention, and internally by impulse control. Inhibition may be manifest in not only affective expression or emotional reactivity, but also the language of the body (e.g., posture).

Warmth versus Frigidity

You do not have to be a psychologist to tell a warm person from one who is chronically frigid, angry or, worse, hostile. Most people gravitate toward the warm and friendly, and avoid emotional refrigerators or volcanoes.

Concept pair	Heightened Sensibilities	Psychic Numbing/ Turmoil
General idea	Positive feelings and affect predominate: heightened aesthetic sensibilities and depth of feelings; tranquillity; spontaneity.	Negative feelings and affect predominate: discontent, embitterment; psychic numbing; turmoil; or inhibition. (Probably not all of these negative feelings all experienced at the same time. A person may fluctuate between psychic numbing and turmoil.)
Item 1	*Aesthetic Sensibilities* Aesthetic sensibilities are heightened in visual, kinesthetic, musical, linguistic or other modalities.	*Sensory Overstimulation* Seeks excitement through sensory overstimulation.

Item 2	*Contentment*	*Discontent*
	Content with what one already has; count one's blessings; gratitude to nature's bounty, God.	Driven by greed: Directs one's attention to what one does not have; registers loss, not gain; sees a bottle as half empty, rather than half full.
Item 3	*Delight*	*Embitterment*
	Capacity for experiencing simple, unabashed delight; joy at ordinary moments, or in just being alive; enthusiastic.	Accumulated anger, feelings of being repeatedly and unfairly treated or harmed; blaming others; a strong sense of injustice of unfairness; feelings of undeserved defeat, or of unreached goals.
Item 4	*Depth of Feelings*	*Psychic Numbing*
	Capacity for experiencing depth of feelings, both positive and negative.	Psychic numbing, inability to feel happiness or unhappiness. Sullen, dejected, despondent; apathetic.

Item 5	Serenity	Turmoil
	Experiences harmony, serenity, tranquillity, or inner peace.	Experiences agitation, confusion, or disorganization; inner turmoil.
Item 6	Spontaneity	Inhibition
	Freedom from constraint, unencumbered by overregulation, social convention; playfulness, humor.	Overly self-conscious, ill at ease; affective or postural inhibition; feelings of obstruction, blockage, or stagnation.
Item 7	Warmth	Frigidity
	Feelings and inner emotions toward people characterized by warmth.	Feelings and inner emotions toward people characterized by frigidity, anger or hostility.

| Examples | Mystical experiences, dramatic conversion, and the like, within or without a religious context; intense, profound, and transcendent, yet difficult to describe; extraordinary experiences (e.g., ecstasy, flash of insight, self-cosmos connectedness) that accompany self-transformation.

"I have a tendency to experience intense emotions in different situations, so much so that tears flow from my eyes." [Item 4] | Indulgences in excitement (e.g., driving fast cars), bombardment by light, color, or sound.

"I feel empty inside, so I need some excitement." [Item 1]

"I have lost the ability to feel anything. Just dead inside." [Item 4] |

Invitation to Self-Exploration

The following invites you to explore your spirituality in the aesthetic-affective dimension.

Describe your emotional reactions and feelings, both positive and negative. I don't mean momentary reactions that change from situation to situation. I mean the general pattern of emotions and feelings that characterize your life.
Describe the deepest emotion you have ever had.

To what extent do you seek sensory stimulation (e.g., driving fast cars, being bombarded by light, color, or sound)?

What special reactions, if any, do you have toward nature, the cosmos? To art, dancing, music, or literature?

Any reactions to simple things, just being alive?

Overall, how would you describe your inner emotional state?

To what extent have you experienced numbing, that is, unable to feel happiness or unhappiness? What about turmoil?

To what extent do you feel overly self-conscious, ill at ease; affective or postural inhibition; feelings of obstruction, blockage, or stagnation? Free, spontaneous, and playful?

To what extent do you feel content with what you already have? Or discontent, because you feel you haven't got enough?

Describe your emotional reactions and feelings toward other people in general?

Have you ever had extraordinary experiences, intense and profound experiences that have deep meanings for your life? ... These may be difficult to describe, because they don't occur in ordinary life. Some people have experienced ecstasy, flash of insight, feeling connected with the cosmos or with God.

Have you ever experienced something like that?

Please feel free to elaborate further.

3. Acceptance versus Denial

Acceptance is quintessential to spirituality: of self, others; of things and conditions that cannot be changed; of inherent limitations, both personal and human; and of death. It goes beyond forbearance, the capacity to endure pain and suffering, which has no necessary foundation in spirituality. It is not fatalism, the belief that your life condition is fixed, regardless of what action is taken to change it.

Denial is nonacceptance or negation of the realities of life. It is manifest in many ways: self-rejection, rejection of others; stubborn persistence in trying to change the unchangeable; failure to recognize and accept limitations; excessive fear of death.

Classically defined in psychoanalytic theory, denial is a defense mechanism: unconscious and maladaptive. It is not deception, but self-deception. It does not refer to conscious attempts to "deny" the seriousness of the plight in which you find yourself. Denial should be distinguished from cognitive avoidance, which refers to a conscious attempt to avoid thinking about something.

Is denial or cognitive avoidance good or bad? That depends on many factors, including frequency, intensity, duration (temporary versus prolonged, entrenched), and the situation(s) or occasion(s) in which you engage in denial or cognitive avoidance. You are in denial when you say (and genuinely think) you are not afraid, but is seen by all to be shivering, sweating, and so forth. So are you when you have a life-threatening illness and refuse to accept medical opinion (consistently expressed by reputable physicians). These are bad.

Suppose you have a terminal illness, understand and accept medical opinion, but say to yourself, "I remain optimistic; I shall endure." You are not in denial; rather, you may be expressing a sentiment of hope, courage, fortitude in the face of great misfortune. You come close to acceptance. Good.

In literature, Faust sold his soul in exchange for youth. In life, the quest for turning back the biological clock now falls on medicine.

Advances in medicine (especially genetics and biotechnology) fuel demands for pushing the frontier of life preservation, even life improvement, to new heights. But humankind will not be satisfied until the gods of death are vanquished. Patients will demand more, even the impossible, from medical practitioners. Insatiable demands, however, signify a lack of acceptance—and of wisdom.

American society is replete with cultural myths, such as the following, that are symptomatic of a lack of acceptance.

1. You have freedom of choice concerning your life over which no one else should circumscribe or exercise control.

2. How you express yourself and fulfill your personal aspirations is your own business: "I do my thing and you do your thing." (Indulgent and socially irresponsible? Individualism misconstrued, banalized?)

3. You can be whatever you want to be, achieve whatever you want to achieve, provided that you believe strongly enough in yourself. (Thus, educators, psychologist, and therapist trumpet "positive thinking" and "self-esteem," rather than hard work and perseverance, as the foundation for success. Can self-esteem be obtained without effort and trial? Do outcomes depend on psychological factors such as self-confidence, without regard to external reality, socioeconomic, political, and environmental?)

4. You are OK just the way you are. (Congruence between the real and the ideal self, in the manner of humanistic psychologists, such as Carl Rogers. By this count, psychopaths are the most congruent.)

5. Everyone can be the President of the United States.

6. The good life is one from which unhappiness is expunged.

7. Medical science and technology will one day succeed in turning back the biological clock, conquering diseases and rid humankind (at least the rich) of suffering completely.

These cultural myths amount to what may be called the illusion of unlimited personal freedom. This illusion is predicated on the failure to acknowledge, on ethical grounds, social responsibility; and on scientific grounds, reality.

Concept pair	Acceptance	Denial
Item 1	*Acceptance of Biological Givens* Accepts one's biological givens (e.g., sex, race), physical characteristics (e.g., appearance). Understands that biological givens do not determine one's destiny.	*Rejection of Biological Givens* Rejects one's biological givens (e.g., sex, race), physical characteristics (e.g., appearance). Feels embarrassed or ashamed.
Item 2	*Acceptance of the Inevitable* Accepts the inevitable facts of life, such as aging, death.	*Nonacceptance of the Inevitable* Preoccupied with or worries excessively over the inevitable facts of life, such as aging, death.

Item 3	*Acceptance of the Unchangeable*	*Nonacceptance of the Unchangeable*
	Accepts other conditions or realities that cannot be changed through individual or collective effort. (Differs from fatalism, believing that it is futile to conditions or realities that may indeed be changed with effort.)	Denial of other conditions or realities (other than those in Item 1) that cannot be changed; stubbornly persists in trying to change the unchangeable.
Examples	"I have been told that I have six months to live. I accept the fact with calmness and dignity." [Item 2]	"All the doctors say that I have a serious disease, but I just don't believe what they say." [Item 3]

Invitation to Self-Exploration

The following concerns your acceptance or nonacceptance of what you are born with, aging, death, and other conditions in life that cannot be changed.

> Some people accept what they are born with (e.g., sex, race); others don't. How do you feel about the givens you were born with? What does acceptance mean to you? Nonacceptance/denial?
> Some men/women do not like being a man/woman; they prefer to be a member of the opposite sex. How do you feel being a man/woman?

Race is not the same as ethnic or cultural identity. For instance, racially a Chinese-American is Chinese; his ethnic-cultural identity may be Chinese, American, or Chinese-American. "Who am I" is a question that I want to put to you now. What is your ethnic or cultural identity? To what extent do you identify with the ethnic or cultural group to which you belong? Are you proud, or ashamed, of being a member of your race? And of ethnic or cultural group? Please explain.

What about aging and death? Your own body (e.g., physical appearance)? Other conditions or realities that cannot be changed?

Please feel free to elaborate further.

4. Humility versus Arrogance

Humility stems from gauging yourself against the collective accomplishments of humankind, the vastness of the cosmos, infinity, some higher being or principle. Humility reflects inner attitudes rather than outer social convention (e.g., maintaining face). For instance, behaviors in face dynamics calculated to show your modesty in front of others do not qualify. Humility does not imply an absence of pride; however, it does imply an absence of arrogance.

Humility is espoused across the world's philosophical-religious traditions. It results from insight into the insuperable limitations of the human mind and, ultimately, the impossibility of comprehending the infinite by the finite. This insight activates the wisdom to accept human limitations, and it is the mother of humility in a deeply spiritual sense. It is metacognitive in nature: "I know my inherent limitations." Spiritual growth parallels depth of humility, following the discovery and acceptance of human ignorance and limitations.

Modesty, a lower form of humility, refers to behaviors that negate arrogance: not showing off your achievements, not seeking the limelight, not expecting others to treat you as "special."

Concept pair	Humility	Arrogance
Item 1	*Personal Limitations* Aware of and accepts personal imperfection and limitations.	*Personal Strengths or Achievements* Arrogance; shows off one's strengths or achievements. (Should not be confused with pride.)
Item 2	*Human Imperfection* Acknowledges human imperfection and limitations.	*Collective Achievements* Arrogance in the collective achievements of humankind or of a particular group (e.g., racial superiority).
Item 3	*Higher Principle* Acknowledges the existence of some higher being or cosmic principle.	*Human Supremacy* Meeting the needs of humankind is the guiding principle for action, without due consideration for other life forms or conservation.

Item 4	*Humility*	*Self-Importance*
	Sense of humility: Feels humble against the collective accomplishments of humankind, the vastness of the cosmos, infinity, some higher being or principle.	Inflated sense of self-importance: Seeks the limelight, or expects others to treat oneself as "special."
Examples	"The more I know, the more I know how much I don't know." [Item 1] "The finite recoils in the face of the infinite." [Item 4]	"Hong Kong people are superior. No question about it. That's why we import domestic helpers." [Item 2] "Given our advances in technology, there isn't any environmental problem that Americans can't solve." [Item 2]

Invitation to Self-Exploration

Tell me something about yourself. In what ways are you proud of your strengths and achievements? How do you show these strengths and achievements?

How do you view your personal imperfection and limitations?

How about the imperfection and limitations of humanity as a whole?

Think of the collective achievements of a particular group of people. Some people believe in racial superiority, that some groups have inborn superiority to other groups. What do you think?

Some believe that there is some higher being (i.e., superior to humans) or cosmic principle? What do you think?

Some people see human beings as supreme in the cosmos; others feel humble. What are your thoughts on this question? Describe your feelings.

Please feel free to elaborate further.

5. Existential Quest versus Hedonistic-Materialistic Pursuits

Spirituality entails an existential quest for a sense of direction; to answer questions about life and death, being and nonbeing. Of course, different people obtain different answers: The crucial thing is to quest for some higher goal in life, and principles that serve as a guide to leading the good life.

To many, hedonistic-materialistic pursuits are more attractive than existential quest. Primacy of hedonistic-materialistic values: Materialism (excessive regard for worldly concerns) and hedonism (pursuit of or devotion to pleasure, especially to the pleasures of the senses) occupy high priority in their scale of values. Excessive hedonistic-materialistic pursuits are symptomatic of spiritual emptiness.

Concept Pair	Existential Quest	Hedonistic-Materialistic Pursuits
Central idea	Primacy of spiritual values: Existential quest occupies high priority in the person's scale of values. (Whether or not spiritual fulfillment is actually attained is not the central issue here.)	Primacy of hedonistic-materialistic values: Materialism and hedonism occupy high priority in the person's scale of values.
Item 1	*Existential Interests* Interested in existential questions.	*Hedonistic-Materialistic Interests* Interested primarily in questions pertaining to hedonistic-materialistic pursuits, to the exclusion of existential questions.
Item 2	*Higher Goals* Quest for some higher goal in life or principles that serve as a guide to leading a good life.	*Hedonistic-Materialistic Goals* Guiding principles concern primarily reaching hedonistic-materialistic goals, or exclude the idea of leading a good or better life.

Item 3	*Spiritual Values*	*Materialistic Values*
	Spiritual values are more important than amassment of personal wealth. (Unlike Item 1, which pertains to interest and curiosity, this one pertains to the priority of values that guide action.)	Excessively materialistic: preoccupation with amassment of personal wealth.
Item 4	*Spiritual Activities*	*Addictive Activities*
	Devotes free or leisure time and energy to activities for spiritual inspiration (e.g., acquiring knowledge about spirituality through reading, discussion, or formal study; engaged in expressive-artistic activities that evoke spiritual experiences; traveling to places of spiritual significance; engaged in actions for the betterment of humankind that has a spiritual dimension to the person).	Devotes free or leisure time and energy to unproductive or, worse, addictive activities (e.g., surfing the Internet; not directly aimed at amassing wealth or consumer products).

Item 5	*Moderation in Material Possessions*	*Addictiveness in Material Possessions*
	Possession of consumer products or other material objects is subject to control and regulation by the person's values and principles.	Preoccupation with possession of consumer products or other material objects; addictive consumer behavior.
Item 6	*Regulated Pursuits of Pleasure*	*Wanton Pursuits of Pleasure*
	Pursuits of pleasure are subject to control and regulation by the person's values and principles.	Preoccupation with pursuing pleasure; pursuits take on a wanton or obsessive-compulsive quality.

| Examples | "I invest emotional or intellectual energy and attach great significance to beliefs concerning human existence." [Item 1]

"I devote time and energy to activities such as reading books or attending workshops on spirituality, listening to music or doing art work, traveling to places for spiritual fulfillment." [Item 4] | "The only things I care about are those I can touch and feel, like sex, drinking, eating good food." [Item 1]

"I spend my free time surfing the Internet, playing pachinko or computer games." [Item 4]

"I shop until I drop dead, purchasing all kinds of things I don't really need." [Item 5] |

Invitation to Self-Exploration

What are your thoughts on the meaning of life? And death?

People have different goals in life and principles that guide them on how to lead their lives. What are your thoughts on this question?

How do you spend your leisure time? What kind of activities?

People have different values and attach different degrees of importance to them. For example, some people think making money, buying consumer goods, pursuit of pleasure are important. What are your thoughts on this question? [Items 4–6]

These days, people can buy all kinds of consumer goods. Please explain what consumer goods mean to you. What are your shopping habits? Do you shop more often when you are down? Shopping addiction?

Some consider spirituality important. What are your thoughts on this question? People have different ideas about spirituality. What does it mean to you?

Please feel free to elaborate further.

6. Transcendence versus Self-Encapsulation

Transcendence is relational spirituality, reached through transcending egocentrism. Relationships are integral to one's meaning and purpose in life. The antithesis of transcendence is self-encapsulation, in which the self derives meaning and purpose solely or primarily from its own individual existence, without reference to a larger context. Self-encapsulation is a form of egoism or self-contained individualism. The following five pairs of component ideas further describe contrasts between transcendence and self-encapsulation.

Self-in-Relations versus Self-Containment

Transcendence entails viewing oneself in a relational context (e.g., self-in-cosmos, personal relationship with God), thus conferring meaning and purpose to one's life. It defines one's relationships with others, society, humanity, nature, cosmos; and (to religious believers) some higher, divine, sacred, or supreme being or beings. In self-containment, attention is focused on one's own individual existence from which meaning and purpose is derived, without reference to a relational context.

Compassion versus Hardheartedness

Compassion occupies a key position in Buddhism: Deep feeling for the suffering of others, extended to humankind. Kindness does not always entail compassion: We may be kind to people who are not in misery. Typical acts of kindness include doing favor and good deeds for others, helping and taking care of them. Devoid of compassion, a person becomes hardhearted, callous, uncaring, and unfeeling.

Selflessness versus Egoism

A selfless person puts the interests of other people above his own, and acts without selfish concerns. The antithesis of selflessness is to act in ways that are motivated solely or primarily by self-interests. Egoism does not necessarily entail selfishness. Egoistic actions are not necessarily illegal or immoral, and do not necessarily infringe on the rights of others.

Altruism versus Selfishness

Altruism is selfless concern for the welfare of others. It may involve great personal sacrifice, even one's life. Selfishness hardly requires commentary. It is not only the absence of altruism, but also the proclivity toward taking actions that benefit oneself at the expense of others.

Universal Love versus Misanthropy

Universal love is the lodestone of ecumenicity. At root, it champions the intrinsic value of human life and cherishing care for one's fellowmen. Misanthropy is the antithesis of the love for humanity.

However, a misanthrope does not necessarily seek to exploit, harm, or destroy his fellowmen. A psychopath does; his actions, therefore, mean an extreme negation of universal love.

Concept pair	Transcendence	Self-Encapsulation
Central idea	Relational spirituality: Views the self in a larger context; spirituality is reached through transcending egocentrism; universal love.	Views the self as self-contained, without reference to a larger context; encapsulates oneself; misanthropy.
Item 1	*Self-in-Relations* Views the self in a relational context (e.g., self-in-cosmos, personal relationship with God); relationships with others, society, humanity, nature, cosmos, or some higher being or beings are integral to one's meaning and purpose in life.	*Self-Independence* Views the self as independent, self-contained, without reference to a relational context. Attention is focused on one's own individual existence from which meaning and purpose is derived.

Item 2	*Compassion*	*Hardheartedness*
	Being kind to others; deep feeling for the suffering of others, extended to humankind.	Hardhearted, callous, uncaring and unfeeling toward the suffering of others.
Item 3	*Selflessness*	*Egoism*
	Considers the interests of other people, acts without selfish concerns.	Acts in ways that are motivated by self-interests.
Item 4	*Altruism*	*Selfishness*
	Selfless concern for the welfare of others; involves personal sacrifice.	Acting in ways that are motivated by only self-interests, often at the expense of others.
Item 5	*Universal Love*	*Misanthropy*
	Champions the intrinsic value of human life and cherishing care for one's fellowmen; respects life in all its forms.	Hatred of humankind; prefers to lead the life of a loner.

Examples	"The life of the individual is incomplete. We all need to relate with others, for the welfare of all." [Item 1]	"I do my thing and you do your thing. No one has the right to interfere with my freedom. It's entirely my own business, if I choose to risk my life in some dangerous sports." [Item 1]

Invitation to Self-Exploration

Some people view life and what it means in terms of one's relationship with others, humanity, nature, cosmos, or God. Others view their life and what it means in terms of one's own existence. What are your thoughts on this question?

> Some people view the world solely or primarily from one's own perspective and act according to one's own self-interests. Others view the world from perspectives of others, and consider their interests first. What are your thoughts on this question? What guides your actions?
> Have you done anything totally out of concern for the welfare of others? Please give examples. Have you ever done anything totally out of self-interest? Please give examples.
> How would you weigh their relative importance?
> Some people believe in universal love; others have negative feelings for humankind. What are your thoughts about the value of humankind? Some people prefer to lead the life of a loner. What do you think?
> Please feel free to elaborate further.

7. Self-Actualization versus Alienation

Self-actualization means the realization of one's potentials, to be the best that one can be. The antecedents of self-actualization are acceptance, humility, existential quest, and transcendence. Having engaged in soul searching, self-actualized persons experience a profound sense of fulfillment and mastery. Alienation is the negation of self-actualization. Its components are social isolation, estrangement, emptiness, meaninglessness, normlessness, and powerlessness.

Concept pair	Self-Actualization	Alienation
Central idea	In touch with oneself; feels closeness to others, nature, divine being(s); regards life as meaningful, purposeful, regulated by norms; has a sense of agency.	Estranged from oneself, others, nature, divine being(s); experiences emptiness, meaninglessness, normlessness, and powerlessness.
Item 1	*Social Connectedness* Feels socially connected with others.	*Social Isolation* Feels socially isolated from others.

Item 2	*Closeness*	*Estrangement*
	Feels close to or being in touch with oneself, nature, God; at home in the cosmos.	Feels estranged from oneself, nature, God; out of place in the cosmos; inward emptiness.
Item 3	*Meaningfulness*	*Meaninglessness*
	Views life as meaningful, purposeful; has a sense of direction; committed to some goal in life.	Views life as meaningless, purposeless; disoriented, lost; not committed to any goal in life.
Item 4	*Normativeness*	*Normlessness*
	Views life as regulated or guided by norms and values.	Experiences norm-lessness, moral void: Norms and values regulating life are absent or not operational.
Item 5	*Agency*	*Powerlessness*
	Experiences oneself as an agent acting in control of one's life-activity; has a sense of mastery.	Feels powerless, unable to control impersonal forces dominating one's life.

Examples	"For a number of years, I have had feelings of being close to the divine." [Item 2]	"I feel like a stranger to myself. I don't know what kind of a person I am." [Item 2]
	"Yes, society has to be regulated by norms. Yet, I am a *free* agent." [Item 4, Item 5]	"I am lost. I don't know what I want to do with my life." [Item 3]
		"Like a jelly fish I am, controlled by the currents of the sea." [Item 5]

Invitation to Self-Exploration

Let's explore how you view some of the most important aspects of life, particularly those of your own.

To what extent do you feel socially connected with, or isolated from, other people?

To what extent do you feel closeness to, being in touch with yourself? Or estranged from yourself? What about Nature? God?

To what extent do you feel at home, or out of place, in the cosmos? Feelings of emptiness? Explain further.

To what extent do you view life as meaningful, purposeful, or as meaningless, purposeless?

Sense of direction, or disoriented, lost?

Is there a goal in life to which you are committed? Explain.

Some people view life as regulated or guided by norms and values; others experience normlessness, like there is a moral void. What are your thoughts on this question?

To what extent do you experience yourself as a person acting in control of your life-activity, or as a person who feels powerless, unable to control the forces dominating your life?
Please feel free to elaborate further.

Appendix B:
Strategies of Coping

Below I guide you through an exploration of strategies for coping with life's misfortunes (trauma, major illness, loss, and so forth). I've created a structure involving four pairs of contrasting strategies:

Forbearance versus Intolerance
Forgiveness versus Vengefulness
Hope versus Despair
Meaning Reconstruction versus Entrenchment

For each pair, I offer questions for you to consider as part of your self-exploration. Answering the questions will help you determine what coping strategies you use and whether they are helpful or harmful to you.

I have had my share of misfortunes. I have experienced despair and depression. But I've managed to emerge from the depths of despondency with renewed hope and passion for life. Central to my strategy is to direct attention away from my own misery to helping others. That's why I feel the urge to share with fellow travelers my experiences in coping with life's misfortunes.

Next, I engage you in dialogues such that therapeutic movement from the negative to the positive direction may be realized. Invitation to change following self-exploration is always there, gently but surely. The appeals of approaching life's problems based on positive strategies are highlighted. Negative strategies are under attack, relentlessly if necessary. With the aid of tables, I illustrate how techniques of therapeutic intervention may be applied. Note that principles underlie techniques. Emphasis is placed on taking action and on directing attention away from the self, toward others.

I have assumed the role of a counselor in these dialogues. However, in line with Dialogic Action Therapy, nothing would be better than to engage yourself in internal dialogues and thus act as your own therapeutic agent. Let us now see how you may do so across the four pairs of coping I offer.

1. Forbearance versus Intolerance

Forbearance is the capacity to endure pain, suffering, or ill fortune without complaint. Often, forbearance is dictated by necessity, as when people fall victim to natural calamities, harsh socioeconomic or political realities beyond one's control, or are threatened, fearful of punishment or retaliation, under duress or, in the extreme, bondage of slavery. Forbearance may or may not entail fortitude, the moral courage to stand up for one's conviction in the face of threat or danger to oneself. Intolerance, in the present context, refers to unwillingness or inability to endure frustration, pain, suffering, or ill fortune, coupled with a tendency to complain.

Invitation to Self-Exploration

> People experience pain and suffering at some time or another. How have you reacted to your own experiences? What if the pain and suffering were inflicted upon you by the deliberate acts of others (e.g., provocation, insults, oppression)?
> People around you are likely to see that you suffer. How do you deal with this situation?
> Suppose you are threatened and you find yourself in danger when you stand up for your convictions (i.e.,

strong beliefs in some principle). What then? Would you give up your convictions, or endure the pain and suffering? Please consider carefully and explain.

Please feel free to elaborate further. You might have left something out; now is the time to add to what you have said.

Approaches and Attacks

Invitation to self-examination and change is always there, gently but surely. No matter what the traveler says or does, invitation sticks onto him like an octopus aimed at its prey. There is really "no way out" of it. This may evoke anger in the traveler, which presents another opportunity for emotional education.

Note that principles underlie techniques. Emphasis is placed on taking action and on directing attention away from the self to others.

In the following table, the therapeutic process calculated to enhance forbearance and to reduce intolerance is illustrated.

Strategy pair	Forbearance	Intolerance
Central idea	Capacity to endure pain and suffering.	Intolerance of pain and suffering.
Item 1	Endures pain and suffering due to ill fortune (e.g., sickness, natural calamities, harsh socioeconomic or political realities beyond one's control).	Responds to pain and suffering due to ill fortune (e.g., sickness, natural calamities, harsh socioeconomic or political realities beyond one's control) with impatience, irritability, anger, resentment, or bitterness; tends to complain, whine, or have emotional outbursts; blames others, the world, God.

Dealing with impatience, irritability, anger, resentment, bitterness	You have gone through a painful experience. You feel you have suffered enough…. You have also been impatient, irritable, resentful. You complain a lot. You have emotional outbursts…. These responses are not helpful. They make life more miserable for you and others around you. I wonder what's behind them. [Explore and deal with possible feelings of guilt, inadequacy, and the like.] No one is asking you to just rid yourself of negative emotions. You have a right to feel angry, after what you have gone through. But, I am asking you to contain your anger, and prevent it from doing more harm…. Better still, turn your anger into strength, to do something positive.
	Complaining and blaming have not made things better. So why not do something else more useful. For example….

Strategy pair	Forbearance	Intolerance
Item 2	Endures pain and suffering inflicted upon oneself by the deliberate acts of others such as provocation, insults, oppression. (Reflects an inner attitude, not merely inhibition of outward expression.)	Responds to pain and suffering inflicted upon oneself by the deliberate acts of others (e.g., provocation, insults, oppression) with impatience, irritability, anger, or resentment, or bitterness (the outward expression of which may be inhibited due to fear of punishment or retaliation); tends to complain, whine, or have emotional outbursts; blames others, the world, God.

| Coping with provocation, insults, oppression | You have suffered because *you feel* other people have done something horrible to you. [The first order of intervention is to ascertain if there is a realistic basis for the feeling. We now assume there is.]

You feel angry inside. Yet, you dare not show your anger…. Of course, showing your anger may be dangerous. You may be punished even more. Understandably, you are afraid…. Bottling up your anger is not a good option, because the anger can eat you up and make you feel worse. So, let's talk about other options…. [Exercises in self-assertion would be useful here.]

[Now comes the hardest part. There is no escape, realistically speaking. This may be difficult for Americans to understand. The fact remains that there are plenty of bullies in the world who inflict pain on others without the slightest compunction and who wouldn't go away.]

This is really hard. You suffer, repeatedly, with no end in sight. You can't fight against something that powerful…. Does it mean there is nothing you can do? No. At the very least, stop feeling sorry for yourself, because that would compound the suffering. It's not your fault…. I would go further: Give yourself credit. You have endured a great deal of pain, more than your fair share. Now, that's strength in its own right. |

Strategy pair	Forbearance	Intolerance
Item 3	Directs one's attention to reduce the pain and suffering of others (which may be caused by one's own).	Becomes intolerant of others because of one's own pain and suffering.
Redirecting attention to others	You seem to have become intolerant of others, because of the pain and suffering you have had. In turn, your intolerance may cause pain and suffering to others. This is a vicious cycle.... Restore yourself, and reverse the vicious cycle. The best way of doing this is to direct your attention to reduce the pain and suffering of others, to make life better for them.... You see, in the end, you make your life better by making life better for others. That's the Dao.	
Item 4	Endures pain and suffering with fortitude or moral courage to stand up for one's convictions in the face of threat or danger to oneself.	Retreats from one's convictions in the face of threat or danger to oneself.

Affirming fortitude	It's hard to hold onto your convictions in the face of such pressures and threats to yourself. Harder still to stand up for them. You may have to pay a heavy price for it.... If you do, however, you will live in the knowledge that you have lived with moral courage, and hold your head up high.... The decision is yours. [Some of you might say that this goes beyond therapy to the domain of ethics. No, it is still therapy, because clarifying the different consequences of different decisions is part of therapy. Yes, the traveler is indeed encouraged to engage in ethical deliberations. Why not?]

2. Forgiveness versus Vengefulness

Forgiveness has two directions: To forgive someone, and to ask for forgiveness from someone. Forgiving oneself stands in a dialogic relation with both forgiving someone and asking for forgiveness. Forgiving oneself and forgiving others are mutually reinforcing. Asking for forgiveness from others without forgiving oneself is incomplete forgiveness. Forgiving oneself without forgiving others is a mark of egocentrism; it negates the right to ask for forgiveness.

The antithesis of forgiveness takes two forms. Vengefulness: to harbor resentment or hatred, resort to personal vindictiveness, get even or seek revenge against the offender. Irresponsibility: to admit no responsibility for harm done to another, feel no remorse, and take no action that may undo at least in part the harm done.

Counseling practitioners have not attended sufficiently to self-other dialogic relations in forgiveness: They tend to dwell on forgiving others, and do not give due attention to forgiving oneself, asking for forgiveness, even less to reparation or restitution.

Invitation to Self-Exploration

People react differently to being offended, harmed, or unfairly treated by others. Think of some experiences you have had. Normally how do you react?

Some people pardon or forgive their offenders. Some seek vengeance. What about yourself?

What does it mean for you to pardon/forgive/revenge? How would you feel afterwards?

Suppose the offence is repeated, again and again. How would you react? What if the offender deliberately inflicts pain and suffering on you? How would you react?

We have been talking about your being offended. What if you are the offender? Think of some experiences you have had.

To what extent do you assume responsibility? Repent? What actions have you taken, if any, to make up?

What about forgiving (or refusing to forgive) yourself? What does it mean? How would you feel afterwards?

What do you think is the relation between forgiving (refusing to forgive) yourself and forgiving (refusing to forgive) others?

Please feel free to elaborate further. You might have left something out; now is the time to add to what you have said.

Approaches and Attacks

It is important to assess the nature of the alleged committed act in question. To ask for forgiveness presumes that a wrongful act, of commission or omission, has indeed been committed, as judged according to prevailing ethical norms. If no wrongful act has been committed, then the real issue relates not to forgiveness, but to feelings of guilt that have no realistic basis. The task is then to reduce guilt, rather than to ask for forgiveness. Therefore, before talking about forgiving or asking for forgiveness, it is essential to establish if indeed an offence has been committed and clarify the apportioning of responsibilities. This point cannot be emphasized enough. There are plenty of people who make a profession of unconditional self-blaming. God help our self-blaming fellow travelers when they seek help from religious or pastoral counselors who, overzealous to practice forgiveness, commence counseling on the false presumption of culpability.

It is also important to attend to sins of commission as well as omission (negligence or failure to act when action is dictated by moral obligation or human decency).

If the spiritual traveler is unwilling to forgive, redirect intervention toward letting go of fixations (e.g., of past traumas, revenge) and moving forward in life: "I understand that you are not willing to forgive, at least not yet. But life goes on, and you will not allow bitterness and vindictiveness to lessen the value of your life." The therapeutic-redeeming aim is often no less than the alleviation, even elimination, of self-torment that has been buried deep within your dialogic self for years.

Strategy pair	Forgiveness	Vengefulness
Item 1	Repentance: Assumes responsibility for one's wrongdoings; feels remorse, contrition, or self-reproach.	Irresponsibility: Refuses to assume responsibility for one's wrongdoings; feels no remorse, contrition, or self-reproach.
Guilt reduction versus repentance	Before talking about asking for forgiveness, we should examine first what you had in fact done.... No one thought what you did was wrong. You yourself have a tough time explaining why what you did was wrong. Yet, you feel guilty.... [The task here is guilt reduction, not repentance.] *Sins of commission* How do you feel about what you did? ... Do you think it is right, or wrong? What do your friends think? ... I would like to invite you to consider the effects of what you did, not only on other people but also on yourself.... Taking moral responsibility for your actions is a big step forward. This takes courage. Repent. Otherwise, I don't know what further I can do for you.... *Sins of omission* You failed to act when action was called for, resulting in causing injury to others. Have you reflected on this? ... Assuming responsibility and repenting for your failure to act is the first step toward a resolution.	

Item 2	Ask for forgiveness from someone whom one has offended.	Refuses to ask for forgiveness from someone whom one has offended.
Asking for forgiveness	You have been troubled by what you did to your friend for a long time. The question is, however, what you have done about it.... Have you thought of asking her for forgiveness? ... You are afraid that she may reject your asking. You may not be able to know for sure.... But, if you have the courage to ask, you would have at least done your part.... You have done something that is difficult to do for most people. You said sorry and you asked for forgiveness from your friend. Now you feel much better. What else have you learned? ... How can you make sure that you will not repeat the same error? ... In what ways have you changed as a person?	
Item 3	Makes reparation or restitution as an attempt to undo, at least in part, the damage done to someone.	Makes no reparation or restitution as an attempt to undo, at least in part, the damage done to someone.
Making reparation	Asking for forgiveness may not be enough. You haven't made any reparation to make up for the damage done.... Making reparation would give substance to your asking for forgiveness. What are you prepared to do?	

Item 4a	Grants a pardon to the offender(s), involving merely permitting the offender(s) to go unpunished.	Refuses to pardon: Tries to get even or seek revenge against the offender(s).
Pardoning the offender(s)	You refuse to pardon the offenders. You want them punished. Does it help to undo what has already been done? Or make things better for yourself? … It's time to pardon.	
Item 4b	Grants a pardon to oneself, involving merely permitting oneself to go unpunished.	Refuses to pardon: Continues to torment or punish oneself.
Pardoning oneself	You refuse to pardon yourself. You continue to punish yourself. What will that do to yourself and others around you? Does it help to undo what has already been done? Or make things better for the person(s) you have wronged? … It's time to stop punishing yourself.	
Item 5a	Conditional forgiveness: Excuse the offender(s) from an offence.	Refuses to forgive: Continues to harbor resentment or hatred toward the offender(s); vindictive.

Forgiving the offender(s)	You have been dwelling on the hurt caused by your friend. This bitterness is eating you up. When is the time to let go? ... No, I don't mean forgetting; I mean forgiving.... At least, give him a second chance....	
Item 5b	Conditional forgiveness: Excuse oneself from an offence.	Refuses to forgive: Continues to feel guilty, blame oneself.
Forgiving oneself	You have no hesitation in forgiving others. Yet, the thought of forgiving yourself never occurs to you. Why not? ... It is time for you to learn to be kind toward yourself.	
Item 6a	Full or unconditional forgiveness of the offender(s), in thought and action.	Refuses to forgive: Continues to harbor resentment or hatred toward the offender(s); vindictive.
Forgiving the offender(s) unconditionally	You say you have forgiven your offenders. Yet, deep down you still blame them for what they have done; your attitude is condescending; you wouldn't let go of resentment....	
Item 6b	Full or unconditional forgiveness of oneself, in thought and action.	Refuses to forgive: Continues to feel guilty, blame oneself.

Forgiving oneself unconditionally	You say you have forgiven yourself. Yet, deep down you still blame yourself for what you have done.... It's time to let go of the past, totally.	
Item 7	The act of forgiving occasions moving and inspiring oneself to be a better person.	Refuses to forgive: Continues to harbor resentment or hatred toward the offender(s), vindictive; or to feel guilty, blame oneself.
Inspiring the traveler to be a better person through forgiving	You have taken a courageous step of letting go of your bitterness. You have forgiven your friend, *and* yourself. Where do we go from here? ... Have you let your friend know you have forgiven him? ... What changes have occurred in yourself and in your relationship with him? ... You may even set an example of forgiveness, and inspire others to forgive.	
Item 8	The act of forgiving occasions moving and inspiring the offender(s) to be a better person(s).	Refuses to forgive: Continues to harbor resentment or hatred toward the offender(s); vindictive.

Inspiring the offender(s) to be a better person(s)	You may even inspire your offender(s) to be a better person(s). You may say something like this to him: "There is no need for you to ask for forgiveness. But that doesn't mean no demands are put on you. Are you assuming responsibility for what you have done? Are you sorry? Have you repented? Have you asked for forgiveness? Made reparations? ... What have you learned? What are you going to do to avoid making the same error? In what ways will you change for the better as a person? ... How?"

3. Hope versus Despair

Hope is the mother of the will to live and of actions for change. Hope is oriented toward the future: What is bad will pass and what is good will be preserved or restored. It differs from optimism, a general orientation that the future will be better than what it is now. Hope maintains that orientation even in the face of calamity or great adversity. It derives from various sources, including religious faith, political ideology, personal conviction and fortitude, and social support; it may also derive from seeing hope in and through others, one's children, students, friends, humanity. Though future oriented, hope impacts the present. Despair is the archenemy of hope. It is extreme pessimism, believing that all is lost and that there is no way out of the present predicament or misfortune.

Invitation to Self-Exploration

Some people react to misfortune, such as major illness and natural or man-made calamity, with despair; others maintain hope. What about yourself? What does hope mean to you? Despair?

Think of the most serious difficulty you have to face in your life. Is there a way out? Or no way out at all? Will things get better, or worse? What would the darkest moment be like? Do you tend to dwell on the past or look forward to the future?

What inner resources or external support (e.g., family, friends) is available to help you? Have you felt helpless? Have you felt jinxed? Abandoned by God (or some other divine being)? Despair of other people? Have you thought that it is futile to continue to struggle? Have you had thoughts of suicide?

What actions, if any, have you taken to help yourself? Or to help others?

Approaches and Attacks

To combat despair, negative feelings and thoughts (as in feeling forsaken by God or some other divine being) are first accepted, rather than being labeled as "irrational" or "superstitious," to be extirpated. Even suicidal thoughts are acknowledged, validated as "honest." However, the basis for the negative feelings and thoughts are attacked through incisive questioning and invitations to reconsideration. In particular, brought to the traveler's attention is the rigidity and absolutism of convictions that underlie his despair.

No effort is spared to rekindle, sustain, and magnify hope. This entails activating your moral courage and inner resources to overcome despair and to embrace life again.

Strategy pair	Hope	Despair
Item 1	Believes there is a way out of the present predicament.	Believes there is no way out of the present predicament.
Pointing to a way out	Of course, you despair. You believe there is no way out…. Think again. Is there really no way out? … There is a way out. Now is the time to explore what that is.	
Item 2	Feels that inner resources are available to confront the present predicament.	Feels that inner resources are unavailable to confront the present predicament.
Activating inner resources	You feel you just don't have what it takes to deal with your present situation. Right? … What makes you so sure that you don't? … Look to your past where you did have what it took to overcome difficulties…. Feel the inner strength within you. Rekindle it. Let it grow. You need all the strength you have. So just let it grow and grow.	
Item 3	Feels that external support (e.g., family, friends) is available.	Feels that external support (e.g., family, friends) is unavailable.

Accepting external support	*Perception of unavailable support may be inaccurate* Family and friends are not here to help you. That's what you think…. They don't want to help you? Or, closer to the truth is that you don't want to accept their help. What makes it so difficult for you? Your family and friends want to help you. That should give you more strength…. Accept their help. Everyone needs support from other people sometimes. *Perception of unavailable support may be accurate* You feel that family and friends are not here to help you…. There are reasons for that…. Right now, the important thing is that there are/may be other people who are ready to help. For example…. Are you ready to accept their help?	
Item 4	"God [Bodhisattva or some other divine being] will not abandon me."	Feels abandoned, forsaken by God or some other divine being.
Combating feelings of being abandoned	You feel abandoned. That's a horrible feeling…. But, more important, are you abandoning yourself? Heaven abandons those who have abandoned themselves. Have you thought about that? … It's great that you no longer feel abandoned. You have faith. Now, will you abandon yourself?	

Item 5	Believes that fortune or some higher or supernatural force is favorable toward oneself: For example, "Heaven has no paths of desperation for people."	Believes that fortune or some higher or supernatural force is unfavorable toward oneself: For example, "I am jinxed."
Combating feelings of being doomed	So, you feel doomed? That would make things worse…. Has your fortune always been unfavorable to you? You count the negatives, and ignore the positives. That would make anybody feel doomed…. So do another counting. Think about the positives…. Now, you no longer believe you are doomed. That's a good feeling. You can move on.	
Item 6	Future orientation (looks beyond the present).	Fixation on the present (does not look beyond the present).
Look beyond the present	You haven't looked beyond the present. Kind of fixated…. There is always another day, tomorrow. Nobody knows for sure what tomorrow will bring. What makes you so sure of yourself? … What happens tomorrow may depend on what you do today. So, what are you going to do now? … It's great that you are now looking beyond the present. What does the future hold for you?	

Item 7	Sense of self-efficacy: "I shall overcome."	Feels helpless.
Enhancing sense of self-efficacy	You feel helpless. That's understandable, given what has happened to you…. But do you have to continue to feel helpless? The more you feel helpless, the more you may become helpless…. Think of an example where you were able to handle a difficult situation…. Now, you have more confidence. That gives you more strength.	
Item 8	Optimism: Believes that the future will be better; sense of a bright future; encouraged.	Pessimism: Believes that the future will be worse; sense of a foreshortened future (e.g., does not expect to have a career, marriage, children, or a normal life span); discouraged.
Combating pessimism	You are pessimistic. You are convinced that things will get worse…. You sound so sure of that you are right. Is this a pattern? … Your newfound optimism is very encouraging.	

Item 9	Will to live, to survive.	Will to live, to survive, is lacking or absent; suicidal ideation.
Activating the will to live	You wallow in self-pity.... You want to die. Here, we have emotional honesty, at least.... You owe to yourself to ask the question, "Is suicide the *only* way out?" ... If you have the guts to kill yourself, you don't mind waiting a bit longer to answer that question.... Give yourself more time. That's not too much to ask for.... I sense you now have a will to live, to survive. Great. That's a key to solution.	
Item 10	Refuses to give up, continues to struggle.	Giving or has given up; sense of futility sets in.
Don't give up	You seem to have given up. You think it's futile to keep on struggling.... This may be cruel. But I have to ask what would happen if you really give up. Is it an option? ... Just don't give up. That's the beginning of finding a solution.	
Item 11	Sees hope in and through other people (e.g., one's children, students, friends, humanity).	Despairs of other people (e.g., one's children, students, friends) and in humanity.

Seeing hope in and through others	*Perception of others may be inaccurate* You despair of other people. You feel they have let you down.... Have they really let you down? Do you bear some responsibility? ... Think of others, even if you no longer care about yourself....	
	Perception of others may be accurate To despair of other people is an awful feeling. But you still have a choice: to *accept* reality, or to keep on torturing yourself on account of other people's failings. To go a step further, you can still find hope in people, despite their failings. [The idea here is to accept the proclivity to disappoint as part of human nature.] ... There may still be others who will not fail you. Don't tell me that everyone has failed you, and will continue to fail you in the future. [The task here is to combat overgeneralization.] You can find hope in and through them.	
Item 12	Takes action to help oneself; proactive, engaged.	Takes no action to help oneself; passive, disengaged.
Taking action to help oneself	You haven't taken action to help yourself. There is no cure for laziness, but there is cure for despair. Now you know what you must do.... Describe how you have taken action to help yourself.... Keep it up.	

Item 13	Takes action to help others; proactive, engaged.	Takes no action to help others; passive, disengaged.
Taking action to help others	One of the best ways of helping yourself is to do something for others. I suggest that you start to help others, not just yourself. If you do, don't be surprised that you will be rewarded.... Describe how you have taken action to help others.... That can be more powerful than helping yourself.	

4. Meaning Reconstruction versus Entrenchment

People reconstruct meaning in response to adverse life events, make sense of what appears to be unfair or, worse, senseless. Unlike forbearance, which entails merely or primarily endurance, meaning reconstruction is a dynamic process that seeks to restore loss of meaning and purpose, even to create new meanings. This process involves cycles of construction, deconstruction, and reconstruction, and the dialectics of thought and action.

Entrenchment, in the present context, refers to unwillingness or inability to find new meanings or purpose. Mental conservatism, fixation, or rigidity inhibits meaning reconstruction, and renders entrenchment more likely. The result is that old constructions are left untouched.

Invitation to Self-Exploration

Let's talk about how you respond to adverse life events, and what meanings you make of them.

Think of an adverse event or unfortunate experience in your life. What are your thoughts about it now? Talk about your thoughts at different points in time. What factors have contributed to changes/lack of changes? What have you learned?

People attach different meanings to their unfortunate experiences. Looking back, in what ways have you examined the way you previously look at your own experience? What changes have occurred in the way you look at this experience? When? How? Please explain. In what ways have you made sense of this experience?

What new meanings to your life, if any, have emerged from this experience? When? How? What are their implications for acting and relating with people? Plans for action?

So how do you relate with others now? In what ways, if any, are you relating differently from before?

And how do you act (or behave) now? In what ways, if any, are you behaving differently from before? Are there things you do now that you have never or rarely done before?

What have you learned from these new ways of relating and acting? What new meanings have emerged? In what ways have you changed or not changed as a person?

Please feel free to elaborate further. You might have left something out; now is the time to add to what you have said.

Approaches and Attacks

Several principles provide guidance to meaning reconstruction. The first is the need to be sensitive to the pain that reconstruction may bring and to overcome it. The second is to be reminded, again in line with Dialogic Action Therapy, that all the reconstruction will do little if no effective actions follow. The third is to be aware that reconstructed meanings devoid of spiritual values may be negative, thus worsening life. Finally, closure has to be achieved: There should be no unended or unending deconstructions.

Strategy pair	Meaning Reconstruction	Entrenchment
Central idea	Attempts to reconstruct meaning and purpose in response to adverse life events.	Mental rigidity or fixation on previous or existing meaning constructions; deconstruction without learning or reconstruction, leaving the person worse off; or construction of meanings, though new, represent accentuations of unhealthy or destructive tendencies in previous constructions.

Item 1	Engages in *deconstruction*, examining and altering previous or existing constructions of meaning. Learn from accumulation and summation of experience.	Maintains existing constructions; leaves previous or existing constructions of meaning untouched.
Invitation to decon- struction	You have gone through an ordeal. You have been looking at it in the same old way for a long time.... This hasn't been helpful. It continues to trouble you.... A misfortune means different things to different people. There are different ways of looking at it. How about a reexamination of how you have been looking at yours? I'm saying that a fixed, entrenched way of looking at the past can be a part of the problem.... What can you learn from your misfortune and the way you have been looking at it?	
Item 2	Attempts to make sense of the adverse life event(s); to restore loss of meaning and purpose.	Sees the adverse life event(s) only as unfair, or worse, senseless.

Making sense of adverse life event(s); restore meaning and purpose	You only see what has happened to you as unfair, or worse, senseless. You can't make sense out of it…. I bet you are bitter. You say you have lost your purpose in life. Wouldn't that make you even bitterer in the long run? Leading a life without purpose is no way to live…. There is no necessary connection between misfortune and loss of purpose. I encourage you to restore meaning and purpose to your life. So, let's start with….	
Item 3	Seeks to *construct* new, healthy meanings and purpose.	Deconstructs without construction, without learning or benefiting from previous experiences; or constructs new meanings that accentuate unhealthy or destructive tendencies in previous constructions.
Finding new ways of relating	Yes, I see that you look at things differently now. You seem to have become gloomier. You have filtered out color from your life. That can't go on…. Now, I invite you to take another look at how you may look at your misfortune. A healthier look this time….	

Item 4	Relates with others differently following the emergence of new meanings.	Maintains previous ways of relating, or getting worse.
Finding new ways of relating	It's great that you have started to explore new meanings about your unfortunate experiences, to restore purpose to your life. How does that translate into new ways of relating with other people? For instance….	
Item 5	Engages in actions prompted by new meanings; acts according to plans.	Maintains previous patterns of action, or getting worse.
Finding new ways of acting	You've been talking about new meanings and purpose. What about new ways of acting?	
Item 6	Meaning *reconstruction*. Evaluates and reflects on new patterns of relating (Item 4) and acting (Item 5), leading to more new meanings, learning, and plans for action.	Existing constructions are entrenched; unhealthy or destructive tendencies strengthened further.
Reflection and recon- struction	Let's reflect on your new patterns of acting and relating…. In what ways have they gone astray and made things worse for your life? … In what ways have they been helpful, constructive?	

More books from Dignity Press and World Dignity University Press

www.dignitypress.org

Mark Tarver
CONVERSATIONS OF TAOIST MASTER FU HSIANG

George W. Wolfe
MEDITATIONS ON MYSTERY

Michael H. Prosser, Mansoureh Sharifzadeh, Zhang Zhengyong
FINDING CROSS-CULTURAL COMMON GROUND

Cui Litang, Michael Prosser (eds.)
SOCIAL MEDIA IN ASIA

Li Mengyu, Michael H. Prosser
CHINESE COMMUNICATING INTERCULTURALLY

Victoria Fontan
DECOLONIZING PEACE

Ada Aharoni
RARE FLOWER

Francesco Cardoso Gomes de Matos
DIGNITY – A MULTIDIMENSIONAL VIEW

Hilary Roseman
GENERATING FORGIVENESS AND CONSTRUCTING PEACE
THROUGH TRUTHFUL DIALOGUE: ABRAHAMIC PERSPECTIVES

Kathy W. Beckwith
A MIGHTY CASE AGAINST WAR

Evelin G. Lindner
A DIGNITY ECONOMY

Howard Richards, Joanna Swanger
GANDHI AND THE FUTURE OF ECONOMICS

Howard Richards
THE NURTURING OF TIME FUTURE

Deepak Tripathi
A JOURNEY THROUGH TURBULENCE

Arctic Queen
THE PEARL

Arctic Queen
MAGIC OF THE EVERYDAY

Kenday Kamara
ONLINE COLLABORATIVE LEARNING

in French:

Pierre-Amal Kana
AFGHANISTAN - LE RÊVE PASHTOUN
ET LA VOIE DE LA PAIX

in German:

Helmut Starrach
EIN LIEBENDES UND RUHELOSES HERZ

Petrus Ceelen
HALT DIE OHREN STEIF
99 FRIEDHOFSGESCHICHTEN

Petrus Ceelen
MEHR ALS DU DENKST
77 NAMENSGESCHICHTEN

in Turkish:

Hayal Köksal
ÇEKIRDEKTEN YETIŞTIRME

CPSIA information can be obtained at www.ICGtesting.com
Printed in the USA
BVOW05s0808120615

404406BV00002B/29/P